W. H. G. Kingston

A Yacht Voyage Round England

W. H. G. Kingston

A Yacht Voyage Round England

ISBN/EAN: 9783743316416

Manufactured in Europe, USA, Canada, Australia, Japa

Cover: Foto ©Andreas Hilbeck / pixelio.de

Manufactured and distributed by brebook publishing software
(www.brebook.com)

W. H. G. Kingston

A Yacht Voyage Round England

A

YACHT VOYAGE ROUND ENGLAND

BY

WILLIAM H. G. KINGSTON

AUTHOR OF

'CAPTAIN COOK; HIS LIFE, VOYAGES, AND DISCOVERIES;' 'THE VOYAGE OF THE STEADFAST'
'THE GOLDEN GRASSHOPPER,' ETC., ETC.

NEW EDITION, REVISED AND ENLARGED

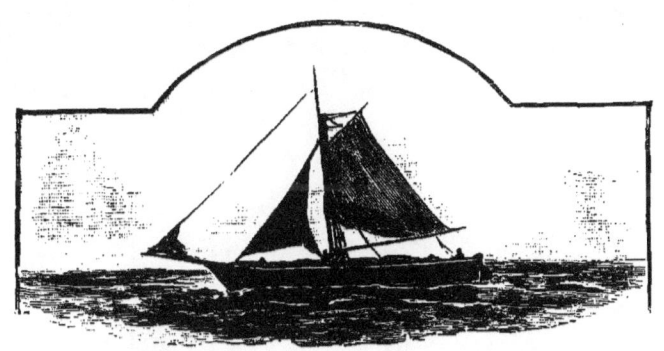

THE RELIGIOUS TRACT SOCIETY

56 PATERNOSTER ROW; 65 ST. PAUL'S CHURCHYARD
AND 164 PICCADILLY

CONTENTS

ILLUSTRATIONS.

WEST COWES.

A YACHT VOYAGE ROUND ENGLAND.

CHAPTER I.

THE START.

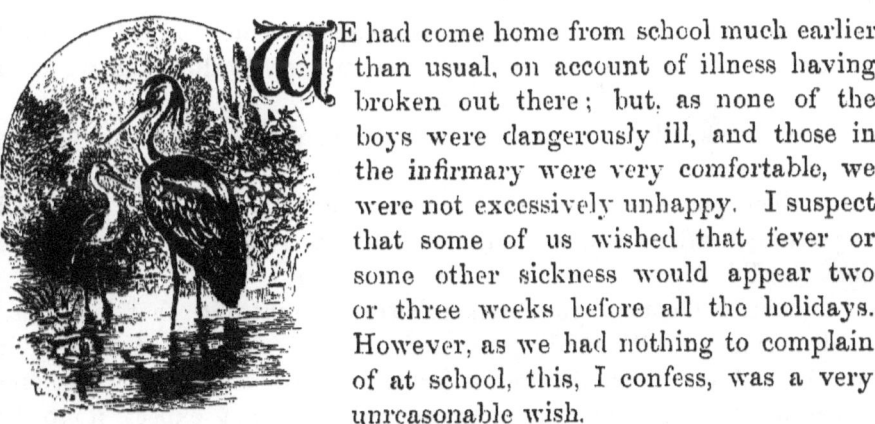

WE had come home from school much earlier than usual, on account of illness having broken out there; but, as none of the boys were dangerously ill, and those in the infirmary were very comfortable, we were not excessively unhappy. I suspect that some of us wished that fever or some other sickness would appear two or three weeks before all the holidays. However, as we had nothing to complain of at school, this, I confess, was a very unreasonable wish.

The very day of our arrival home, when we were seated at dinner, and my brother Oliver and I were discussing the important subject of how we were to spend the next ten or twelve weeks, we heard our papa, who is a retired captain of the Royal Navy—and who was not attending to what we were talking about—say, as he looked across the table to mamma:

'Would you object to these boys of ours taking a cruise with me round England this summer?'

We pricked up our ears, you may be sure, to listen eagerly to the reply. Looking at Oliver, then at me, she said:

'I should like to know what they think of it. As they have never before taken so long a cruise, they may get tired, and wish themselves home again or back at school.'

'Oh no, no! we should like it amazingly. We are sure not to get tired, if papa will take us. We will work our passage; will pull and haul, and learn to reef and steer, and do everything we are told,' said Oliver.

'What do you say about the matter, Harry?' asked papa.

'I say ditto to Oliver,' I replied. 'We will at all events *try* to be of use;' for I knew from previous experience that it was only when the weather was fine, and we were really not wanted, that we were likely to be able to do anything.

'Then I give my consent,' said mamma; on which we both jumped up and kissed her, as we had been accustomed to do when we were little chaps; we both felt so delighted.

'Well, we shall be sorry to be away from you so long.' said Oliver, when we again sat down, looking quite grave for a moment or two. 'But then, you know, mamma, you will have the girls and the small boys to look after; and we shall have lots to tell you about when we come back.'

'I cannot trust to your remembering everything that happens,' said mamma. 'When I gave my leave I intended to make it provisional on your keeping a journal of all you see and do, and everything interesting you hear about. I do not expect it to be very long; so you must make it terse and graphic. Oliver must keep notes and help you, and one complete journal will be sufficient.'

'That's just the bargain I intended to make,' said papa. 'I'll look out that Harry keeps to his intentions. It is the most difficult matter to accomplish. Thousands of people intend to write journals, and break down after the first five or six pages.'

On the morning appointed for the start a little longer time than usual was spent in prayer together, a special petition being offered that our Heavenly Father would keep us under His protection, and bring us safely home again. Soon afterwards we were rattling away to Waterloo Station, with our traps, including our still blank journals, our sketch-books, fishing-rods, our guns, several works on natural history, bottles and boxes for specimens, spy-glasses, and lots of other things.

Papa laughed when he saw them. 'It would not do if we were going to join a man-of-war; but we have room to stow away a good number of things on board the Lively, although she is little more than thirty-five tons burden.'

In a quarter of an hour the train started for Southampton; and away we flew, the heat and the dust increasing our eagerness to feel the fresh sea-breezes.

'Although the Lively can show a fast pair of heels, we cannot go quite so fast as this,' said papa, as he remarked the speed at which we dashed by the telegraph posts.

On reaching the station at Southampton, we found Paul Truck, the sailing-master of the cutter, or the captain, as he liked to be called, waiting for us, with two of the crew, who had come up to assist in carrying our traps down to the quay. There was the boat, her crew in blue shirts, and hats on which was the name of the yacht. The men, who had the oars upright in their hands while waiting, when we embarked let the blades drop on the water in smart man-of-war style; and away we pulled for the yacht, which lay some distance off the quay.

'I think I shall know her again,' cried Oliver: 'that's her, I'm certain.'

Paul, who was pulling the stroke oar, cast a glance over his shoulder, and shaking his head with a knowing look, observed:

'No, no, Master Oliver; that's a good deal bigger craft than ours. She's ninety ton at least. You must give another guess.'

'That's the Lively, though,' I cried out; 'I know her by her beauty and the way she sits on the water.'

'You're right, Master Harry. Lively is her name, and lively is her nature, and beautiful she is to look at. I'll be bound we shall not fall in with a prettier craft—a finer boat for her size.'

Paul's encomiums were not undeserved by the yacht; she was everything he said; we thought so, at all events. It was with no little pride that we stepped on deck.

Papa had the after-cabin fitted up for Oliver and me, and he himself had a state cabin abaft the forecastle. There were besides four open berths in which beds could be made up on both sides of the main cabin. The forecastle was large and airy, with room for the men to swing their hammocks, and it also held a brightly polished copper kitchen range.

Everything looked as neat and clean 'as if the yacht had been kept in a glass case,' as Paul observed.

Papa, having looked over the stores, took us on shore to obtain a number of things which he found we should require. We thus had an opportunity of seeing something of the town.

The old walls of Southampton have been pulled down, or are crumbling away, the most perfect portion being the gateway, or Bar Gate, in the High Street. On either side of it stand two curious old heraldic figures, and beside them are two blackened pictures—one representing Sir Bevis of Hampton, and the other his companion, Ascapart. Sir Bevis, who lived in the reign of Edgar, had a castle in the neighbourhood. It is said he bestowed his love on a pagan lady, Josian, who, having been converted to Christianity, gave him a sword called Morglay, and a horse named Arundel. Thus equipped he was wont to kill four or five men at one blow. Among his renowned deeds were those he performed against the Saracens, and also his slaughter of an enormous dragon.

The extensive docks at the mouth of the river Itchen, to the east of the town, have, of course, greatly increased its wealth. We saw

BIRTH-PLACE OF ISAAC WATTS, SOUTHAMPTON.

a magnificent foreign-bound steamer coming out of the docks. The West India ships start from here, as do other lines of steamers running to the Cape, and to various parts of the world; so that South-ampton is a bustling seaport. There is another river to the west of the town, called the Test ; and that joining with the Itchen at the point where the town is built, forms the beautiful Southampton Water.

But perhaps the most interesting fact about Southampton is that Isaac Watts, the Christian poet, was born here in 1671. The house

ST. MICHAEL'S GAOL, SOUTHAMPTON.

in French Street is still standing, and we went to look at it. There he passed his play-days of childhood ; there the dreamy, studious boy stored up his first spoils of knowledge ; there he wrote his first hymns ; and thither he went to visit his parents, when he himself was old and famous. We also went to see the remains of St. Michael's Gaol, in which Watts' father had been confined for his nonconformity.

IN THE NEW FOREST.

And as we looked on the old prison we thanked God that nowadays, in England at least, religious persecution is unknown.

When we returned on board, we noticed with surprise on each side of the river what had the appearance of green fields, over which the water had just before flowed; they were, however, in reality mud flats covered by long sea-weed.

Soon after tea we turned into our berths, feeling very jolly and quite at home, though Oliver did knock his head twice against the deck above, forgetting the size of our bed-room. We lay awake listening to the water rippling by, and now and then hearing the step of the man on watch overhead; but generally there was perfect silence, very different from the noise of London.

We were both dressed and on deck some time before papa next morning, for as the tide was still flowing, and there was no wind, he knew that we could not make way down the river. So we had time for a dive and a swim round the vessel, climbing on board again by means of a short ladder rigged over the side.

Soon after this we saw a few of the other vessels hoisting their sails; and then Captain Truck, Oliver, and I pulled and hauled until we got our mainsail set. The men then washed down the decks, though really there was no dirt to wash away, and we tried, as we had promised, to make ourselves useful.

When papa appeared he looked pleased at our being so hard at work. As there was just then a ripple on the water, he ordered the anchor to be got up; and it being now full tide, we began, almost imperceptibly, to glide away from among the other vessels. On the right was the edge of the New Forest, in which William Rufus was killed; although I believe that took place a good way off, near Lyndhurst; and very little of the eastern side of the forest now remains.

On the left we passed Netley Abbey, a very pretty, small ruin, and near it a large military hospital and college, where medical officers of the army study the complaints of the troops who have been in tropical climates. On the opposite side, at the end of a point stretching partly across the mouth of the water, we saw the old grey, round castle of Calshot, which was built to defend the entrance, but would be of little use in stopping even an enemy's gun-boat at the present day. However, papa said there are very strong fortifications at both ends of the Solent, as the channel here is called. No enemy's gun-boat could ever get through, much less an enemy's fleet; at any rate, if they did, he hoped they would never get out again.

Some way to the left of Calshot rose the tall tower of Eaglehurst among the trees. The wind was from the west. We stood away towards Portsmouth, as papa wished to visit an old friend there, and to give us an opportunity of seeing that renowned seaport as well. We caught a glimpse of Cowes, and Osborne to the east of it, where the Queen frequently resides, and the town of Ryde, rising up on a hill surrounded by woods, and then the shipping at Spithead, with the curious cheese-shaped forts erected to guard the eastern entrance to the Solent.

Papa told us that these curious round forts, rising out of the sea, are built of granite; that in time of war they are to be united by a line of torpedoes and the wires of electric batteries. They are perfectly impregnable to shot, and they are armed with very heavy guns, so that an enemy attempting to come in on that side would have a very poor chance of success.

As we were anxious to see them, we had kept more in mid-channel than we should otherwise have done. We now hauled up for Portsmouth Harbour. Far off, on the summit of the green heights of Portsdown Hill, we could see the obelisk-shaped monument to Nelson, an appropriate landmark in sight of the last spot of English ground on which he stepped before sailing to fight the great battle of Trafalgar, where he fell. We could also trace the outline of a portion of the cordon of forts—twenty miles in length—from Langston Harbour on the east to Stokes' Bay on the west. Along the shores, on both sides of the harbour, are two lines of fortifications; so that even should a hostile fleet manage to get by the cheese-like forts, they

would still find it a hard matter to set fire to the dockyard or blow up the Victory. That noble old ship met our sight as, passing between Point Battery and Block House Fort, we entered the harbour.

She did not look so big as I expected, for not far off was the Duke of Wellington, which seemed almost large enough to hoist her on board; and nearer to us, at the entrance of Haslar Creek, was the gallant old St. Vincent, on board which papa once served when he was a midshipman. We looked at her with great respect, I can tell you. Think how old she must be. She has done her duty well,— she has carried the flag of England many a year, and now still does her duty by serving as a ship in which boys are trained for the Royal Navy.

Further up, in dim perspective, we saw ships with enormous yellow-painted hulls; noble ships they were, with names allied to England's naval glory. They were all, however, far younger than the St. Vincent, as we discovered by seeing the apertures in their stern-posts formed to admit screws. Some fought in the Black Sea, others in the Baltic; but papa said 'that their fighting days are now done, though they are kept to be employed in a more peaceful manner, either as hospital ships or training schools.'

Shortening sail, we came to an anchor not far from the St. Vincent, among several other yachts. On the Gosport side we could see across the harbour, away to the dockyard, off the quays of which were clustered a number of black monsters of varied form and rig. Papa said—though otherwise we could not have believed it—'that there were amongst them some of the finest ships of the present navy.' I could hardly fancy that such ships could go to sea, for they are more like gigantic coal barges with strong erections on their decks, than anything else afloat.

Of course I cannot tell you all our adventures consecutively, so shall describe only some of the most interesting. We first visited the St. Vincent, which, as we had just left our little yacht, looked very fine and grand. Papa was saying to one of the officers that he had served on board her, when a weather-beaten petty officer came up, and with a smile on his countenance touched his hat, asking if papa remembered Tom Trueman. Papa immediately exclaimed, 'Of course I do,' and gave him such a hearty grip of the hand that it almost made the tears come into the old man's eyes with pleasure, and they had a long yarn about days of yore. After this papa met many old shipmates. It was pleasant to see the way in which he greeted them and they greeted him, showing how much he must have been beloved, which, of course, he was; and I'll venture to say it will be a hard matter to find a kinder or better man. I'm sure that he is a brave sailor, from the things he has done, and the cool way in which he manages the yacht, whatever is happening.

After we had finished with the St. Vincent we went on board the Victory, which looks, outside, as sound as ever she did—a fine, bluff old ship; but when we stepped on her deck, even we were struck by her ancient appearance, very unlike the St. Vincent, and still more unlike the Duke of Wellington. There was wonderfully little ornamental or brass work of any sort; and the stanchions, ladders, and railings were all stout and heavy-looking.

Of course we looked with respect on the brass plate on her deck which marks the spot where Nelson fell. We then went far down into the midshipmen's berth, in the cockpit. How dark and gloomy it seemed; and yet it was here Nelson, while the guns were thundering overhead, lay dying. How very different from the mess-rooms of young officers of the present day! Here another inscription, fixed on the ship's side, pointed out where the hero breathed his last. Going into the cabin on the main deck, we saw one of the very topsails—riddled with shot—which had been at Trafalgar. After being shifted at Gibraltar, it had been for more than half a century laid up in a store at Woolwich, no one guessing what a yarn that old roll of canvas could tell.

We also saw an interesting picture of the 'Death of Nelson,' and another of the battle itself. We felt almost awe-struck while seeing

THE FORTS AT SPITHEAD.

these things, and thinking of the gallant men who once served on board that noble ship. Papa said that he hoped, if the old ship is not wanted for practical purposes, that she may be fitted up exactly as she was at Trafalgar.

We afterwards called on an old lady—a friend of papa—who told us that she clearly recollected going off from Ryde in a boat with her father and mother, and pulling round the Victory when she arrived from Gibraltar at Spithead, on the 4th of December, 1805, with the body of Nelson on board. In many places the shot were still sticking in her sides, her decks were scarcely freed from blood, and other injuries showed the severity of the action.

After this, the Victory was constantly employed until the year 1812, from which time she was never recommissioned for sea; but from 1825 until within a few years ago, she bore the flags of the port-admirals of Portsmouth.

Late in the evening we crossed the harbour to the dockyard, where papa wanted to pay a visit. A curious steam ferry-boat runs backwards and forwards between Portsmouth and Gosport. We passed a number of large ships coated with thick plates of iron; but even the thickest cannot withstand the shots sent from some of the guns which have been invented, and all might be destroyed by torpedoes. We could hardly believe that some of the ships we saw were fit to go to sea. The most remarkable was the Devastation. Her free-board— that is, the upper part of her sides—is only a few feet above the water. Amidships rises a round structure supporting what is called ' a hurricane deck.' This is the only spot where the officers and men can stand in a sea-way. At either end is a circular revolving turret containing two thirty-five ton guns, constructed to throw shot of seven hundred pounds. These guns are worked by means of machinery.

Contrasting with the ironclads, we saw lying alongside the quays several enormous, white-painted, richly-gilt troop-ships, also iron-built, which run through the Suez Canal to India. The night was calm and still; and as we pulled up the harbour a short distance among the huge ships, I could not help fancying that I heard them talking to each other, and telling of the deeds they had done. Papa laughed at my poetical fancy, which was put to flight when he told me that scarcely any of them, except those which were engaged in the Baltic and Black Sea, had seen any service.

Pulling down the harbour on the Gosport side, to be out of the way of passing vessels, we soon reached the yacht, feeling very tired, for we had been wide awake for the last sixteen hours. As we sat in our little cabin, it was difficult to realise that outside of us were so many objects and scenes of interest connected with the naval history of England. Papa told us a number of curious anecdotes. Not many hundred yards from us, about a century ago, was to be seen a gibbet on Block House Point, at the west entrance of the harbour, on which hung the body of a man called Jack the Painter. Having taken it into his very silly head that he should forward the cause of freedom by burning the dockyard, he set fire to the rope-house, which was filled with hemp, pitch, and tar. Jack, having performed this noble deed, escaped from the yard, and was making his way along the Fareham Road, when, having asked a carter to give him a lift, he pointed out the cloud of smoke rising in the distance, observing that he 'guessed where it came from.' The carter went his way; but shortly afterwards, when a hue and cry was raised, he recollected his passenger, who was traced, captured, tried, and executed.

Another story we heard was about the mad pranks played by naval officers in days of yore. At that time, a sentry-box, having a seat within, stood on the Hard, at Portsmouth, so that the sentry could sit down and rest himself. It happened that a party of young captains and commanders, coming down from dinner to embark, found the sentry at his post, but drunk and sound asleep in his box! Punishment was his due. They bethought themselves of a mode of astonishing him. Summoning their crews, box and sentry were carried on board one of their boats and transported to Gosport, and then placed in an upright position facing the water. When the relief came to the spot where the sentry was originally stationed, what was their astonishment and alarm to find neither sentry nor box! The captain of the guard reported the circumstance to the fort-major. 'The enemy,' he averred, 'must be at hand.'

The garrison was aroused, the drawbridges were hauled up. Daylight revealed the box and the position of the sentry, who protested that, although as sober as a judge, he had no idea how he had been conveyed across the harbour.

Numerous 'land-sharks' used to be in waiting to tempt those who were generally too ready to be tempted into scenes of debauchery and vice. This state of things continued until a few years ago, when it was put into the heart of a noble lady—Miss Robinson—to found an institute for soldiers and sailors. There they may find a home when coming on shore, and be warned of the dangers awaiting them. After great exertion. and travelling about England to obtain funds, she raised about thirteen thousand pounds, and succeeded in purchasing the old Fountain Hotel, in the High Street, which, greatly enlarged, was opened in 1874 as a Soldiers' and Sailors' Institute, by General Sir James Hope Grant.

Dear me, I shall fill up my journal with the yarns we heard at Portsmouth, and have no room for our adventures, if I write on at this rate. After our devotions, we turned in, and were lulled to sleep, as we were last night, by the ripple of the water against the sides of the yacht.

CHAPTER II.

IN THE SOLENT.

NEXT morning, soon after breakfast, we went on shore to pay a visit to the dockyard. On entering, papa was desired to put down his name; and the man seeing that he was a captain in the navy, we were allowed to go on without a policeman in attendance, and nearly lost ourselves among the storehouses and docks. As we walked past the lines of lofty sheds, we heard from all directions the ringing clank of iron, instead of, as in days of yore, the dull thud of the shipwright's mallet, and saw the ground under each shed strewed with ribs and sheets of iron ready to be fixed to the vast skeletons within. Papa could not help sighing, and saying that he wished 'the days of honest sailing ships could come back again.' However, he directly afterwards observed, 'I should be sorry to get back, at the same time, the abuses, the wild doings, and the profligacy which then prevailed. Things have undoubtedly greatly improved, though they are bad enough even now.'

Tramways and railways, with steam locomotives, run in all directions. Formerly, papa said, the work was done by yellow-coated convicts with chains on their legs. They have happily been removed from the dockyard itself, and free labourers only are employed.

Convicts, however, are still employed in various extensive public works.

Of course we visited Brunel's block machinery, which shapes from the rough mass of wood, with wonderful accuracy and speed, the polished block fit for use. Huge lathes were at work, with circular saws and drills, sending the chips of wood flying round them with a whizzing and whirring sound. So perfect is the machinery that skilled artisans are not required to use it. Four men only are employed in making the shells, and these four can make with machinery as many as fifty men could do by hand. On an average, nineteen men make one hundred and fifty thousand blocks in the course of the year.

Leaving the block-house, we went to the smithy, where we saw Nasmyth's steam hammer, which does not strike like a hammer, but comes down between two uprights. On one side is a huge furnace for heating the material to be subjected to the hammer. Papa asked the manager to place a nut under it, when down came the hammer and just cracked the shell. He then asked for another to be placed beneath the hammer, when it descended and made but a slight dent in the nut.

Soon afterwards a huge mass of iron, to form an anchor, was drawn out of the furnace; then down came the hammer with thundering strokes, beating and battering it until it was forced into the required shape, while the sparks flying out on all sides made us retreat to a safer distance.

One of the largest buildings in the dockyard is the foundry, which is considered the most complete in the world. We looked into the sheds, as they are called, where the boilers for the ships are constructed, and could scarcely hear ourselves speak, from the noise of hammers driving in the rivets. Many of the boilers were large enough to form good-sized rooms. We walked along the edge of the steam basin. It is nine hundred feet long and four hundred broad. The ships, I should have said, are built on what are called the building slips, which are covered over with huge roofs of corrugated iron, so that the ships and workmen are protected while the building is going forward.

Before leaving we went into the mast-house, near the entrance to the yard. Here we saw the enormous pieces of timber intended to be built into masts—for masts of large ships are not single trees, but composed of many pieces, which are bound together with stout iron hoops. Here also were the masts of ships in ordinary. They would be liable to decay if kept on board exposed to the weather. Each mast and yard is marked with the name of the ship to which it belongs. The masts of the old Victory are kept here, the same she carried at Trafalgar. Not far off is the boat-house, where boats from a large launch down to the smallest gig are kept ready for use.

We looked into the Naval College, where officers go to study a variety of professional subjects. When papa was a boy the Naval College was used as the Britannia now is—as a training-school for naval cadets. Finding an officer going on board the Excellent— gunnery ship—we accompanied him. We were amused to find that the Excellent consists of three ships moored one astern of the other, and that not one of them is the old Excellent, she having been removed. Our friend invited us to accompany him on board an old frigate moored a little way up the harbour, from which we could see some interesting torpedo experiments.

As we pulled along he gave us an explanation of the fish torpedo— a wonderful instrument of destruction which has been invented of late years. It is a cylinder, which carries the explosive material at one end and the machinery for working the screw which impels it at the other. It can be discharged through a tube with such accuracy that it can strike an object several hundred yards off. On getting on board the old frigate, we found a large party of officers assembled. We were to witness the explosion of two other sorts of torpedoes. One was used by a steam launch, the fore part of which was entirely covered over by an iron shield. The torpedo was fixed to the end of a long pole, carried at the side of the launch. At some distance from the ship a huge cask was moored, towards which the launch rapidly made her way. The pole, with the torpedo at the end, was then thrust forward; the concussion ignited it the instant it struck the cask and blew it to fragments.

Another launch then approached a large cask floating with one end out of the water, to represent a boat. An officer stood up with a little ball of gun-cotton in his hand, smaller than an orange, to which was attached a thin line of what is called lightning cotton, the other end being fastened to a pistol. As the launch glided on he threw the ball into the cask. The boat moved away as rapidly as possible, when the pistol being fired, in an instant the cask was blown to atoms. What a fearful effect would have been produced had the innocent-looking little ball been thrown into a boat full of men instead of into a cask !

Another experiment with gun-cotton was then tried. A piece not larger than a man's hand was fastened to an enormous iron chain fixed on the deck of the ship. We were all ordered to go below, out of harm's way. Soon afterwards, the gun-cotton having been ignited by a train, we heard a loud report; and on returning on deck we found that the chain had been cut completely in two, the fragments having flown about in all directions.

The chain of a boat at anchor was cut by means of a piece of gun-cotton fixed to it, and ignited by a line of lightning cotton fired from one of the launches. This showed us how the chain-cable of a ship at anchor might be cut; while a torpedo boat might dash in, as she was drifting away with the tide and the attention of her officers was engaged, to blow her up.

The chief experiments of the day were still to come off. We saw a number of buoys floating in various directions some way up the harbour. A launch advanced towards one, when the buoy being struck by the pole, the charge of a torpedo some twenty yards away was ignited, and the fearful engine exploding, lifted a huge mass of water some thirty or forty yards into the air.   How terrible must be the effects when such a machine explodes under a ship!   As soon as the torpedoes had exploded, the boats pulled up to the spot, and picked up a large number of fish which had been killed or stunned by the concussion—for many did not appear to be injured, and some even recovered when in the boats.

Papa, though very much interested, could not help saying that he was thankful these murderous engines of war had not been discovered in his time.   It is indeed sad to think that the ingenuity of people should be required to invent such dreadful engines for the destruction of their fellow-creatures.   When will the blessings of the gospel of peace be universally spread abroad, and nations learn war no more?

We next pulled over to the Gosport side, to visit the Royal Clarence Victualling Establishment, which papa said was once called Weovil.   Here are stored beef and other salted meats, as well as supplies and clothing; but what interested us most was the biscuit manufactory.   It seemed to us as if the corn entered at one end and the biscuits came out at the other, baked, and all ready to eat.   The corn having been ground, the meal descends into a hollow cylinder, where it is mixed with water.   As the cylinder revolves a row of knives within cut the paste into innumerable small pieces, kneading them into dough.   This dough is taken out of the cylinder and spread on an iron table, over which enormous rollers pass until they have pressed the mass into a sheet two inches thick.   These are further divided and passed under a second pair of rollers, when another instrument cuts the sheets into hexagonal biscuits, not quite dividing them, however, and at the same time stamping them with the Queen's mark and the number of the oven in which they are baked.   Still joined together, they are passed into the ovens.   One hundred-weight of biscuits can be put into one oven.

On the Gosport side we went over some of the forts, which are of great extent.   The longest walk we took was to Portsdown

Hill, for the sake of visiting the Nelson Monument. On it is an inscription :—

𝕿𝔬 𝖙𝖍𝖊 𝕸𝖊𝖒𝖔𝖗𝖞 𝔬𝖋

LORD VISCOUNT NELSON.

BY THE ZEALOUS ATTACHMENT OF ALL THOSE WHO

FOUGHT AT TRAFALGAR—TO PERPETUATE

HIS TRIUMPH AND THEIR REGRET.

MDCCCV.

We had a magnificent view from the top of the monument, looking completely over Gosport, Portsmouth, and Southsea, with the harbour at our feet, and taking in nearly the whole line of the Isle of Wight, with the Solent, and away to the south-east, St. Helen's and the English Channel. Later on we pulled five miles up the harbour, to Porchester Castle, built by William the Conqueror. For many centuries it was the chief naval station of the kingdom, modern Portsmouth having sprung up in the reign of Henry the First, in consequence of Porchester Harbour filling with mud.

It was here, during the war with Napoleon, that several thousands of French prisoners were confined, some in the castle, and others on board the hulks. They, of course, did not like to be shut up, and many attempting to escape were suffocated in the mud. They were but scantily supplied with provisions, though they were not actually starved; but a French colonel who broke his parole wrote a book, affirming that on one occasion an officer who came to inspect the castle, having left his horse in the court-yard, the famished prisoners despatched the animal, devouring it on the spot; and, by the time the owner returned, the stirrup-irons and bit alone remained!

Portsmouth is a very healthy place, although from its level position it might be supposed to be otherwise. It has a wide and handsome High Street, leading down to the harbour.

The Fountain, at the end of the High Street, no longer exists as an inn, but has been converted by Miss Robinson into a Soldiers' and

Sailors' Institute. We went over the whole establishment. At the entrance are rooms where soldiers and sailors can see their friends; and then there is a large bar, where, although no intoxicating drinks can be obtained, tea, coffee, and beverages of all sorts are served. Near it is a large coffee-room. Passing through the house, we entered a very nice garden, on the right of which there is a bowling-green and a skittle-alley; and we then came to a very handsome hall which serves for religious meetings, lectures, concerts, teas, and other social gatherings. There were also rooms in which the men can fence or box. A large reading-room (with a good library) and Bible-class-room are on the second floor; and at the top of the house are dormitories, making up a considerable number of beds for soldiers, as also for their wives and families, who may be passing through Portsmouth either to embark or have come from abroad. There is a sewing-room for the employment of the soldiers' wives. A Children's Band of Hope meets every week. There is even a smoking-room for the men, and hot or cold baths. Indeed, a more perfect place for the soldier can nowhere be found. Miss Robinson herself resides in the house, and superintends the whole work, of which I have given but a very slight description. I should say that this most energetic lady has also secured several houses for the accommodation of soldiers' families, who would otherwise be driven into dirty or disreputable lodgings.

Another philanthropist of whom Portsmouth is justly proud is John Pounds, who though only a poor shoemaker, originated and super-intended the first ragged school in the kingdom. Near the Soldiers' Institute is the John Pounds' Memorial Ragged School, where a large number of poor children are cared for. It is very gratifying to know that many of our brave soldiers and sailors are also serving under the great Captain of our salvation, and fighting the good fight of faith, helped in so doing by good servants of God.

The town of Portsmouth was until lately surrounded by what were called very strong fortifications; but the new works have rendered them perfectly useless, and they are therefore being dis-mantled—a great advantage to the town, as it will be thrown open to the sea breezes.

A light breeze from the eastward enabled us to get under weigh just at sunrise, and to stem the tide still making into the harbour. Some-times, however, we scarcely seemed to go ahead, as we crept by Block House Fort and Point Battery on the Portsmouth side.

Once upon a time, to prevent the ingress of an enemy's fleet, a chain was stretched across the harbour's mouth. We had got just outside the harbour when we saw a man-of-war brig under all sail standing in. A beautiful sight she was, her canvas so white, her sides so polished!—on she stood, not a brace nor tack slackened. Papa looked at her with the affection of an old sailor. It was an object which reminded him of his younger days. 'You don't see many like her now,' he observed. Presently, as she was starting by us, a shrill whistle was heard. Like magic the sails were clewed up, the hands, fine active lads—for she was a training vessel—flew aloft, and lay out on the yards. While we were looking, the sails were furled; and it seemed scarcely a moment afterwards when we saw her round to and come to an anchor not far from the St. Vincent. 'That's how I like to see things done,' said papa. 'I wish we had a hundred such craft afloat; our lads would learn to be real seamen!'

He and Paul were so interested in watching the brig, that for the moment their attention was wholly absorbed. As we got off the Southsea pier we began to feel the wind coming over the common; and being able to make better way, quickly glided by the yachts and small vessels anchored off it, when we stood close to one of those round towers I have described, and then on towards Spithead.

Spithead is so called because it is at the end of a spit or point of sand which runs off from the mainland. We passed close over the spot where the Royal George, with nine hundred gallant men on board, foundered in August, 1782. She was the flag-ship of Admiral Kempenfeldt. He was at the time writing in his cabin, where he was last seen by the captain of the ship, who managed to leap out of a stern port and was saved, as was the late Sir Philip Durham, port-admiral of Portsmouth, then one of the junior lieutenants. The accident happened from the gross negligence and obstinacy of one of the lieutenants. In order to get at a water-cock on the starboard side, the ship had been heeled down on her larboard side, by running her guns over until the lower deck port-sills were just level with the water. Some casks of rum were being hoisted on board from a lighter, bring-ing the ship still more over. The carpenter, seeing the danger, reported it to the lieutenant of the watch, who at first obstinately refused to listen to him. A second time he went to the officer, who, when too late, turned the hands up to right ship, intending to run the guns back into their former places. The weight of five or six hundred men, however, going over to the larboard side completely turned the hitherto critically balanced scale ; and the ship went right over, with her masts in the water. The sea rushing through her ports quickly filled her, when she righted and went down, those who had clambered through the ports on her starboard side being swept off. Two hundred out of nine hundred alone were saved. Among these was a midshipman only nine years old, and a little child found fastened on to the back of a sheep swimming from the wreck. He could not tell the names of his parents, who must have perished, and only knew that his name was Jack, so he was called John Lamb. None of his relatives could be found, and a subscription was raised and people took care of him, and having received a liberal education, he entered an honourable profession.

Some years ago the remains of the ship were blown up by Sir C. Pasley, and many of the guns recovered. Close to the spot, in the days of bluff King Harry, the Mary Rose, after an action with a French ship, went down with her gallant captain, Sir George Carew, and all his men, while his crew were attempting to get at the shot-holes she had received.

In 1701, the Edgar, 74 guns, which had just arrived from Canada, blew up; her crew and their friends were making merry when they, to the number of eight hundred, miserably perished.

While at anchor here also, the Boyne, of 91 guns, caught fire. All efforts to put out the flames were unavailing; but the greater number of her crew escaped in boats. As she drifted from Spithead towards Southsea, her guns continued to go off, until touching the shore, she blew up with a tremendous explosion.

THE MINOTAUR.

The ships at Spithead now are of a very different appearance from those formerly seen there. Among them was the Minotaur, which, in consequence of her great length, is fitted with five masts. Just as we were passing her she got under weigh, papa said, in very good style; and certainly, when all her canvas was set, she looked a fine powerful sea-going craft.

The Devastation came out of the harbour, and stood on towards St. Helen's. She certainly looked as unlike our notions of a man-of-war as anything could be, though, as Paul Truck observed, 'she would crumple up the Minotaur in a few minutes with her four thirty-five ton guns, powerful as the five-masted ship appears.'

Though she looked only fit for harbour work, Paul said that she had been out in heavy weather, and proved a fair sea-boat. The only place that people live on, when not below, is the hurricane-deck. In this centre structure are doorways which can be closed at sea. They lead down into the cabins below, as well as to the hurricane-deck, out of which rise the two funnels and an iron signal-mast. This is thick enough to enable a person to ascend through its inside to a crow's-nest on the top, which serves as a look-out place. From it also projects the davits for hoisting up the boats. On the hurricane-deck stands the captain's fighting-box, cased with iron. Here also is the steering apparatus and wheel. When in action, all the officers and men would be sent below except the helmsmen, who are also protected, with the captain and a lieutenant, and the men inside the turrets working the guns. These are so powerful that they can penetrate armour six inches thick at the distance of nearly three miles.

We brought-up for a short time at the end of Ryde Pier, as papa wished to go on shore to the club. The pier-head was crowded with people who had come there to enjoy the sea-breeze without the inconvenience of being tossed about in a vessel. The town rises on a steep hill from the shore, with woods on both sides, and looks very picturesque. To the west is the pretty village of Binstead, with its church peeping out among the trees.

We were very glad, however, when papa came on board, and we got under weigh to take a trip along the south coast of the island. The wind and tide suiting, we ran along the edge of the sand-flats, which extend off from the north shore, passing a buoy which Paul Truck said was called 'No Man's Land.' Thence onwards, close by the Warner light-ship.

As we wanted to see a light-ship, the yacht was hove-to, and we went alongside in the boat. She was a stout, tub-like, Dutch-built-looking vessel, with bow and stern much alike, and rising high out of the water, which is very necessary, considering the heavy seas to which she is at times exposed. The master, who knew Paul Truck, was very glad to see us, and at once offered to show us all over the vessel.

The light was in a sort of huge lantern, now lowered on deck ; but at night it is hoisted to the top of the mast, thirty-eight feet above the water, so that it can be seen at a distance of eight miles. It is what is called a reflecting light. I will try and describe it..

Within the lantern are a certain number of lights and reflectors, each suspended on gimbals, so that they always maintain their perpendicular position, notwithstanding the rolling of the vessel. Each of these lights consists of a copper lamp, placed in front of a saucer-shaped reflector. The lamp is fed by a cistern of oil at the back of the reflector. This being a revolving light, a number of reflectors were fixed to the iron sides of a quadrangular frame, and the whole caused to revolve once every minute by means of clockwork. The reflectors on each side of the revolving frame—eight in number—are thus successively directed to every point in the horizon ; and the combined result of their rays form a flash of greater or less duration, according to the rapidity of their revolution. In the fixed lights eight lamps and reflectors are used, and are arranged in an octagonal lantern ; they do not differ much in appearance from the others.

The master told us that the invention was discovered very curiously. A number of scientific gentlemen were dining together at Liverpool— a hundred years ago—when one of the company wagered that he would read a newspaper at the distance of two hundred feet by the light of a farthing candle. The rest of the party said that he would not. He perhaps had conceived the plan before. Taking a wooden bowl, he lined it with putty, and into it embedded small pieces of looking-glass, by which means a perfect reflector was formed ; he then placed his rushlight in front of it, and won his wager. Among the company was Mr. William Hutchinson, dock-master of Liverpool, who seizing the idea, made use of copper lamps, and formed reflectors much in the same way as the gentleman before mentioned.

Everything about the ship was strong, kept beautifully clean, and in the most admirable order. The crew consists of the captain and mate, with twelve or fourteen men, a portion of whom are on shore off duty. The life is very monotonous; and the only amusement they have is fishing, with reading and a few games, such as draughts and chess. They had only a small library of books, which did not appear very interesting. Papa left them a few interesting tracts and other small books, and gave them a short address, urging them to trust to Christ, and follow His example in their lives. They listened attentively, and seemed very grateful. They have a large roomy cabin, and an airy place to sleep in. The captain has his cabin aft, besides which there is a large space used as a lamp-room, where all the extra lamps and oil and other things pertaining to them are kept. They seemed happy and contented; but when a heavy gale is blowing they must be terribly tossed about. Of course there is a risk—although such is not likely to occur—of the vessel being driven from her moorings. In case this should happen, they have small storm sails, and a rudder to steer the vessel. When this does happen it is a serious matter, not only to those on board, but still more so to any ships approaching the spot, and expecting to find guidance from the light.

Standing on, we passed close to the Bembridge or Nab light-vessel. This vessel carries two bright fixed lights, one hoisted on each of her masts, which can be seen at night ten miles off, and of course it can be distinguished from the revolving Warner light. Farther off to the west, at the end of a shoal extending off Selsea Bill, is another light-ship, called the Owers.

Having rounded Bembridge Ledge, we stood towards the white Culver cliffs, forming the north side of Sandown Bay, with lofty downs rising above Bembridge. Near their summits are lines of fortifications, extending westward to where once stood Sandown Castle,

THE UNDERCLIFF.

near which there is now a large town, although papa said he remembered when there was only a small inn there, with a few cottages. On the very top of the downs is a monument erected to Lord Yarborough, the king of yachtsmen, who died some years ago on board his yacht, the Kestrel, in the Mediterranean. He at one time had a large ship as his yacht, on board which he maintained regular naval discipline, with a commander, and officers who did duty as lieutenants. It was said that he offered to build and fit out a frigate, and maintain her at his own expense, if the government would make him a post-captain off-hand, but this they declined to do.

Standing across the bay, we came off a very picturesque spot, called Shanklin Chine, a deep cut or opening in the cliffs with trees on both sides. Dunnose was passed, and the village of Bonchurch and Ventnor, climbing up the cliffs from its sandy beach. We now sailed along what is considered the most beautiful part of the Isle of Wight,—the Undercliff. This is a belt of broken, nearly level ground, more or less narrow, beyond which the cliffs rise to a considerable height, with valleys intervening; the downs in some places appearing above them. This belt, called the Undercliff, is covered with trees and numerous villas.

At last we came off Rocken End Point, below St. Catherine's Head. This is the most southern point of the island. On it stands a handsome stone tower, 105 feet high, with a brilliant fixed light upon it. The village of Niton stands high up away from the shore.

It now came on to blow very fresh. There was not much sea in the offing; but, owing to the way the tide ran and met the wind, the bottom being rocky, the water nearer the shore was tossed about in a most curious and somewhat dangerous fashion, for several 'lumps of sea,' as Truck called them, came flop down on our deck; and it was easy to see what might be the consequences if an open boat had attempted to pass through the Race. Paul told us that good-sized vessels had been seen to go down in similar places. One off Portland is far worse than this in heavy weather.

Farther on is a curious landslip, where a large portion of the cliff once came down, and beyond it is Blackgang Chine, a wild, savage-looking break in the cliffs, formed by the giving way of the lower strata. Farther to the west, towards Freshwater Gate, the cliffs are perpendicular, and of a great height, the smooth downs coming to their very edge.

Some years ago a picnic party, who had come over from Lymington, had assembled on that part of the downs, having come by different conveyances. Among them was a boy, like one of us—a merry fellow, I dare say. After the picnic the party separated in various directions. When the time to return had arrived, so many went off in one carriage, and so many in another. In the same way they crossed to Lymington in different boats. Not until their arrival at that place was their young companion missed, each party having supposed that he was with the other. What could have become of him? They hoped against hope that he had wandered far off to the east, and had lost his way. Then some of the party recollected having seen him going towards the edge of the cliff. He was a stranger, and was not aware how abruptly the downs terminated in a fearful precipice. It was too late to send back that night. They still hoped that he might have slipped down, and have lodged on some ledge. At daybreak boats were despatched to the island. At length his mangled remains were found at the foot of the highest part of the cliff, over which he must have fallen and been dashed to pieces. Papa said he recollected seeing the party land, and all the circumstances of the case.

Here, too, several sad shipwrecks have occurred, when many lives have been lost. A few years ago, two ladies were walking together during a heavy gale of wind, which sent huge foaming billows rolling on towards the shore. One, the youngest, was nearer the water than the other, when an immense wave suddenly broke on the beach, and surrounding her, carried her off in its deadly embrace. Her companion, with a courage and nerve few ladies possess, rushed into the seething water, and seizing her friend, dragged her back just before the hungry surge bore her beyond her depth,

Papa gave us these anecdotes as we gazed on the shore. We had intended going completely round the island; but the wind changing, we ran back the way we had come, thus getting a second sight of many places of interest.

It was dark before we reached the Nab; but steering by the lights I have described, we easily found our way towards the anchorage off Ryde. At length we sighted the bright light at the end of the pier, and we kept it on our port bow until we saw before us a number of twinkling lights hoisted on board the yachts at anchor. It was necessary to keep a very sharp look-out, as we steered our way between them, until we came to an anchorage off the western end of the pier.

The next morning, soon after daybreak, when we turned out to enjoy a swim overboard, we saw, lying close to us, a fine sea-going little schooner, but with no one, excepting the man on watch, on deck. We had had our dip, and were dressing, when we saw a boy spring up through the companion hatch, and do just what we had done—jump overboard.

'I do declare that must be Cousin Jack!' cried Oliver. 'We will surprise him.'

In half a minute we had again slipped out of our clothes, and were in the water on the opposite side to that on which the schooner lay. We then swam round together; and there, sure enough, we saw Jack's ruddy countenance as he puffed and blew and spluttered as he came towards us.

'How do you do, Brother Grampus?' cried Oliver.

In another moment we were all treading water and shaking hands, and laughing heartily at having thus met, like some strange fish out in the ocean. Greatly to our delight, we learned that the schooner we had admired was Uncle Tom Westerton's new yacht, the Dolphin; and Jack said he thought it was very likely that his father would accompany us, and he hoped that he would when he knew where we were going.

This, of course, was jolly news. We could not talk much just then, as we found it required some exertion to prevent ourselves being drifted away with the tide. We therefore, having asked Jack

THE DOLPHIN.

to come and breakfast with us, climbed on board again. He said that he would gladly do so, but did not wish to tell his father, as he wanted to surprise him.

A short time afterwards, Uncle Tom Westerton poked his head (with a nightcap on the top of it) up the companion hatchway, rubbing his eyes, yawning and stretching out his arms, while he looked about him as if he had just awakened out of sleep. He was dressed in a loose pair of trousers and a dressing-gown, with slippers on his feet.

'Good morning to you, Uncle Tom!' shouted Oliver and I.

'Hullo! where did you come from?' he exclaimed.

'From Portsmouth last. This is papa's new yacht; and we are going to sail round England,' I answered.

Just then papa, who had no idea that the Dolphin was close to us, came on deck. The surprise was mutual.

Uncle Tom and Jack were soon on board; and during breakfast it was settled that we should sail together round England, provided papa would wait a day until uncle could get the necessary provisions and stores on board; and in the mean time we settled to visit Beaulieu river and Cowes, and at the latter place the Dolphin was to rejoin us next day.

We, as may be supposed, looked forward to having great fun. We had little doubt, although the Lively was smaller than the Dolphin, that we could sail as fast as she could, while we should be able to get into places where she could not venture.

As soon as breakfast was over, while the Dolphin stood for Portsmouth to obtain what she wanted, we got under weigh, and steered for the mouth of Beaulieu river. On our way we passed over the Mother Bank, a shoal off which vessels in quarantine have to bring up; and here are anchored two large mastless ships,— one for the officers and men of the quarantine guard, the other serving as a hospital ship. We next came off Osborne, where the Queen lives during the spring,—a magnificent-looking place, with trees round three sides, and a park-like lawn descending to the water's edge. Before the Queen bought it, a good-sized private house stood here, belonging to a Mr. Blackford, whose widow, Lady Isabella, sold it to Her Majesty. A small steam yacht lay off the land, ready to carry despatches or guests.

Rounding Old Castle Point, we opened up the harbour, and

came in sight of the West Cowes Castle, and the handsome club-house, and a line of private residences, with a broad esplanade facing the sea, and wooded heights rising above it; and beyond, looking northward, a number of villas, with trees round them and a

OSBORNE HOUSE.

green lawn extending to the water. The harbour was full of vessels of all descriptions, and a number of fine craft were also anchored in the Roads.

We thought Cowes a very pleasant-looking place. It was here that the first yacht club was established. The vessels composing it are known *par excellence* as the 'Royal Yacht Squadron;' and a regatta has taken place here annually for more than half a century.

Ryde, Southampton, and Portsmouth, indeed nearly every seaport, has now its club-house and regatta. The chief are Cowes, Ryde, Torquay, Plymouth, Cork, Kingston, and the Thames. Each has its respective signal flag or burgee. That of Cowes is white, of Ryde red, and most of the others are blue, with various devices upon them. At Cowes, some way up the harbour, on the west side, are some large ship-building yards. Here a number of fine yachts and other vessels are built. Mr. White, one of the chief shipbuilders, has constructed some fine life-boats, which are capable of going through any amount of sea without turning over; and even if they do so, they have the power of righting themselves. He has built a number also to carry on board ships, and very useful they have proved on many occasions. Ships from distant parts often bring up in the Roads to wait for orders; others, outward bound, come here to receive some of their passengers. Very frequently, when intending to run through the Needle passage, they wait here for a fair wind, so that the Roads are seldom without a number of ships, besides the yachts, whose owners have their head-quarters here, many of their families living on shore.

We agreed, however, that we were better off on board our tight little yacht, able to get under weigh and to go anywhere without having to wait for our friends on shore.

Leaving Cowes harbour on our port quarter, we stood for Leep Buoy, off the mouth of the Beaulieu River. Hence we steered for the village of Leep, on the mainland. Truck knowing the river well, we ran on until we came to an anchor off the village of Exbury. Here it was thought safer to bring up, and proceed the rest of the distance in the boat. The river above Exbury becomes very narrow, and we might have got becalmed, or, what would have been worse, we might have stuck on the mud.

We pulled up for some miles between thickly-wooded banks,—indeed, we were now passing through a part of the New Forest. Suddenly the river took a bend, and we found ourselves off a village called Buckler's Hard. The river here expands considerably, and we saw two or three vessels at anchor. In the last great war there was a dockyard here, where a number of frigates and other small men-of-war were built from the wood which the neighbouring forest produced. Now, the dockyard turns out only a few coasting craft. How different must have been the place when the sound of the shipwright's hammer was incessantly heard, to what it now is, resting in the most perfect tranquillity, as if everybody in the neighbourhood had gone to sleep! No one was to be seen moving on shore, no one even on board the little coasters. Not a bird disturbed the calm surface of the river.

As it was important that we should be away again before the tide fell we pulled on, that we might land close to Beaulieu itself. The scenery was picturesque in the extreme, the trees in many places coming down to the water's edge, into which they dipped their long hanging boughs. About six miles off, the artist Gilpin had the living of Boldre, and here he often came to sketch views of woodland and river scenery. We landed near the bridge, and walked on to see Beaulieu Abbey. Passing through a gateway we observed the massive walls, which exist here and there almost entire, in some places mantled with ivy, and at one time enclosing an area of sixteen acres or more.

A short way off was a venerable stone building, now called the Palace House, once the residence of the abbot, who being too great a man to live with the monks, had a house to himself. When convents were abolished, this was turned into a residence by the Duke of Montague, to whose family it had been granted. He enlarged and beautified it, enclosing it in a quadrangle with walls, having a low circular tower at each angle, encompassed by a dry moat crossed by a bridge. The whole building is now fitted up as a modern residence.

A short distance to the east stands a long edifice, with lofty rooms, which was undoubtedly the dormitory, with large cellars beneath it. At the south end the ancient kitchen remains entire, with its vaulted stone roof and capacious chimney, proving that the monks were addicted to good cheer; indeed, the remains of the fish-ponds, or stews, not far off, show that this was the case.

They also took care to supply themselves with fresh water, from a fine spring issuing from a cave in the forest about half a mile away, which was conveyed to the abbey in earthen pipes. That they were not total abstainers, however, is proved by the remains of a building evidently once containing the means of manufacturing wines; and close to it, in some fields having a warm southern aspect, still called the Vineyards, grew their grapes.

This abbey, indeed, stands on just such a spot as sagacious men, considering how best they might enjoy this world's comforts, would select;—a gentle stream, an ample supply of water, a warm situation, extensive meadow and pasture land, sheltered from keen blasts by woods and rising hills. The monastery was built, we are told, in the time of King John, by a number of Cistercian monks. A monkish legend, which, like most other monkish legends, is probably false, asserts that the abbots of that order being summoned by the king to Lincoln, expected to receive some benefit, instead of which the savage monarch ordered them to be trodden to death by horses. None of his attendants were willing, however, to execute his cruel command. That night the king dreamed that he was standing before a judge, accompanied by these abbots, who were commanded to scourge him with rods. On awakening he still felt the pain of his flagellation; and being advised by his father-confessor to make amends for his intended cruelty, he immediately granted the abbots a charter for the foundation of the abbey.

The monks, as usual, practising on the credulity of the people, grew rich, and obtained privileges and further wealth from various sovereigns; while the Pope conferred on their monastery the rights of a sanctuary, exemption from tithes, and the election of its abbot without the interference of king or bishop. In 1539 there were within their walls thirty-two sanctuary men for debt, felony, and murder. Unpleasant guests the monks must have found them, unless a thorough reformation had taken place in their characters.

Here Margaret of Anjou took shelter after the fatal battle of Barnet; and Perkin Warbeck fled hither, but being lured away, perished at Tyburn. On the abolition of monasteries, Beaulieu Abbey was granted to the Earl of Southampton, whose heiress married the Duke of Montague, from whom it descended to his sole heiress, who married the Duke of Buccleuch. The family have carefully preserved the ruins, and prevented their further destruction.

'The abbeys have had their day; but, after all, we cannot help holding them in affectionate remembrance for the service' they rendered in their generation,' observed Oliver, in a somewhat sentimental tone, which made me laugh.

'They may have done some good; but that good could have been obtained in a far better way,' said papa; 'they were abominations from the first; and the life led by the monks was utterly at variance with that which Scripture teaches us is the right life to lead. We might as well regret that Robin Hood and Dick Turpin do not now exist, because they occasionally behaved with generosity to the poor, and showed courtesy to the ladies they robbed. The monasteries were the result of the knavery of one class and the ignorance and superstition of another. Do not let the glamour of romance thrown over them ever deceive or mislead you as to their real character. When we hear of the good they did, remember that the monks were their own chroniclers. We have only to see what Chaucer says of them, and the utter detestation in which they were held by the great mass of the people, not only in Henry the Eighth's time, but long before, to judge them rightly. There are weak and foolish people, at present, urged on by designing men, who wish for their restoration, and have actually established not a few of these abominable institutions in our free England, where girls are incarcerated and strictly kept from communicating with their friends, and where foolish youths play the part of the monks of the dark ages. I am not afraid of your turning Romanists, my boys, but it is important to be guarded on all points. Just bring the monastic system to the test of Scripture, and then you will see how utterly at variance it is from the lessons we learn therein.'

We felt very nervous going down the river, for fear we should stick on the mud, as the tide had already begun to ebb, and we might have been left high and dry in a few minutes; but, through Paul's pilotage and papa's seamanship, we managed to avoid so disagreeable an occurrence, and once móre passing the beacon at the mouth of the river, we steered for Cowes Roads, where we brought up at dark.

Next morning we saw the Dolphin anchored not far from us. To save sending on board, we got out our signals, and the instruction book which enables us to make use of them.

We first hoisted flags to show the number of the yacht in the club, and waited until it was answered from the Dolphin. We next hoisted four numbers without any distinguishing flag, which showed the part of the book to which we referred, and meant, 'Are you ready to sail?' This was answered by a signal flag which meant 'Yes;' whereupon we ran up four other numbers signifying, 'We will sail immediately.'

As the Dolphin, which was to the east of us, began to get under weigh, we did so likewise; and she soon came close enough to enable us to carry on a conversation as we stood together to the westward.

The shores both of the mainland and of the Isle of Wight are covered thickly with woods, the former being portions of the New Forest, which at one time extended over the whole of this part of Hampshire, from Southampton Water to the borders of Dorsetshire. On our left side we could see high downs rising in the distance, the southern side of which we had seen when going round the back of the island.

In a short time we came off Newton River, now almost filled up with mud. Some way up it is a village, which, once upon a time, was a town and returned a member to parliament. The hull of a small man-of-war is anchored, or rather beached, on the mud near the mouth of the river, and serves as a coast-guard station.

The wind shifting, we had to make a tack towards the mouth of Lymington Creek, which runs down between mud-banks from the town of Lymington, which is situated on the west side of the river. On a height, on the east side, we could distinguish an obelisk raised to the memory of Admiral Sir Harry Burrard Neale. He was a great favourite of George the Third, as he was with all his family, including William the Fourth. He was a very excellent officer and a good, kind man, and was looked upon as the father of his crew. At the mouth of the river is a high post with a basket on the top of it known as Jack-in-the-basket. Whether or not a sailor ever did get in there when wrecked, or whether on some occasion a real Jack was placed there to shout out to vessels coming into the river, I am not certain.

Passing the pleasant little town of Yarmouth, the wind once more shifting enabled us to lay our course direct for Hurst Castle. We passed the village of Freshwater, with several very pretty villas perched on the hill on the west side of it. Here also is the commencement of a line of batteries which extend along the shore towards the Needles. The ground is high and broken, and very picturesque, with bays, and points, and headlands. On our starboard, or northern side, appeared the long spit of sand at the end of which Hurst Castle stands, with two high red lighthouses like two giant skittles. Besides the old castle, a line of immensely strong fortifications extend along the beach, armed with the heaviest guns, so that from the batteries of the two shores an enemy's ship attempting to enter would be sunk, or would be so shattered as to be unable to cope with any vessel of inferior force sent against her.

The old castle is a cheese-like structure of granite, and was considered, even when it stood alone, of great strength. Its chief historical interest is derived from its having been the prison of Charles the First when he was removed from Carisbrook Castle. After the failure of the treaty of Newport, Charles was brought from Carisbrook, which is almost in the centre of the Isle of Wight, to a small fort called Worsley Tower, which stood above Sconce Point, to the

CARISBROOK CASTLE.

westward of the village of Freshwater. Here a vessel was in waiting, which carried him and a few attendants over to Hurst, where he was received by the governor, Colonel Eure, and kept under strict guard, though not treated unkindly. From thence he was removed to Windsor, and afterwards to London, where his execution took place.

As we were examining with our glasses the powerful line of
fortifications, both on the Hurst beach and along the shore of the Isle
of Wight, papa remarked that he wished people would be as careful
in guarding their religious and political liberties as they are in
throwing up forts to prevent an enemy from landing on our shores.
Many appear to be fast asleep with regard to the sacred heritage we
have received from our forefathers, and allow disturbers of our peace
and faith, under various disguises, to intrude upon and undermine
the safeguards of our sacred rights and liberties.

Presently we found ourselves in a beautiful little spot called Alum
Bay.   The cliffs have not the usual glaring white hue, but are striped
with almost every imaginable colour, the various tints taking a
perpendicular form, ranging from the top of the cliff to the sea.   If we
could have transferred the colours to our pallet, I am sure we should
have found them sufficient to produce a brilliant painting.   West of
the coloured cliffs is a line of very high white cliffs, extending to the
extreme west point of the island, at the end of which appear the
Needle Rocks, rising almost perpendicularly out of the sea.   Once upon
a time two of them were joined with a hollow, or eye, between them,
but that portion gave way at the end of the last century.   On the
outer rock, by scraping the side, a platform has been formed, on which
stands a high and beautifully-built lighthouse, erected some years
ago.   Formerly there was one on the top of the cliff, but it was so
high that it was frequently obscured by mist, and was not to be seen
by vessels steering for the Needles passage.

As we stood close into the shore, and looked up at the lofty cliffs,
we agreed that it was the grandest and most picturesque scene we
had yet visited.

On the other side of the channel are the Shingles, a dangerous sandbank, on which many vessels have been lost.   A ledge of rocks
below the water runs off from the Needles, known as the Needle
Ledge.   When a strong south-westerly wind is blowing, and the tide
is running out, there is here a very heavy sea.   Vessels have also

THE NEEDLES.

been wrecked on the Needles; and Paul Truck told us how a pilot he once knew well saved the crew of a vessel which drove in during the night on one of those rocks, which they had managed to reach by means of the top-gallant yard. Here they remained until the pilot brought a stout rope, which was hauled up by a thin line to the top of the rock, and by means of it they all descended in safety. The pilot's name was John Long.

SCRATCHELLS BAY.

Years before this a transport, with a number of troops on board, was wrecked just outside the Needles, in Scratchells Bay. Being high water, she drove close in under the cliffs, and thus the sailors and crew were able to escape; and the next morning the cliff appeared as though covered with lady-birds, footprints of the poor fellows who had been endeavouring to make their way up the precipitous sides.

Further round is a large cavern, in which it is said a Lord Holmes —a very convivial noble and Governor of Yarmouth Castle—used to hold his revels with his boon companions. But were I to book all the stories we heard, I should fill my journal with them.

When we were a short distance outside the Needles, a superb steam frigate passed us with top-sails and top-gallant sails set, steering down channel. Papa looked at her with a seaman's eye. 'Well—well, though she is not as beautiful as an old frigate, she looks like a fine sea boat, and as well able to go round the world as any craft afloat, and to hold her own against all foes.'

Just at sunset, a light wind blowing, we took the bearings of the Needles and Hurst lights, and stood for Swanage Bay, on the Dorsetshire coast.

SWANAGE BAY.

CHAPTER III.

HEN we turned in, the yacht was speeding along with a gentle breeze towards Swanage. The Needle light showed brightly astern, and the two lights on Hurst Point were brought almost into one, rather more on our quarter. Oliver and I wanted to keep watch, but papa laughed at us, and said we had much better sleep soundly at night, and be wide awake during the day; and that if anything occurred he would have us called.

Though Oliver and I said we would get up once or twice, to show that we were good sailors, we did not, but slept as soundly as tops until daylight streamed through the small skylight overhead into our berths.

We had now learned not to knock our skulls against the beams; and both of us turning out slipped into our clothes, and thanked God for having kept us safely during the night. On going on deck, what was our surprise to find the Needle Rocks still in sight, with a high point of land on our starboard beam, which Paul Truck told us was Christchurch Head.

It was a perfect calm, not a ripple played over the surface of the water, the sails scarcely giving even a flap. Not far off lay the

Dolphin, equally motionless. The sun had not yet risen, but the atmosphere was perfectly clear, and we could see objects to a great distance. To the west of the head we observed a tower, which Truck told us was that of the Priory; and from thence to Hurst we observed a line of cliffs of considerable height, with several villages on their summit.

We got out our mackerel lines, hoping to catch some fish for breakfast; but there was not way enough on the vessel to give the bait play, and none would bite. Paul walked up and down whistling for a breeze; but it did not come a bit the faster for that, as you may suppose. Sailors have a notion—derived from some heathen custom—that by whistling the spirit of the wind will be propitiated. This is not surprising, when we remember that people on shore have a still greater number of foolish notions derived from the same source.

When papa came on deck, he told us that Sir Harry Burrard Neale, who commanded the San Firenzo, was at school at Christchurch before he went to sea, that on one occasion, when playing a game of 'follow my leader,' he, being the leader, mounted to the top of the tower, and managed to scramble down again outside, few, if any, of the boys daring to follow him.

The whole of the coast along which we were now sailing was in the days of restrictive duties the scene of numberless smuggling transactions. The smugglers were a bold, daring race—one part accomplished seamen; the other, though accustomed to go afloat, possessors of small farms and holdings on shore. The goods, either spirits, tobacco, or silks, were brought across generally in large powerful luggers, many of them in war-time strongly armed; and when interfered with by the king's ships they often fought desperately, and managed to get away. The spot on which a cargo was to be landed was fixed on beforehand. Generally, several were chosen, so that should the Coastguard be on the watch near one, the smugglers, warned by signals from the shore, might run to another. There, a party of armed men, numbering some hundreds, would be ready to receive them. As soon as the goods were landed, they were carried up the cliffs on men's shoulders, and placed in light carts and wagons.

CHRIST CHURCH AND NEIGHBOURHOOD.

which drove off with a mounted escort, who seldom failed to give battle to the Revenue men if an attempt was made to stop them.

Often severe fighting took place, and—except when a strong force of military were brought down upon them—the smugglers generally made their escape. The goods were either stowed away in secret places or farm-houses in the neighbourhood, or carried off to London, where they were handed over to the wealthy firms which supplied the means for the trade.

In later years the smuggling vessels were smaller and unarmed, the smugglers trusting to their cunning for success. Sometimes only large boats or galleys were employed, which pulled across the Channel, timing themselves so as to reach the English coast some time after dark. If a Revenue cutter was seen approaching, the casks of spirits were loaded with stones, and being thrown overboard, were sunk, the smuggler having first taken the bearings of the land, so as to be able to return to the spot and drag for them. Sometimes the Revenue cutter saw what was done, and performed that operation instead of the smuggler, the officers and crew thus obtaining a rich prize at slight cost. So enormous was the profit, that if two or three cargoes out of seven were run, the smugglers were content.

Smuggling of any sort is of course illegal. The Government puts duties on commodities for the good of the State, which duties must be paid, and the smuggler is cheating not only the Government but his countrymen; yet many people formerly did not see it in its true light, and even some gentlemen, blind to its dishonourable character, encouraged the smugglers by buying their goods. Papa said that he remembered in his boyish days a person of excellent position, knowing that a cargo was to be run near his house, having invited the Revenue officers to dinner, made them all tipsy, and not letting them go until he was informed that the cargo was safe on shore. He received a portion as a reward for the service he had rendered. The greatest knaves, however, were the merchants whose capital bought the goods and whose warehouses were supplied by them. At one time the greater portion of the population of the sea-board of Hampshire and Dorsetshire were engaged more or less in the trade.

While we were at breakfast we heard the mainsail give a loud flap, and soon afterwards a pleasant rippling sound told us that the yacht was moving through the water. In a short time we were close in with the shore, just off Bournemouth, a watering-place which has gained considerable popularity during the last few years.

BOURNEMOUTH.

We clearly saw a large number of houses and villas, with two churches standing on the side of the hill, backed by dark pine groves. A few years ago there were only a few cottages on a sand-bank, a small stream, and a decoy pond in the neighbourhood. By keeping out of the tide we made some way. and now standing to the southward on the port tack we came off Poole Harbour, looking up which we could see the woods and a house on Branksea Island, and the tower of what was once a castle erected for the defence of the place.

We were told that this island was purchased several years ago by a colonel who married a rich heiress. The place was believed to contain valuable clay and other productions; and a firm of bankers, having begged the colonel to become one of their directors, allowed him to draw whatever amount he chose. Believing himself to be possessed of unbounded wealth, he built a superb house and laid out the grounds in splendid style, giving all sorts of expensive entertainments. At length the bank broke, the bubble burst, and the unhappy man was reduced to the extreme of penury, while numbers of unfortunate people who had invested their money in the bank were ruined.

We did not sail up the harbour; but Paul Truck told us that the town is of considerable size, and that it sends out a large number of trading vessels.

Passing two high white rocks rising out of the water, called Old Harry and his Wife, we stood on into Swanage Bay, where we brought-up just off the little town. The boat was lowered, and we pulled to the end of the wooden pier, on which we landed; although Oliver said we could not call it landing, seeing that it was not land. However, we soon got on to the shore. As we looked about we agreed that it was one of the prettiest little places we had been in.

To the left was a bright lawn, with trees here and there, and villas dotted about. Some houses extend along the shore to the right, while an old-fashioned looking street runs up the hill. We observed large quantities of slabs of stone, which are quarried from the hills in the neighbourhood. The ground beyond the town is completely burrowed, like a huge rabbit-warren, and near the mouth of each quarry are huts and sheds, where the stone, which is brought up in the rough, is worked into shape. The men, instead of being blackened like coal-miners, are covered with white dust.

This portion of the country is called the Isle of Purbeck, although it is in reality a peninsula. It is bounded on the north by Poole Harbour and the river which passes Wareham, while the sea is on the

KEEP OF CORFE CASTLE.

two other sides; and a small river, called Luxford Lake, rises from some hills not far from the south shore, so that the place is almost surrounded by water.

About six miles off is Corfe Castle, on a hill almost in the centre of Purbeck Island. It is a picturesque ruin, and full of interesting associations. It was here that Edward, the dupe of the wily Dunstan, was murdered in the year 979, at the instigation of Elfrida, the widow of Edgar, and Edward's mother-in-law, who wished to have her own son, poor 'Ethelred the Unready,' upon the throne. A far more interesting event connected with it was the defence made by Lady Bankes, the wife of the owner, in 1643, against the Parliamentary forces. It must have been in those days a very strong place, for Lady Bankes, with her daughter and her maid-servants, assisted by five soldiers, successfully defended the middle ward against the attack of one of the storming divisions, the whole defensive force not exceeding eighty men, unprovided with cannon. It would probably have fallen, however, had not Lord Carnarvon raised the siege.

Near Swanage also, in the middle of an open heath, is the celebrated Aggle Stone, or holy stone, though it is more generally known at present as the Devil's Night-cap. It is a long stone poised on a single point. We agreed that it was something like a giant mushroom. The country people say it was thrown from the Isle of Wight, with the intention of destroying Corfe Castle, but that, falling short, it descended where we found it, on the top of the hill, eighty or ninety feet high. We could not decide whether it was placed here by art or Nature, for similar stones exist in other places where water and the atmosphere have cleared away the surrounding earth. Papa was of opinion that it was formed by natural causes.

Getting under weigh from Swanage, we stood round Peveril Point and Durlestone Head. The wind being off shore, we kept close in with the coast, which consists of high cliffs full of fossils, we were told. As we were passing St. Alban's, or St. Aldhelm's Head, we got out our mackerel lines. We had half a dozen each, about forty fathoms long. To each line were fastened eight or ten snoods : a snood is a short line with a hook at the end. At first we baited with pieces of white linen, as the mackerel is a greedy fish, and will bite at any glittering object in the water.

'Two lines overboard will be enough, or they will be fouling each other,' observed Truck.

Oliver took charge of one, I of the other. They had not been in the water two minutes when Oliver cried out, 'Hurrah, I've hooked a fish!' He was hauling in his line, when two more were seen skipping along on the surface, glittering in the sunlight. At the same time I felt several tugs at my line, and on hauling it in I found that I had four fish on—long, elegantly shaped fish they were, with blue grey backs and white bellies. In half an hour we had caught two dozen—more than enough for all hands for supper and breakfast.

The next morning, the wind having been very light, we ran into a little harbour of rare beauty called Lulworth Cove. The entrance is very narrow, with rugged abrupt cliffs rising far above the mast-head; and when we were once in we appeared to be in a perfect basin, the sides consisting of high white walls towering to the sky, with cottages in an opening on one side; while the sandy bottom could almost be seen through the tranquil water, clear as crystal. The cliffs consist of Portland stone. The strata in some places have a curious appearance, resembling huge twisted trees. In one side are caves of various sizes, and here also fossils in great numbers are found. Landing, we walked about two miles to Lulworth Castle, belonging to Mr. Edward Weld, the son of the owner of the celebrated yachts the Lulworth and Alarm. The castle is a square-shaped building, with a tower at each corner; it has long, narrow windows, and is handsomely fitted up. Both James the First and Charles the Second at different times inhabited it, as did several later sovereigns down to William the Fourth. It formerly belonged to Cardinal Weld, who left it to his brother, the late owner.

Though interested with what we saw on shore, we were always glad to get on board and enjoy the open sea. Sailing on, we in a short time reached Weymouth Roads, and hove to off the mouth of the river Wey, on both sides of which the town is built, with a fine esplanade extending along the shore for a considerable distance. Good old King George the Third used to reside here in a house built by his brother, the Duke of Gloucester, now turned into the 'Gloucester Hotel.' One object in his coming was to sail on board a frigate commanded by his favourite captain, Sir Harry Neale.

The king frequently wanted to go much further out to sea than was considered prudent. On such occasions the captain used to propose either whist or chess. As soon as His Majesty was observed to be absorbed in the game, the ship was put about and headed back towards the shore. When the king got tired of playing, and was about to return on deck, the ship's head was put off shore again. He either did not find out the trick played him, or was well aware that it was done for his advantage, and said nothing. The king and Sir Harry often played chess together, when the king, who played very badly, was generally beaten. Sometimes His Majesty played with some of the courtiers, on which occasions he was nearly always successful; when, however, the courtiers played with Sir Harry, they beat him. The king observing this, remarked, one day, with a smile:

'It does seem very odd, when I play with Sir Harry he beats me; when Lord So-and-So plays with him, he gets the worst of it; but when Lord So-and-So plays with me, I gain the day. Very strange—very strange.'

On one occasion the frigate was going from Portsmouth to Weymouth, when she was hailed by a boat which had come off from the shore. The captain hove-to, and an old Scotch couple came up the side. On the object of their visit being enquired, they stated that they had come all the way from Scotland to look for their son, who was on board a man-of-war; and that they had been at Portsmouth, and had searched for him in vain at a number of other seaports.

On asking the name, 'David Campbell,' was the answer. Sir Harry enquired whether such a man was on board. 'Yes,' was the reply. Davy Campbell being called, a fine youth made his appearance, who was immediately recognized by the old couple, and received a fond embrace.

The captain carried them to Weymouth, where the king, hearing their story, spoke to them kindly, and made them a handsome present; while Sir Harry promised to look after their boy; and they went home rejoicing in the success of their efforts to see him once more. I hope he promised to write to them in future, and to let them know of his welfare, and that he got back to Scotland again to see them before they died.

The king used to speak to the officers and men in the kindest way, and frequently to call up the young midshipmen and give them fatherly advice. Papa's father was a midshipman on board, so that he had heard a great deal about the king and Queen Charlotte.

One day Sir Harry, who had months before received a present of bottled green peas, recollecting them, ordered them to be prepared for dinner. On the queen being helped, Sir Harry, who had forgotten when green peas were in season, observed to Her Majesty, ' These peas have been in bottle a whole year.'

' So I did think,' answered the queen, pressing one of them with her fork, and sending it flying out of her plate and hitting His Majesty on the nose. They were almost as hard as swan-shot. In those days the way of preserving vegetables was not so well understood as at present.

The king was often sadly ill-treated, according to his own account, by those in authority, and would complain amusingly about trifles. One grievance was that he never had the satisfaction of wearing soft linen, for that as soon as his shirts had worn smooth they were taken away, and their places supplied with new harsh ones. So that, after all, sovereigns are not more free from the discomforts of life than are other people !

We heard these anecdotes as we were standing towards Portland Harbour, formed by a magnificent breakwater of granite, which runs out from the shore to the east, and then circles round with an opening about the centre. It was built to form a harbour of refuge, as no other exists along the coast which can be entered at all times between the Needles and Plymouth.

We were struck by the enormous blocks of stone of which it is constructed. They were all quarried from the Isle of Portland, which forms one side of the harbour, by convicts who are confined in a large stone prison at the top of the hill. Both on the breakwater and on shore are strong stone forts for the defence of the harbour, in which, in time of war, would also be stationed some heavy ironclads; so that a large squadron alone would venture to annoy the shipping within.

The yachts brought-up, and we went on shore to walk along the breakwater and to inspect some of the fortifications. Near us were two enormous ironclads; and as we pulled by them we could not help remarking what magnificent-looking craft they appeared, though Uncle Tom said that he would just as soon go round the world in the Dolphin as he would in one of those huge monsters.

A railway is laid along the top of the breakwater to carry stones and guns to the further end. Papa told us that some years ago, while it was in the course of construction, he came to see it; that as he was looking towards the end he perceived an engine coming along. He stepped on one side to avoid it, when, as it drew near, he observed the driver making a signal to him. He had just time to spring on to a wooden platform at the edge, when another engine, coming from the opposite direction, passed over the spot on which he had been standing. In an instant he would have been crushed to death. 'How grateful did I feel to God that I had been thus mercifully preserved!' he said.

At the outer end of the breakwater there is a lighthouse, with a single fixed red light, so that it cannot be mistaken for any other of the neighbouring lights. At the end of the south pier-head of Weymouth Harbour is also a single red fixed light; but it is far

THE ISLE OF PORTLAND.

away to the northward of the breakwater light, and cannot be seen at any great distance.

The Portland Breakwater is indeed a magnificent work. The plans were designed by Mr. Rendel, and the estimated cost was six hundred thousand pounds. The first stone was laid by Prince Albert, in July, 1849. The whole length is nearly a mile and a half. It first runs out from the Isle of Portland for 1,800 feet, when it is finished by a circular head of solid masonry. Then, for about four hundred feet, there is an opening through which vessels may enter or run to sea in case of necessity. Then comes another circular head similar to the first, from which the principal part of the breakwater extends in the same straight line for about three hundred feet, and then curves round to the north for 5,400 ft. It was formed—in the first instance—by extending stages in the direction required, on which rails were laid down to support the stone-wagons pushed by locomotives to the outer end. The wagons, on reaching their destination, were tilted up, and the stone dropped down to the bottom. Thus the work was continued gradually until the outer end was reached. The stones after they were thrown down were placed in the required position by divers, who worked with crowbars. A dangerous employment it must have been. A man employed on the breakwater who accompanied us told us that on one occasion the air-pipe burst, and that, although the diver immediately gave the signal, when he was hauled up he was nearly dead. Another poor fellow did not answer the tug, which a man in a boat above gave every half-minute. When he was hauled in it was found that the water had run under the joints of his helmet and drowned him. There were five lines of rail laid down, each carrying trucks pushed by locomotives. We were told that 2,500 tons of stone were by this means dropped every day into the ocean; and though thus actively working, it was long before the artificial rock appeared above the surface. Sometimes several weeks passed, load after load being dropped in, before the mass was of sufficient size to rise above the water.

After having been left some time to consolidate, the summit was capped by blocks of hewn stone, rising from low-tide mark to many feet above that of high water, so that the sea during the fiercest gale could not force its way over it. The piles to support the stage were what are called screw piles; they were ninety feet in length, and soaked in creosote to preserve them, the weight of each being about seven tons. One of the most curious operations was that of forcing the creosote into the piles. It was done by placing them in an iron cylinder one hundred feet in length, and six feet in diameter. Out of this the air was first pumped, and then the creosote was pumped in.

All the stones were brought from the neighbouring hill, where they were quarried by about eight hundred convicts. The trucks descended from the hill down an incline, the full trucks dragging up the empties by means of ropes and blocks. Upwards of five million tons of stone were thus employed.

While visiting the prison we heard a number of anecdotes about the convicts. Notwithstanding all the vigilance of the warders and guards, several have contrived to make their escape. On a dark night, during exceedingly thick weather, a daring fellow managed to scale the walls and drop down outside unperceived. He at once made his way to the shore, where he in vain searched for a boat. Being no sailor, had he found one, he would have been unable to manage her. He knew that should he attempt to make his way over-land he would, to a certainty, be re-taken. Finding a piece of wreck, with some broken oars, and other drift-wood, and a coil of rope, he contrived to put together a raft, on which seating himself, he shoved off, expecting to be picked up by some passing vessel. Instead of this, he was—fortunately for himself—discovered by the active coastguardmen, and brought back to prison. Had he succeeded in getting to a distance, in all probability he would have been drowned or starved to death.

Climbing to the top of the hill, we obtained a view to the northward of the crescent-shaped line of shingle, ten miles long, called Chesil Bank, which joins Portland to the main land. At the Portland end the pebbles are of the size of a hen's egg, gradually diminishing to that of a bean at the other extremity. This enabled smugglers to ascertain on the darkest night the part of the shore they had reached. The west side of the bank is known as Dead Man's Bay, from the number of persons who have perished there. The most disastrous event occurred in 1794, when a fleet of transports, under convoy of Admiral Christian, bound out for the West Indies, stranded in the bay, and one thousand persons were drowned. In this century, the Abergavenny and Alexander (Indiamen) were driven on this treacherous shore, and upwards of two hundred persons perished; and as late as 1838, the Columbine was wrecked on the bank, and many of her crew lost. In those days there were no life-boats to hasten to the rescue of the helpless seamen.

Passing amid quarries, we observed enormous square blocks of stone hewn out and ready to be transported to the shore by carts, with long teams of horses harnessed—often nine together. In the upper layer of the quarries was discovered a fossil pine-tree, upwards of thirty feet in length, and a foot in diameter, with two or three branches.

Next morning we and the Dolphin again got under weigh, and the wind being off shore stood close round the Bill of Portland, having the Shambles light vessel, which has a single fixed light, on our port beam. The Shambles is a large shoal, so called from the number of vessels lost on it with all hands. A fine Indiaman was wrecked there many years ago, coming home full of passengers, not one of whom was saved. In another day they expected to be re-united to their friends, from whom they had long been absent. How sad it seems! We who were sailing over the comparatively tranquil sea could scarcely believe it possible that so many of our fellow-creatures had thus perished within sight of land.

In former years many ships were lost in consequence of the masters not knowing their exact position. In the present day the coast is much better lighted than formerly. The character of every part of the bottom of the Channel is well known, so that a ship may grope her way up with the lead going, the mud, sand, or shells, which are brought up sticking to the grease in a little hollow at the end of the lead, showing whereabouts she is. Then the quadrants, chronometers, and other nautical instruments are of superior construction, and their use better understood ; and, lastly, compasses indicate more truly the direction in which the ship is sailing. Not that compasses themselves are at fault, but that—as papa explained to us—every compass of a ship is influenced by the iron on board the vessel. Now, before a ship sails she is swung round in all directions, so that the exact amount of the influence exercised by the iron is ascertained, and allowance made accordingly. There are also a large number of careful pilots on the look-out for ships coming up Channel. However, after a long course of thick weather and contrary winds, the most experienced master is unable to be certain of his true position ; and, notwithstanding all the precautions taken, ships are sometimes carried out of their course, or caught on a lee shore, and driven on the rocks and wrecked. I have been speaking of sailing vessels. Steamers have an advantage; but even they, from the effects of currents and tides, sometimes get out of their course, or an accident happens to the machinery, or a gale comes on and drives them, in spite of all efforts of paddle or screw, on shore.

We kept inside the Race, which in stormy weather, with the wind meeting the tide, is excessively dangerous. The seas rise up as if some power is moving the water from beneath, and letting it suddenly fall down again. When it thus falls down on the deck of a small vessel, all steerage-way being lost, she is drifted along, utterly helpless, by the tide, and if heavily laden, possibly sent to the bottom. Vessels, however, when passing the Bill of Portland, keep outside the Race, or, when the wind is off the land, close to the shore, as we were doing. When they are caught by a current in a calm, they are drifted through it.

The men at the lighthouses have on several occasions seen a vessel suddenly disappear beneath the foaming water, which, leaping up, had carried her to the bottom exactly as if she had been dragged down by the tentacula of some marine monster.

Near the end of the Bill are two white towers, of different heights, one thirty-two and the other eighty-six feet high. They are the lighthouses, and in each of them is a bright fixed light. They stand over fifteen hundred feet apart, and both lights can be seen at a great distance,—the highest being visible four miles further off than the lowest.

Close to the summit of the cliffs stand two castles, overlooking the wide expanse of the Channel. One, surrounded by embattled walls, is Pennsylvania Castle. It was built by the grandson of the great William Penn, the founder of Pennsylvania in America, and was so called after it. Its large windows show that it was not intended as a fortification, and, of course, a few shot from a modern gun would knock it to pieces. On the further side of a dip or valley, on the summit of a point of rock commanding a magnificent view along the coast, stands a far more ancient edifice, a tower in the shape of a pentagon, commonly said to have been built by William Rufus, and called Bow and Arrow Castle from the small circular apertures pierced in the walls for shooting arrows. There are large brackets above them, from which were suspended planks for the protection of the garrison when hurling their missiles at the foe.

We talked a good deal about the Quaker Penn, who, being the son of the renowned Admiral Sir William Penn, sacrificed all the advantages which his social position afforded him for the sake of the gospel, and with the hope of spreading its benign truths among the heathen of the New World, and of affording refuge to those driven forth from their native land by persecution.

On getting round the Bill of Portland we saw a-head the sandy cliff of Bridport, two hundred feet in height, with dark and rugged eminences beyond, the Golden Cap of brighter hue rising above them.

We now stood across West Bay, towards Torquay. Finding the tide against us, we kept close enough in shore to be able to distinguish places with our glasses. The first harbour off which we came was Bridport, a town of considerable size. The port is formed by two piers, with a basin further in. A number of vessels for the Newfoundland fishers are fitted out here. About a couple of miles from the entrance is the Pollock Shoal; but our craft drew so little water that we might have passed over it without danger of striking.

To the west of Bridport we saw Charmouth, with its lovely wooded heights, and next to it Lyme Regis, which has a breakwater running out of it called the Cobb, within which there is shelter for vessels. Once upon a time it was a place of considerable trade. During Cromwell's days the town was strongly Republican, and held out gallantly against Prince Maurice, who came to invest it, even the women putting on red cloaks and men's hats, to look like soldiers. It was here also that the unfortunate Duke of Monmouth landed, to try and gain a kingdom, but ere long to lose his head.

Still further west, we came off the white and lofty cliff known as Beer Head. Near to it is Beer, a fishing village possessing 'an ancient and fish-like smell.' The inhabitants are primitive in their habits, and were at one time as daring smugglers as any on the coast.

As the wind fell we dropped anchor, and pulled on shore, to visit a curious cavern, partly natural and partly a stone quarry. We carried with us all the lanterns we could muster from both vessels. We could not at first see the mouth, owing to a cloud produced by the different temperature of the outer air and that from within. The entrance is under a rocky archway, over which hung in rich festoons wreaths of green foliage. For some distance we had to grope our way through a narrow low passage, with the water dripping down on. our heads. At last we found ourselves in a huge cavern supported by substantial pillars. In the more ancient part, from which stone was quarried by picks, the sides and roof were perfectly smooth. In one place there was a dome, with four well-formed arches, not unlike the interior of a cathedral crypt. From hence we were told the stone was hewn for the building of Exeter Cathedral. The modern portions of the cavern have been excavated by gunpowder, which has of course torn off huge masses without any regard to symmetry.

When we returned on board, Paul Truck told us that in days of yore a smuggler bold—Jack Rattenbury by name—took possession of the cavern, in which to store his goods after he had safely landed them from his lugger. For some time he carried on his trade undiscovered, for, being a cautious man, he dug a vault, in which his cargoes of brandy and bales of lace and silks were concealed, covering the floor over again with heaps of stone. The Revenue officers, however, at length got scent of Jack's doings, and came in strong force, hoping to capture him and take possession of his property. But he had received timely notice, and nothing could be found within the cavern.

Of course they did not fail to pay many a subsequent visit. Once more Jack—hearing that they were coming when his vault was full of goods, and that they had an inkling of the true state of the case— managed to carry off a considerable portion. The remainder fell into their hands as the reward of their perseverance. Shortly afterwards Jack himself was captured by the Revenue officers, who got possession of all his contraband goods. In the larder of his house was a fat goose, which they were anxious to possess, in order to have a feast to commemorate their success, but the goose not being contraband, they dared not take possession of it, so they offered to purchase the bird at a large price. Jack and his wife, however, were firm. Nothing would induce them to sell the goose, though money might be useful to Jack, who was to be carried off to prison ; and the officers were fain to be content with the bread and cheese and cider with which he supplied them. Jack used to tell the story with great glee, observing that the goose was well stuffed with point lace, every yard of which was worth ten times as much as the bird.

The smuggler sometimes turned the tables on his pursuers. A daring Revenue officer having suddenly come upon him, Jack and his companions seized the unfortunate man, and kept him fast bound until they had removed all their merchandise. Though supposed to be unusually successful, and looked upon as the prince of smugglers in those parts, Jack did not manage to save money, and ultimately died a poor man. Papa said that such a clever, ingenious fellow must have made his fortune in any honest business.

We were becalmed off Sidmouth while attempting to reach Exmouth, at the mouth of the river Exe, some way up which stands the large town of Exeter. Though some distance from the shore, we could hear plainly the rumble of the trains as they passed along the railway, the water being a great conductor of sound. We had a lantern with a bright light hanging from the forestay, to show our position to any passing steamer which might otherwise have run us down. This was the only danger to be apprehended, for no sailing vessel could have come near us, and at the distance we were from the land there was no risk of being drifted on the rocks.

Uncle Tom hailed us, and we went on board the Dolphin to supper. Of course we heard many anecdotes about that part of the country. Uncle Tom, who had spent some time at Sidmouth, described it to us. The surrounding scenery is highly picturesque. It was while residing here, for the sake of his health, that the Duke of Kent died. In the same house the Queen spent much of her childhood.

At a village near Beer, where the women are employed in manufacturing lace, Her Majesty's wedding dress was made. The country people throughout the district are employed in the manufacture of lace.

On the shore hereabouts, all sorts of marine curiosities can be picked up, such as petrified wood, madrepores, jaspers, agates, and a variety of shells.

Near Sidmouth is a very interesting house, which is thrown open occasionally to public view by the proprietor. In the garden are glass houses, in which oranges, vines, pines, and the most beautiful orchids grow, with pineries, and ferneries, and formerly there were aviaries, and a menagerie of curious animals, and in the cottage are preserved a number of rare things.

Further inland is Budleigh Salterton, so named after its buddle, or stream, which running through the village makes its way slowly down to the sea. Near here is a homestead called Hayes Barton, at which

TEIGNMOUTH PIER.

Sir Walter Raleigh was born. The house remains much as it was in his days, and in the parlour the wide hearth is still to be seen at which he used to sit and smoke his pipe. It was here that the servant, coming in—never having before seen his master so employed —threw a tankard of water over Sir Walter, fancying that he was on fire.

As we returned on board the Lively, we observed two white fixed lights, which marked the entrance to Teignmouth Harbour, showing us clearly our position.

When the morning broke we were still off the ruddy cliffs which line the shore. A person first seeing this part of the coast would consider that Albion was a misnomer for England, as no walls of white chalk are to be seen rising from the blue ocean. As far as the eye can reach, various tints of red prevail.

A light breeze carried us into Babbicombe Bay, and we were again becalmed off some curiously-shaped rocks, which lie off a point called

THE BEACH, BABBICOMBE.

Bob's Nose. It was rather tantalising not to be able to get in to see more of the scenery of that most picturesque bay. We could, however, distinguish the houses among the rich groves on the top of the cliffs, in which were openings, with pretty cottages perched on projecting ledges, while others were built close down to the water. Two yachts were at anchor in the bay, which we agreed must be a capital yachting place, as a vessel can get in or out at all times, and it is sheltered from every wind except from the east. We had our mackerel lines out whenever the vessel was moving through the water. Though, as before, we at first baited with pieces of white linen, yet as soon as a mackerel was caught, we put a bit of it on to our hooks, at which its relatives eagerly bit. The ends of the lines were fastened either to the backstay or the taffrail, allowing them to pass over our finger, so that the moment a mackerel took the bait we could feel it. We then hauled in, the fish appearing at the surface skipping and jumping like a mass of silver. We caught a dozen fine fish before breakfast, and they were immediately frizzing away on the fire. As we could not move along, we amused ourselves with our spy-glasses, observing what was going forward on shore.

While thus employed a party came off in a couple of boats to picnic on one of the green islands off Bob's Nose. The first thing most of the people did, as soon as they had deposited their baskets on a comparatively level space at the bottom, was to try and climb up to the summit, which is of considerable height. The sides are steep, and present a surface of soft green grass. We saw one fat old lady, evidently ambitious of vying with her younger companions, making an attempt to reach the top with the aid of a boatman and one of the gentlemen of the party. Up she went some distance, when she stopped, though not for long, and panted for breath; then on again she proceeded, though not so quickly. But the task was clearly beyond her power. Again and again she stopped. In vain her two supporters tugged. We saw her making gestures, as if imploring to be let alone. At length down she plumped on the turf, signing to her friends to leave her. For some time she appeared to be tolerably comfortable, though we saw her fanning herself, and puffing and blowing, while her companions quickly went on and joined the rest of the party, who had gained the summit. It would have been prudent in her to remain quiet, but unwisely she moved onwards.

'She's gathering way!' exclaimed Uncle Tom; and, sure enough, down she began to slide, at first very slowly, but as an impetus was gained, she went faster and faster. In vain she screamed for help. The soft grass afforded no hold to the frantic grasps she made at it. Her cries reached us. Her companions must have been very hard of hearing, for it was not until she had slid two-thirds of the way down that any of them seemed to attend to her, and then the whole party set off rushing down the hill-side, at the bottom of which they stood ready to receive her. Though much frightened, she was not, I think, much hurt.

TORBAY.

Tom and Jack came on board to luncheon, and we agreed to row in to Torquay, and to allow the yachts to follow; but just as we were shoving off a breeze sprang up, so we jumped on board again, and, rounding Bob's Nose, we were able with a few tacks to make our way into the harbour. We brought-up in the inner harbour, but the Dolphin remained at anchor outside.

Torquay is one of the prettiest sea-side places in England. From the water we observed the houses on the hill-sides, with beautiful villas scattered about in all directions amid groves of green trees.

TORQUAY.

The shore along the north side of the bay is indented by numerous little bays called coves; the water is deep and clear, so that they are much frequented by bathers. One is appropriated to ladies, another to gentlemen. At the end of the last century Torquay consisted only of a few fishermen's cottages scattered about the beach.

We took an interesting walk on shore, which we greatly enjoyed. We visited a curious natural cavern called Kent's Cavern. The scenery round the entrance is thickly wooded and wild in the extreme, probably just as it has been for centuries. We were told that it runs for upwards of six hundred feet into the bowels of the earth, and has numerous branches and ramifications. We had brought a guide and lights with us, so that we could explore it without risk. We could see, imbedded in the rock, bones of animals which at some remote period made it their abode; and naturalists, who dig them out, say that they belong to tribes which are only found in tropical climates. Our guide showed us that there are three distinct layers or floors of earth in the cavern. In the topmost are found beads and various instruments manufactured by the Saxons, as well as the bones of foxes and badgers. In the next strata are the bones of elephants, of rhinoceroses, of lions and hyenas, of wolves and elks. In the third layer are the bones of bears, which must have been of great size, as also of a nondescript animal said to be between a lion and a bear. Curiously enough, judging from the remains found in them, the branches on one side indicate the favourite habitation of elephants, while on the other, packs of wolves were in the habit of taking up their abode. Probably the more savage beasts of prey dragged in the carcases of the creatures they had killed; and they in their turn dying, left their bones mingled with the others. We were told that flint knives were found along with the bones of animals which for ages have become extinct, pointing to a period when the country must have been inhabited by races of men as uncivilised as the South Sea Islanders. Possibly it might have been at a period antecedent to the flood, when our island was joined to the Continent.

The next morning we got under weigh, and stood across to Brixham, on the south side of Torbay. There is a wide beach all the way along the whole sweep of the bay, except near Brixham, where the cliffs again rise, and extend to the southern point called Bury Head. Brixham is one of the largest fishing villages on the coast. The inhabitants own a number of vessels. At few places is a greater quantity of shells to be picked up of all descriptions, of which we collected a number in a few minutes, when we pulled ashore. Some of the shells were four or five inches long. The occupant has the power of working itself rapidly into the soft sand, to get out of harm's way. We saw some, but they suddenly popped down, and were far out of our reach when we attempted to dig them up.

Brixham will ever be memorable as the place where the Prince of Orange landed. We looked at the stone on which he placed his foot when he first stepped on shore. It was a glorious day for liberty when his fleet of seventy ships, carrying fourteen thousand men, stood in the bay. The inhabitants were inclined to look askance at the invaders when they landed, recollecting the horrors they had endured at the hands of Judge Jeffreys after the death of Monmouth; but when they saw the banner of the prince unfurled, bearing the inscription of 'God and the Protestant religion,' and he addressed them, saying, with a Dutch accent, 'Mein people, mein goot people! Be not afraid! I am come for your goot, and for all your goots;' and when they saw the gallant array by which he was surrounded, their courage revived, and loud acclamations rent the air. It was the dawn of a new era; and England owes a deep debt of gratitude to the memory of the gallant prince by whose means our civil and religious liberties have been secured on a basis which can never be undermined unless by our own folly and supineness, although treacherous enemies within are insidiously making the attempt.

Papa made these remarks, and we all heartily agreed with him. Torbay affords excellent anchorage except when the wind is to the east, towards which direction it is perfectly open; and fearful accidents have occurred when gales have suddenly sprung up from that quarter. Some years ago upwards of sixty vessels—some of large size—had stood into the bay during a strong westerly wind. During the night it suddenly veered round to the east, and blew a tremendous gale, the rain pouring in torrents. Having brought-up close to one another, they were unable to beat out, and some breaking loose drove against others. One large vessel drove against the pier with a tremendous crash, which awakened the inhabitants from their slumbers. The brave fishermen—knowing what had occurred—rushed out to render assistance, and were the means of saving many of the crew. A little boy was thrown by a seaman from the ship, and caught in the arms of a fisherman. Several vessels went down at their anchors, others were cast on shore. When morning broke many others were seen to founder with all hands, there being no possibility of rendering their crews any assistance. The whole shore was strewn with dead bodies thrown up by the foaming seas.

THE BEACH, SIDMOUTH.

CHAPTER IV.

T an early hour the next morning, the Dolphin and we got under weigh, with a northerly breeze, and rounding Berry Head stood for Froward Point, at the eastern side of Dartmouth Harbour. We had to keep at a distance from it, to avoid a reef of rocks which runs off that part of the coast. The entrance of Dartmouth Harbour is picturesque, with high rocks on both sides. It is, or rather once was, guarded by a castle on either hand. That on Dartmouth is still held as a military post. The castle on the King's Wear side is now fitted up as a private residence. In the days of Edward the Fourth the men of Dartmouth received thirty pounds a year on condition of their building a mighty defensive tower, and extending a long chain to reach across to King's Wear. Running up the Dart, we came to an anchor opposite the town, which stands on a level space. Few rivers in England have so picturesque an entrance as the Dart, the scenery of which, though less bold as we proceeded higher up, is very pretty.

From the Dart sailed the fleet of Cœur de Lion, when he led the Crusaders to the Holy Land. In this neighbourhood also was born John Davis, the Arctic explorer, whose name is given to the strait at the entrance of Baffin's Bay, which he discovered when on his expedition in his two small vessels, the Sunshine and the Moonshine, —the one of fifty tons, and the other of thirty-five tons burden, carrying respectively twenty-three and nineteen men.

A few miles up the Dart another Arctic navigator—Sir Humphrey Gilbert—was born. Here also Sir Walter Raleigh resided ; and from the Dart he led forth those expeditions against the Spaniards, in his

DARTMOUTH.

ship the Roebuck, in which the Madre de Dios and other argosies laden with treasure, rich spices, and jewels rewarded the valour of his followers.

The most interesting person connected with Dartmouth of late years is Newcomen, the inventor of the steam engine. He carried on business in the town as an ironmonger. All honour is due to his memory, although others perfected the work which he commenced.

Dartmouth contains many picturesque, highly ornamented old houses, although a large number have been pulled down to make room for modern residences. Amongst the most interesting of the former is the curious old Butter Row. Some little way up the

BUTTER ROW, DARTMOUTH.

harbour, on the west side, is King's Wear, where the Dart Yacht Club have their headquarters. Near the mouth of the harbour is the Britannia school and training ship for Royal Naval Cadets. Here they remain until they have attained a sufficient knowledge of navigation and seamanship to become midshipmen, and make them-

selves really useful. Their regular schooling goes on all the time.
Officers in the navy are far more highly educated than they used to
be in days of yore, when a knowledge of navigation and seamanship
was all that was required.

THE RIVER DART.

Papa knew one of the officers, so we went on board the ship. It is
fitted up with a large school-room, class-rooms, and dormitories.

She has only the few guns necessary for exercising. Though once a line-of-battle ship—being built of wood—she would be unable to compete with ironclads, and of course her fighting days are over.

The wind being fair, we stood out of the Dart in the afternoon, and steered for the Start. At the end of the Start is a lofty tower. It was visible at sunset, when the wind fell almost calm. The tide was favourable, however, and we made some way. In a short time a brilliant revolving light flashed across the waters. It can be seen nineteen miles off, the tower being two hundred and four feet above high water. In the tower is a bell, which is rung during fogs, to warn ships from approaching too near. The light is a dioptric or lens-light of the first order. The apparatus consists of a central powerful lamp; round this is placed an arrangement of glass, so formed as to refract these beams into parallel rays in the required directions.

Lenses were employed in lighthouses at a very early period. When they were first made they were used for burning instruments, by collecting the rays of the sun. It was seen, however, that they would equally collect the rays of a lamp. They have of late years been very greatly improved by a celebrated glass manufacturer. Great indeed has been the improvement in lighthouses. Once upon a time they were simply high towers, which had on their summits open fireplaces, in which either wood or coal fires were burned. They were often unserviceable at the very time their services were most required. During a heavy gale, for instance, when the wind was blowing towards the land, it drove the flames of an open fire away from the direction in which they were most wanted to be seen. Sometimes, in fog or rain, the glare of the fire was visible by refraction in the atmosphere, although the fire itself could not be seen. Such was the tower of the North Foreland. This lighthouse existed in 1636, and merely had a large glass lantern fixed on the top of a timber erection, which, however, was burnt in 1683. Towards the end of the same century a portion of the present structure was raised, having an iron grate on the summit. It being found difficult to keep a proper flame in windy or rainy weather, about 1782 it was covered in with a roof and large sash windows, and a coal fire was kept alight by means of enormous bellows, which the attendants worked throughout the night.

This very primitive means of maintaining a light was exchanged in 1790 for a lantern, with lamps and other apparatus. The Eddystone lighthouse was from the first illuminated by means of a chandelier, containing twenty-four wax candles, five of which weighed two pounds. The Liverpool lighthouses had oil lamps, with rude reflectors. Down to the year 1823 coal fires were used in several lighthouses. Really good lights have come into universal use only during the last few years; and it is said that on the west coast of Sweden a coal fire is still used at an important lighthouse.

The Argand lamp is generally employed in lighthouses. It was the greatest advance in artificial lighting until the introduction of gas. It was discovered by Monsieur Argand, a citizen of Geneva. He was trying experiments with a common lamp he had invented. A younger brother describes its accidental discovery. He says: 'My brother had long been trying to bring his lamp to perfection. The neck of a broken flask was lying on the chimney-piece. I happened to reach across the table, and to place it over the circular flame of the lamp. Immediately it rose with brilliancy. My brother started from his seat in ecstasy, rushed upon me in a transport of joy, and embraced me with rapture.' Thus was the new form of lamp discovered.

Various forms of cylindrical wick lamps are employed for illuminating lighthouses. For reflectors the wick is nearly an inch in diameter. For the lens light a more powerful and complicated lamp is used. The oil is made to flow into the burners by various means. The most simple is by placing the reservoir higher than the lamp, the oil thus flowing by its own gravity to the level required. Mineral oil is now generally used, as being superior to rape-seed or sperm oil. Olive oil is used in some foreign lighthouses; and at the Cape of

Good Hope oil produced from the tails of Cape sheep is employed. It is said to be far superior to all other oils for its brilliancy in burning.

Attempts have been made to introduce the limelight, that being of far greater brilliancy than any other. We read of a curious experiment connected with it. A limelight was placed on the summit of a hill, called Slievesnaught, in Ireland, which was always enveloped in haze by day. Between it and the observing station was a church tower, twelve miles distant, and on this station an ordinary reflector was fixed, while the hill itself was seventy miles distant. Notwithstanding the great difference in the distances, the limelight was apparently much nearer and brighter than the light twelve miles off.

Great as are the difficulties of keeping up a continuous flame, they have been almost overcome by an arrangement introduced by Mr. Renton, which preserves the cylinder of lime from cracking. Gas has lately been introduced in the lighthouse at Hartlepool. Hopes were entertained that electric lights might be introduced, but the great difficulty is to maintain an equable force, as the battery gradually declines in power. There are also other difficulties to be mastered. The most successful experiments have been carried on in the South Foreland lighthouse, by an arrangement of powerful magnets. The current thus produced passing through the carbon pillars, produces a splendid light, entirely eclipsing all other modes of illumination. Years ago a limelight was so arranged as to be used on board ship for illuminating objects at a great distance. By its means, an intended attack of torpedo vessels could be detected. It was employed also in the Abyssinian expedition, for illuminating the advance camp when there was a possibility of it being attacked by Theodore's troops. Now, however, electric lights are used on board all the first-class men-of-war, incandescent lamps being fitted for internal use, and arc lights for signalling and searching purposes.

All this information we obtained while slowly gliding by the

Start. The Start light, from its height and brilliancy, can be seen much further off than the Eddystone light, which we sighted just before morning. A head wind springing up, and the tide being against us, we ran back past Bolt Head into Salcombe Range. The sun had not risen as we entered the harbour. The scenery of the entrance is wild and romantic. High and rugged rocks appeared above our mast-head. We brought-up on the eastern side of the harbour. As soon as the anchor was down we piped to breakfast.

Just beneath Bolt Head we observed the ruins of an old castle, once a stronghold of importance, which held out bravely for the Royalists under the governor, Sir Edward Fortescue. For four months he and his gallant followers withstood the numberless cannon-shot poured in from the heights above, and at length only yielded on honourable terms to the leader of the Parliamentary forces, who allowed them to walk out with their arms and colours flying.

Uncle Tom and Jack came on board to breakfast, and we spent a jolly morning, in spite of the pouring rain. I could never fancy taking a cruise alone in a yacht, especially without a crew, as two or three gentlemen have done; but nothing is more pleasant than sailing in company with another yacht, with a merry party on board each vessel, and exchanging visits, sometimes 'mealing'—as Uncle Tom called it—on board the one, sometimes on board the other, as we always did when in harbour. At sea this, of course, could not be done, except in calm weather. Although Salcombe Range is rugged and wild in the extreme at its mouth, there are some beautiful country houses higher up the harbour; one belongs to the Earl of Devon, and another to Lord Kinsale. So genial is the climate, that myrtles, magnolias, oleanders, and aloes grow in profusion, and fill the air with their fragrance. Vines and all sorts of fruit-trees also flourish—the apple-tree especially yielding a rich crop. We agreed that for a winter residence there could not be a more delightful spot in England.

The following evening, the weather clearing, we made sail, the

Dolphin leading. As we stood out, we passed a fine large schooner —a fruit vessel, I believe—which had put in here. Paul Truck hailed her as we passed slowly by, and he found that he knew her master, who said that she had put in to land her owner and his family, and that she was bound up the Straits of Gibraltar. The very next night she was driven on shore near the Lizard—either on the Stags or some other rocks—and was dashed to pieces, all hands perishing.

The wind, though light, was sufficiently to the southward to enable us to stand for Plymouth; but we kept close-hauled, that we might have a good offing, should the wind shift to the westward, when it would be in our teeth. Darkness was creeping over the face of the water. The Dolphin was about two cables length ahead of us. We had just gone down to tea, and Oliver was pouring out a cup for papa, when we were startled by a loud shout uttered by Truck:

' A man overboard from the Dolphin!'

Oliver, in his agitation, let go the teapot, which was capsized. We all rushed on deck, papa leading, and Oliver butting me with his head behind.

' Where is he?' asked papa, running forward to look out. ' Keep her as she goes,' he shouted.

The Dolphin was in stays, coming about, an operation she took some time to perform. It was evident we should be up to the spot where the man—whoever he was—had fallen into the water before she could reach it. We peered through the gloom, but could perceive nothing amid the leaden seas flecked over with snowy foam.

' Stand by to lower the boat; trice up the main tack!' cried papa.

' I see him, sir!' cried Ned and Ben, in one voice, pointing to a black spot which appeared now in the hollow of the sea, now with the foam curling round it.

' If it's a man, he's swimming well,' cried papa.

' I do believe it's Jack!' exclaimed Oliver.

'Haul up the foresail, down with the helm, let fly the jib sheet!' shouted papa.

At that moment a cry reached our ears, 'Help! help!'

The cutter was now hove to. While papa had been giving his orders he had been throwing off his coat and waistcoat. No sooner did he hear Jack's voice than overboard he sprang, striking out towards our cousin, who was on the point of sinking, being seized with cramp. He was a good swimmer, and but for this might have kept up until he had reached the Lively, for the Dolphin was much further off from him than we were. We saw papa making his way towards Jack. I felt inclined to jump overboard; but Truck sang out to Oliver and me to assist in getting the boat in the water, when the two men, Ned and Ben, jumped into her.

'Pull away in the wake of the captain,' shouted Truck; 'he'll hand Master Jack to you when he gets hold of him. Take care you don't capsize the boat. The captain will look after himself; but listen, and do as he tells you.'

There was a good deal of sea on, and the boat tossed about fearfully. There seemed a great risk of her bows striking Jack, had the men attempted to pull directly towards him. They soon overtook papa, but wisely kept at an oar's length on one side of him. My heart beat as if it would jump into my throat. It seemed to me that at any moment papa himself might sink. I could barely distinguish Jack's head, and sometimes I thought it was only a lump of sea-weed. He had prudently not attempted to swim, but thrown himself on his back. The Dolphin's boat was by this time in the water, and was also making its way towards the spot; but papa was very much nearer. I almost shouted with joy when I saw that he had got hold of Jack, and was keeping his head, which I could now more clearly distinguish, above the white foam.

'Pull round, lads,' I heard him shout, 'and back in towards me!'

The men obeyed the order.

'Now, one of you come aft, and catch hold of the boy.'

With intense relief we saw Jack hauled on board over the stern ; but papa was still in the water.   For a moment I thought of sharks, remembering how often those horrible monsters had carried off people just about to get into a boat.   Then I recollected that they were seldom if ever seen so far north.   Papa just held on to the stern until Jack had been carried by Ben a little way forward, and then we saw him climb in, Ben just lending him a hand, which was all he required.   Doubly thankful we were when we saw him also safe in the stern-sheets.

'Praise God!' exclaimed old Truck.   'If the captain had gone it would have broken my heart.'

The boat, instead of returning to us, pulled on to the Dolphin, and there was just light sufficient for us to see Jack lifted on board, both vessels remaining hove-to.   Presently the Dolphin's boat came along-side with a message from papa, desiring us to go back in her.   We jumped in at once, and were quickly on board.   Papa had gone below to change his wet clothes, when we found that Jack had been placed on a mattress on deck, wrapped up in a blanket.   Uncle Tom was kneeling by his side, exposing his face and chest to the breeze, while one of the men stood by with a lantern.   Jack was as pale as death —indeed, as we watched him with intense grief, he appeared to be dead.

'He's got too much water in his throat,' said the captain of the Dolphin ; 'better place him on his face, and let it run out.'

This was done, with our assistance, and Uncle Tom placed one of Jack's wrists under his forehead ; but still he showed no sign of life. While we were attempting thus to restore him, papa came on deck. He at once placed Jack on his back, and putting a cloak under his shoulders, slightly raised his chest, while he told me to hold his feet covered up in the blanket.   He then wiped his mouth and nostrils, and drew his tongue out, keeping it projecting beyond the lips.   By slightly raising the lower jaw the tongue was held in the required position by his teeth.   He then raised his arms upwards by the sides of his head, and kept them steadily but gently stretched out, moving them forwards for a few moments. He then turned them down, and pressed them gently and firmly for the same period of time against the sides of the chest. He continued repeating these movements alternately about fifteen times in a minute. By papa's directions, we rubbed both his arms and his legs, from the feet and hands towards the heart; and another blanket having been heated at the galley, he was wrapped up in it. In the meantime, papa having called for a bucket of cold water, dashed it with considerable force over Jack's face. How thankful we felt when, after this operation had twice been performed, we heard a slight sigh escape our cousin's lips!

'Thank God, all is well!' exclaimed papa. 'Cheer up, Tom; Jack is coming to.'

Again the patient sighed, and we observed that he was beginning to breathe. Papa placed his hand on Jack's heart. 'It beats faintly,' he said; 'but the pulsations are becoming stronger and stronger. We may carry him below now without fear,' he added, in cheerful voice; 'he will soon come round.'

Jack now cried out faintly, as if suffering from pain.

'That's a good sign,' said papa.

All this time we had continued rubbing his feet and hands. Papa and Uncle Tom lifted him up, carried him below, and placed him in his berth, having completely dried his head, and wrapped him in a warm blanket. On this the steward brought some broth, which he had been warming up, and a few teaspoonfuls were poured down Jack's throat.

Papa said he had adopted Doctor Sylvester's mode of proceeding, which is that advocated by the Royal Humane Society. The advantages of it are that inspiration may be made to precede expiration. The expansion of the throat is artificially ensured. The patient is not likely to be injured by the manipulation, and the contents of the stomach cannot pass into the wind-pipe, while the tongue is prevented from obstructing inspiration. Both sides of the chest are thus equally inflated, and a larger amount of air is inspired than by other methods. Of course, where medical men with apparatus are at hand, other plans may be adopted ; but papa said he had seen several persons treated as Jack had been, apparently much farther gone, but who yet had completely recovered.

We watched over our cousin for some time, when as both Uncle Tom and papa thought he was quite out of danger, we returned on board the cutter. How he had fallen into the sea no one could positively say, but we knew we should hear all about it on the following day.

The wind had greatly fallen, and the yacht had all this time remained hove-to. As soon as we had got on board, the boat was hoisted up. Papa shouted, ' Let go the fore-sheet ; ' and the cutter moving through the water, the yacht quickly passed the Dolphin. She, however, immediately followed our example, and together we sailed on towards the brilliant light of the Eddystone. We watched it for some time, and at length turned in ; but before getting into our berths we heartily thanked God that by His great mercy our poor cousin had been delivered from a terrible death. When we went on deck again, at early dawn, the Dolphin was astern of us. We hove to, and allowing her to come up with us, enquired after Jack.

' He's going on well, and is fast asleep,' was the answer. We were by this time near enough to the Eddystone lighthouse to distinguish its form and colour. At high water, the rock on which it stands is covered to the depth of fourteen feet, so that it then literally rises out of the sea. Its predecessor was erected by Smeaton in 1759, about fourteen miles south of Plymouth Breakwater ; but the rocks on which it was built were gradually undermined by the waves, and it had to be replaced by a new building on a firmer foundation.

We made but very little way during the night. The sky at this time had assumed a most extraordinary appearance. It appeared to be sprinkled over with flocks of wool of the most brilliant colours—red, yellow, green, pink and gold, indeed, all the hues of the rainbow, with scarcely any blue spaces.

'What a magnificent day we shall have!' I exclaimed.

'I'm not so sure of that, sir,' answered Truck. 'If I mistake not, before we get into Plymouth Sound we shall have a sneeze from the south-west. Fortunately we've got a harbour under our lee. We won't rouse up the captain, though, because he is tired after his swim and his anxiety about Master Jack, but I'll take leave to shorten sail in good time.'

'Four reefs down in the mainsail, lads,' he sang out. 'Be smart about it. Get out the storm jib. In with the big jib.'

'Before many minutes are over the gale will be down upon us!' Paul shouted out to the Dolphin, making signs to show what he expected. We saw her immediately afterwards shortening sail. Scarcely had we set the storm jib than the wind struck it, and away we flew over the now fast-rising seas. In a few seconds the wind was howling and shrieking, and the whole ocean was covered with foam.

A short distance off, on the starboard quarter, was the Dolphin. In an instant, as the squall struck her, she heeled over until the water rushed through the lee scuppers; but the foresail was speedily brailed up, and under a storm jib and closely-reefed mainsail she staggered on, keeping about the same distance from us as at first. Afar off were numberless vessels standing for the harbour; some perhaps had sailed the previous evening, others were standing up Channel, or had previously been making for Plymouth. We dashed on over the now foaming billows. The number of vessels appeared to increase as they approached either the east or the west end of the breakwater: we kept to the former entrance. Some of the outward-bound vessels ran back into Cawsand Bay, on the west side of the harbour, just abreast of the end of the breakwater on which the lighthouse stands. Every moment the wind increased, until it blew a tremendous gale; and thankful we were when we had passed the Newstone and Shagstone, two dangerous rocks at the eastern entrance of the Sound, and had got safe inside the breakwater. This is about a mile up the Sound, running east and west, the two ends inclining to the northward.

We passed by so quickly that we had but little time to examine it; but we could see what a magnificent structure it was, being composed entirely of huge masses of granite. Papa told us that it was commenced in 1812, 'a few years before he was born.' In the first instance enormous blocks of stone were thrown down, such as the tides could not move, until the foundation was formed in the required shape, and nearly a mile in length. When this artificial reef rose almost on a level with the water, after it had had time to settle, blocks of hewn stone were cemented on to it, so that it now has the appearance of a long broad wall with a lighthouse at the western end.

It has stood so many severe gales that there is no probability of its giving way, unless some unexpected movement of the ground below should occur. Until the Portland Breakwater was built, that at Plymouth was considered the finest structure of the sort in the world. In those days engineering skill had not advanced as far as it has at present. The stones were conveyed from the quarries in boats, so contrived that they could be dropped through the bottom, over the spot where it was desired to place them. The whole cost of the work was a million and a half of money, although a third less in length than the Portland Breakwater. Just inside this ocean barrier several large ships were at anchor, perfectly secure from the gale raging outside it; but we continued our course up the Sound, with the tack triced up and the peak dropped, and even then we had as much sail as we could stagger under. We were very glad after rounding the Cobbler Rock to bring up in Catwater, which is the eastern harbour of Plymouth. Passing beneath the citadel, which completely commands the Sound, as soon as we had stowed sails, we went on board the Dolphin. We found our cousin sitting up in bed.

'How are you, Jack?' I asked.

'Somewhat weak, and very queer,' he answered. 'I want to thank you, Uncle Westerton, for saving me; for if you hadn't come when you did, I believe that I should have gone to the bottom.'

'Don't talk about it, Jack,' said papa; 'you are not the first fellow—I'm thankful to say—I've picked out of the water; and for your father's sake, as well as your own, we should have been sorry to lose you. Praise God for His mercy that you are still alive, and are able to serve Him in the way He desires!'

'What did it feel like when you were drowning?' asked Oliver; 'I've heard say that the sensation is very pleasant.'

'I can't say that I found it so, and I doubt if anybody else does. All I remember is that I felt in a horrible fright, and that the water came rushing into my mouth much faster than I liked. I had a terrible pain in one of my legs, which prevented me from swimming a stroke; then I heard a loud roaring noise, while all seemed confusion, except that I felt a most disagreeable choking sensation. I really do not know what else happened; but I would advise you not to follow my example if you can help it.'

'But I say, Jack, how did you manage to tumble into the water?' inquired Oliver.

'That's a puzzle to me,' answered Jack. 'I believe that I had jumped up on the taffrail when the vessel gave a kick, and over I went. I must have sunk, I think, before I knew where I was; and when I came to the surface I instinctively struck out towards the Lively, for I could not see the schooner, as my eyes happened to be turned away from her. I should have been alongside you in a few minutes, had not that dreadful cramp come on. Beyond that I really don't know much more.'

After Jack had had his breakfast he declared that he was well enough to go on shore; but the rain coming down in torrents we remained on board the Dolphin, and amused ourselves by forming plans for the next day, should it clear up. I should have said that we had brought-up among an enormous number of coasters and small trading vessels, as Catwater is the mercantile harbour of Plymouth; while yachts generally betake themselves to Hamoaze, at the mouth of the Tamar, on the west side of Devonport.

All day long the rain continued; but I got on board the cutter, and spent some time in writing up my journal. It was very provoking to be kept prisoners; but such is often the fate of yachtsmen. We might, to be sure, have gone on shore in our waterproofs and south-westers; but we agreed that there would be no fun in paddling about a strange place after the fashion of young ducks; so summoning all the patience we could muster, we made ourselves as happy as we could on board. We had reason to be thankful that we had got into a snug harbour. Vessels were continually arriving with spars carried away and otherwise damaged, and during the night it blew a perfect hurricane.

Before the breakwater was built the sea used to come rolling right up the Sound, and vessels have even been wrecked close under Plymouth, and the town itself often suffered. Even as it was, we could not get across to Drake's Island, on which a fort is situated guarding the entrance to the Tamar. In the afternoon of the next day the weather became bright and beautiful, and we walked through Plymouth to Devonport, which contains the dockyard, and is surrounded by fortifications. We visited the dockyard, which is very similar to that of Portsmouth. We were much interested in going into the rope manufactories, where ropes and hempen cables are spun in rooms twelve hundred feet long. Several ships were building on the slips, and saw-mills and forges were busily at work. We afterwards went to Stonehouse, where the Royal William Victualling Establishment is situated. It covers fourteen acres; and here beer is brewed, wheat is ground, biscuits baked, and cattle and pigs are turned into beef and pickled pork.

Next day was Sunday, when we went to church.

On Monday morning we pulled in the Dolphin's boat across to Mount Edgecumbe, having a good view of the south side of Plymouth and the green slopes of the Hoe, which extend down to the water's edge on the west of the citadel.

From Mount Edgecumbe the noble owner of the estate takes his title. It is indeed a beautiful spot, the hill-side facing the water

PLYMOUTH SOUND, FROM MOUNT EDGECUMBE.

covered with trees, and walks cut amid them. From the hills at the north end we enjoyed beautiful views up the Hamoaze, and looked down into Mill Bay, and watched the fierce tide as the ebb made, rushing out of the Tamar, past the Devil's Point, having a good view also over the whole shore, thickly sprinkled with houses and fortifications.

The inhabitants of few towns in England have a finer place of recreation than the Hoe affords on a summer's evening, where the people of Plymouth can walk up and down enjoying the view of its picturesque shores, and at the same time getting the sea-breeze, which blows up the Sound.

MOUNT EDGECUMBE.

We were just on the point of leaving Mount Edgecumbe when we saw several people ahead of us; and Oliver, who was in front, turned round and said, 'I do believe there's Dick Pepper;' and running on he gave him a slap on the shoulder, when we saw that it was really Dick himself.

Dick stopped till I got up to him.

'I am staying with an old uncle and aunt at Plymouth; but they don't know what to do with me, and, to say the truth, I don't know what to do with myself,' he said.

'Wouldn't it be fun if you could come with us?' exclaimed Oliver.

'That it would!' answered Dick; 'and I'm sure Aunt Deborah will be delighted to get rid of me.'

We introduced him as our schoolfellow to papa, who, guessing what was in our minds, invited him to come and sail with us, as he knew we should like it.

Dick replied that if his uncle and aunt would let him he would come fast enough; and as they were strolling on before, we three ran after them. Dick told them of the invitation he had received. I guessed by the faces of the old lady and gentleman that they would not refuse. I was right; and it was at once settled that Dick should return home and pack up a few traps, and come on board that very evening.

Dropping a little way behind, we were joined by Jack, when we set up a shout, which somewhat astonished Aunt Deborah and her husband. We saw the latter, who was somewhat deaf, enquiring what the noise was about. When Dick joined them he got a scolding for being so improperly hilarious.

While he and his relatives returned across the ferry to Stonehouse, we went to see the steam floating bridge, similar to that used between Portsmouth and Gosport. We much wished that we had had time to pull up the Tamar, the scenery of which is highly picturesque. Small steamboats run up it a considerable distance, and carry excursionists. We went some distance up, to see the beautiful iron bridge which spans it, as also to have a look at the Oreston quarries, from which the material for forming the breakwater was principally procured.

On getting back to Catwater we found Dick and his traps waiting for us, so we quickly transferred him and them on board the Lively;

while Oliver took up his quarters, by Uncle Tom's invitation, on board the Dolphin. As we had still daylight, and the tide suited, we got up our anchors and sailed down the Sound, steering for the western entrance, when we saw a white light burst forth from the lighthouse at the end of the breakwater.

' Why, I thought it was a red light,' I observed.

' So it is when turned seaward ; but by having a white light looking up the harbour, vessels know when they are well inside,' answered papa.

As we ran out we passed a large fleet of fishing-boats also coming out of Cawsand Bay, which, before the breakwater was built, was the most secure anchorage during south-westerly gales. These boats were engaged in the whiting fishery. The fish are not only sold in Plymouth and the neighbouring towns, but are sent up in large quantities to the London market.

Returning on board, we stood northward, that we might obtain a view of the coast as we sailed along. Dick and I remained on deck all the morning. At last we sighted Looe, the first town we had seen on the Cornish coast. Looe stands at the mouth of a valley, at the bottom of which runs a stream. It consists of East and West Looe—romantic foreign-looking places. The houses are grouped together irregularly, with whitewashed walls, stairs outside, green roofs and grey gables, with myrtles, geraniums, and other plants of a warm climate flourishing in their midst. West Looe is inhabited chiefly by fishermen, their humble cottages being scattered about without any respect to order. However, we obtained but a distant view of it.

As the wind freshened up a little we stood on towards Fowey, passing Looe Island and Talland Point. Fowey is a place of far more importance than Looe, although much of its ancient glory has departed. The town rises above the quay, and consists of a number of narrow, crooked streets ; and it has a quiet old market-house, a fine tower, and a building called the *Place* House. The town owes much to a patriotic gentleman, Joseph Treffry, by whose means it has of late years been greatly improved.

Once upon a time, when Liverpool was a mere fishing village, Fowey sent forth a large fleet to aid King Edward—no less than forty-seven ships, with seven hundred and seventy mariners, swelled the king's fleet. Often, too, the men of Fowey beat back their French invaders; indeed, the Place House was built as a fortress.

On going out of Fowey we passed a number of coasters loaded with china clay, which is found in large quantities near this town. Arsenic also is found in many of the Cornish mines. Persons employed in obtaining it suffer greatly from its poisonous fumes.

The flashing light of St. Anthony's Point burst forth when we were about three miles from the entrance of Falmouth Harbour, and enabled us, with the assistance of the green fixed light on the breakwater, to take up a safe berth inside. We had heard much of the beauty of Falmouth, and expected next morning to be delighted with its appearance.

'Well, I really think I shall make a very good sailor,' said Dick, as we sat at supper, while the vessel lay at anchor in the calm harbour. 'I feel as well as I ever did in my life.'

'You must take care not to pitch head foremost overboard, as you were nearly doing this morning,' observed Jack; 'you might not be as fortunate as I was—to be picked up again.'

'Why, I forgot that there was the water between you and me; and when you shouted out I was going to run up and shake hands,' was the answer.

The fact was that Dick, while we were near the Dolphin, was as nearly as possible walking overboard, with the intention of getting on her deck, and would have done so had not Truck hauled him back. Dick had no notion of which was the stem and which the stern of the vessel, or how the wind acted on the sails; nor could he make out why we tacked; and several times he asked how it was that we did not sail directly towards the point to which we wished to go.

'I say, what do you call that stick in the middle of the boat?' he asked, after he had been on board some hours; 'and that other one running out at one end; and why has your uncle's vessel got two sticks and you only one; if one is enough, why should he have two?'

I explained that our vessel was a cutter, and that the Dolphin was a schooner, and that the stick running out at one end was the bowsprit, on which the jib was set to turn the head of the vessel either one way or the other.

'Nothing like asking questions,' observed papa, when we laughed at Dick. 'Stick to the custom, my boy, and you'll soon know as much as these youngsters. A person who is afraid of asking questions remains in ignorance.'

As may be supposed, Dick hit his head pretty hard against the beam above him several times before he learned to roll into his berth after the most approved fashion.

Soon after daybreak we were on deck in our shirts, intending to jump overboard and take a swim. Jack and Oliver made their appearance at the same moment on board the Dolphin, and shouting to us, overboard they went, and came swimming up. I, pulling my shirt over my head, followed their example. Dick, forgetting to pull off his shirt, with wonderful courage—which arose, however, from ignorance—plunged after me, when to our dismay we discovered that he had no notion of swimming. I was already some distance from the side of the vessel.

Poor Dick began splashing about, and striking out as he had seen me do; but, beginning to sink, he shouted out, 'Help, help!'

Fortunately, Captain Truck saw him, and hove a grating close to him with a rope attached to it.

'Hold on to this, young gentleman, until Master Harry comes to help you. Don't be afraid, and you'll be all right.'

Dick caught hold of the grating, and wisely did as he was advised. I, hearing his cries, had in the meantime turned round, and getting up to him, took a rope which Truck hove to me, and fastened it round his waist.

'You are all right now,' I said; 'but before you attempt to do anything else, learn to strike out with your feet with regular strokes. Pull your knees up, and then shove them out horizontally even with the surface of the water. There, that will do capitally; you see how fast you shove the grating ahead.'

Truck on this slackened out more rope; and Dick, delighted, soon carried the rope out as far as it would go. Then, turning the grating round, I made him push it back again towards the vessel.

'Now rest a bit—just as I am doing,' I said; 'don't move, but let your legs and body float up; just touch the grating with your arms stretched out, and as much of your body as possible under the water. There, you see, you float like a cork. Now you observe that, if you remain perfectly quiet, the water will float your body. All the grating now does is to support your head; but if you were to turn on your back, and let your head sink down into the water, with only your face above, the water would support your head.'

Dick did as I suggested, and was quite surprised to find how perfectly he floated.

'Now, you see, when swimming, you require only the movement of your arms to keep your head above water, although they also assist you to progress and to guide yourself; but the feet make most of the onward movement. Just try without the grating, and the rope will bring you up if you sink.'

Dick, who was quite rested again, did as I advised, and managed to get from one end of the vessel to the other, although it must be confessed that more water ran down his throat than he found pleasant. I then showed him how he could tread water, by keeping his body perfectly upright with his arms folded; here was a still greater surprise to him, and he was thus able to keep his chin well out of the water, and sometimes, by striking hard, to raise his shoulders even above the surface.

'This is capital!' he exclaimed. 'Though I had read about swimming, I had no notion how it was done; and I could not have supposed it possible that water could float me so easily. I had tried several times in the ponds, and nearly drowned myself.'

'Ah, but we have got the salt water of the Atlantic here, which is far more buoyant than the fresh water,' I observed.

Dick was so delighted that it was with difficulty we could get him to come on board again and dress for breakfast.

'You'll make a first-rate swimmer in a few days, sir,' said Paul Truck, as he assisted him up the side. 'I'll tell you why—you have no more fear than a Newfoundland dog. The reason people can't swim is that they fancy that they can't; whereas, the Newfoundland dog knows that he can, and goes in and does it.'

Having dried myself, I ran down and brought up a clean shirt for Dick, who asked Truck to fasten his up in the rigging.

'Better souse it out with fresh water first, or you wouldn't find it pleasant to put on again,' answered the captain, laughing; 'the salt would tickle your skin, I've a notion.'

'Not if it is dry, surely?' asked Dick.

'Yes; you see the salt would remain. Why, you'd have as much salt in that shirt as would serve you for dinner for a week if I was to, dry it in the sun without rinsing it out. Haven't you ever seen salt in the holes of the rocks?'

Dick had not, but I very frequently had.

'How do you think that salt comes there?' asked Truck.

Dick could not tell.

'Why, it's just this: the sun draws up the fresh water, and doesn't draw up the salt, but leaves that behind. If it wasn't for that, we should have salt rain; and a pretty go that would be; for all the trees, and plants, and grass would be killed, and vessels, when away from land and hard up for water, would not be able to get any.'

We had been so busy dressing that we had not had time to admire the harbour. We now agreed that it looked a very beautiful spot, with bright green fields and the white houses of the town, with Pendennis Castle on the western point and St. Mawes opposite to it. Facing Falmouth we could see Flushing, and church towers and villas on the shores of the river Fal away to the northward.

On going on shore, however, the place did not appear quite so attractive, and the streets and alleys had a Wapping look about them, and were redolent of the odours of a seaport. But as we got out of the more commercial part, the town improved greatly. One of the most interesting buildings we visited was that of the Cornwall Sailors' Home, though there were many other fine public buildings.

Pendennis Castle chiefly occupied our attention. It is of considerable size. At one part is a round tower—the most ancient portion of the building—erected in the time of Henry the Eighth. The works extend seaward, so that they guard the entrance to the harbour. We wandered from bastion to bastion, gazing over the ocean two hundred feet below us. The paved platforms, the heavy guns, and the magazines for ammunition showed that the fortress was prepared for an enemy. Should one appear, may its garrison hold out as bravely as did that under the command of old John Arundel, a partisan of the Stuarts, when besieged by the Parliamentary army, until the defenders and their brave captain were starved into submission.

We walked on along the shore until stopped by the Helford river—really an arm of the sea—which we crossed in a ferry boat. We caught sight, in the far distance to the southward, of the Manacles, a group of isolated rocks, on which more than one stout ship has been knocked to pieces. All along were fine romantic cliffs, the views rewarding us for our exertions. We returned on board soon after sunset, and I employed the rest of the evening in writing up my journal.

CHAPTER V.

FINE, bright morning found us outside the harbour, with the Manacles on our starboard bow, steering for the Lizard, which we hoped to round before noon, so as to reach Penzance that evening. We passed sufficiently near the Manacles to distinguish their black heads standing with threatening aspect high out of the water.

'It was there, sir, a few years ago, a large ship—The John—was lost during thick weather when making for Plymouth, and upwards of one hundred of her passengers and crew perished,' observed Truck, as he pointed out the rocks to us. 'She had no business to be so close in shore, and that is all I can say. It is sad to think how many stout ships have been cast away on the rocks about here. When we get to the Lizard we shall see the Stags.'

After passing the Lizard we kept the land close on board. As the wind was south-west, we sailed straight for Penzance. We could distinguish high and broken cliffs of a reddish hue extending the whole way to the Lizard; when they disappeared we could perceive a low rocky point running out towards the Stags. On the summit of the cliffs which form the Lizard Head stand two lighthouses, two hundred and twenty-three feet apart. A covered passage runs between them, in the centre of which are the residence and offices attached to the towers, so that the keepers can communicate without being exposed to the fierce gales of winter. Each of the white towers is sixty-one feet high, and contains a brilliant fixed catoptric or reflecting light.

The Lizard is the most southerly point of England, and although it is exposed to heavy gales the climate is very healthy. Just as we were about to round the Stags the wind shifted, and compelled us to stand away to the southward, by doing which we hoped, aided by the next ebb, to be able to steer direct for Penzance.

Had we gone about at that time, we should have run the risk of being driven on the Stags, both wind and tide setting in that direction. The wind became very light, and we made but slow progress.

Our hopes of reaching Penzance gradually decreased as the day wore on, and yet, while the flood was making, it would have been folly to stand towards the shore. At length papa calculated that the tide had turned. We were on the point of putting the vessel's head to the northward when a thick mist, driving up from the chops of the Channel, completely enveloped us, while the wind rapidly increased, as of course did the sea.

Dick, who had been walking about with his hands in his pockets, now suddenly found himself jerked here and there, and was compelled to pull them out to catch hold of anything which came in his way; sometimes a stanchion, sometimes the side of the vessel, now and then Truck, or me, or the man at the helm.

'Take care, my lad, you don't go overboard,' sang out papa. 'You'd better turn in and keep out of harm's way.'

Dick, however, was too proud to do this. 'No, thank you; I'd rather stay on deck,' he answered. 'I'll pull and haul, and help the sailors in any way you like.'

'I won't ask you to do that; only sit down on the skylight, and should a sea strike us hold on with your eyelids.'

Dick did as he was advised; at first he sat up, and looked very bold; but gradually he became paler and paler, and yellower and yellower, while his lip curled, and a groan every now and then escaped his breast.

'Hulloa! what's become of the Dolphin?' I exclaimed, looking round, and not seeing her anywhere.

'She was away to leeward of us when I went down to tea,' observed Truck, who had just then returned on deck. 'Where did you last see her?' he asked of the man at the helm.

'Maybe a couple of hundred fathoms astern, sir; but I don't think more,' was the answer.

We hailed the Dolphin, but there was no reply.

'She was further off than you supposed,' said papa, who had himself gone below for a few minutes.

We could not understand why they did not answer our hail, for they must, we thought, have heard us. As it was important to keep as close to the wind as possible, that we might be sure of weathering the Stags, we could not run down to speak the Dolphin. Papa, however, felt sure that Uncle Tom would also keep as close to the wind as he could, with the same object in view.

We had by this time gone about, and were heading up towards the port we wished to reach. Papa judged that we were already near Mount's Bay. Dick had thrown himself down on deck, completely overcome. I was standing by him, urging him to get up and go below, when what was my dismay to see towering above us the dark hull and wide-spreading canvas of a large ship.

'Steady! keep her as she goes!' papa shouted out.

Had we attempted to keep away, the stranger must have struck us on our quarter. Had we luffed up, she would have run completely over us, and we should have been carried to the bottom. I fully expected even then that such would be the case.

'Run forward, my lads!' he shouted out to Dick and me and the crew, while he himself seized the helm, making the helmsman throw himself flat on his back. All was the work of a moment. In another instant I heard a crashing and rending. Our boat was knocked to fragments, and the davits carried away. I saw the bowsprit sweeping across our deck, tearing the mainsail as it did so, and carrying away back-stays and other rigging.

Dick was shouting out, 'What has happened? What are we going to do?'

'I hope to get rid of this craft!' cried Captain Truck, who having seized an axe, followed by the rest of the crew, was cutting away at the stranger's bowsprit rigging.

Happily, our gaff stood, although our topmast was carried away by her foreyard-arm, and came down with a crash on deck, papa narrowly escaping being struck. The next instant we were free.

'You'll be on shore in a quarter of an hour if you steer your present course!' shouted papa. 'Steer to the south-east.'

'Ay, ay! Thank you,' came from the ship; 'sorry to have run you down, but you've returned good for evil.'

'I pray that I may always do so!' answered papa; and the next instant the stranger was lost to sight in the thick mist.

We immediately hove to, to get in the wreck of the topmast, and to repair damages. A piece of planking was nailed over the side which had been stove in, and the fragments of the boat were stowed on deck.

'I hope the Dolphin will escape that fellow,' observed Captain Truck. 'If he doesn't alter his course he may run her down, and then, maybe, wreck himself on the Stags.'

'I am thankful to believe he has altered his course,' observed papa. 'I heard the order given; but I should like to fall in with the Dolphin, for we must run back to Falmouth and repair damages. She, probably, not knowing what has happened to us, will stand on to Penzance. We can reach Falmouth, however, much sooner than we can get there, and have the work done more rapidly.'

We accordingly kept away, and in a short time the Lizard Lights appeared through the mist at such a height that papa knew we were clear of the Stags. After this we steered for St. Anthony's Light, and soon came in sight of a green fixed light on the Prince of Wales' Breakwater, passing which before midnight we brought up in safety in the harbour.

'We have good reason to be thankful at having escaped the danger to which we were exposed this evening,' observed papa, as we were taking some supper in the cabin before turning in. 'It is one to which yachts as well as other vessels must always be exposed, especially at the present time, when so many steamers are running up and down. I should have been happier had the Dolphin been with us; but I hope we may find her the day after to-morrow, as she is sure to wait at Penzance for us.'

The first thing in the morning we went on shore to get carpenters off to repair the bulwarks and make a new topmast. Papa found a boat exactly the size we required, and purchased her, for it would have taken too much time to repair the damaged one.

The carpenters made quick work. By daybreak the next morning, having all again ataut, we sailed for Penzance. When we were well round the Lizard, we fell in with a fleet of boats which had come off shore. On looking in the direction towards which they were pulling, we saw the water curiously agitated.

'They are after a school of pilchards,' said Captain Truck. 'See how the water glitters with them; if you look through your glasses at the top of the cliffs, you will see a number of people with boughs in their hands waving them. They have been on the look-out to give notice as soon as they caught sight of the school. When they see the first, they sing out "Heva;" but what it means I don't know, except to give notice to the men in the boats.'

Meantime, the rowers were straining their muscular arms to the utmost, until they reached the school, when they immediately united the nets they had on board; and thus starting from the same point, quickly began to cast them out, until they formed a circle not less than two thousand feet in circumference, in the midst of which we could see the shining fish leaping and struggling in a mass together.

Truck told us that the seine was about twelve fathoms deep, that it thus formed a wall, the upper part being supported by corks, and the lower weighted by lead.

While the circle was being formed, a third boat was employed in driving the fish toward the centre of the enclosure, as there was a risk that they might otherwise escape before it was completed. The wind was very light, and the sea calm, so that we could watch the operation at our leisure. The other boats, now fastened with long ropes to the seine, began slowly dragging it towards the shore, the fish, meantime, mostly keeping in its centre. Now and then a few would make their escape by leaping over it, but the greater number did not appear to have the sense to do this.

We followed them, as we knew where there was water for the nets there must be water for us. At length, we saw them approach a sandy beach. Here the rowers ceased exerting themselves; but they did not attempt to drag the net on to the beach, for it would inevitably have been broken through by the vast quantity of fish inside. Several smaller boats had put off, the men in them carrying small nets and baskets. They now commenced what is called 'tucking.'

The small nets were thrown out, each forming a circle, and the fish caught in them were hauled on board in the ordinary way. The other boats ladled out the pilchards with baskets. Each boat as she was laden pulled back to the shore by a passage left open for her to pass through, which was immediately closed again.

A number of women and lads, with creels on their backs, were collected on the beach to carry the fish up to the curing-house, situated some little way off on the top of the downs.

A considerable time was occupied in emptying the seine, for though no fish appeared on the surface of the water, the tucking nets brought up a considerable quantity which were swimming lower down. The whole of the vast net was then dragged up on the beach, when the fish which had been caught in the meshes, or had before escaped capture, were secured.

As the calm continued, papa took us on shore in the boat to visit the curing-house; and we heard a great deal more about the pilchard fishery from the men on the beach. We were surprised to find that the value of the fish caught in that single seine was estimated at fully six hundred pounds. Sometimes a thousand pounds' worth of fish is caught in one seine. If the fishermen were always thus successful they would soon grow rich; but they often meet with misadventures. On one occasion a large net full of fish was caught by the tide before it could be dragged on shore, and carried away against the rocks, when not only did the fish get free, but the net itself was almost destroyed. At another time, when a large school had been encircled, the fish making a dash together at one point, capsized the net and got clear over the top, not a quarter of the number remaining. Just before this, a seine had been securely moored, when a ground swell setting in from the westward before the fish could be taken out, the net was rolled over and over, and every fish escaped, while the net was utterly destroyed.

The fishing boats we met with in Mount's Bay are not only very picturesque, with their brown-tanned sails, but are amongst the finest to be found anywhere; and they often ride out gales in which larger vessels might founder. Their plan is, when caught in a heavy sea, to form a sort of breakwater of planks and spars, under the lee of which they ride with sufficient scope of cable. We were told of one, with a crew of five men, which performed a journey to Australia, having touched at the Cape of Good Hope for water and fresh provisions. Since then, several small craft, with only a couple of men on board, have crossed to America. On one occasion, a man, with his wife, came from the United States to England; but they both suffered severely from the privations to which they were exposed.

In the spring fishery the nets are shot near shore, off some sandy

inlet, at sunset; and it is curious to note that the fish thus meshed
are all on the inside of the net, but when they are meshed in the
morning they are found on the opposite side. This proves that they
come into shallow water during daylight, and go off again into deep
water at night.

The people in this part of the country were at one time greatly
addicted to smuggling, and many of their vessels were commanded by
daring fellows, on whose heads a price had been set. Among the most
desperate of these outlaws was Captain Wellard, who commanded the
Happy-go-Lucky, carrying fourteen guns. For years he had carried
on his trade with impunity, and it was said he had vowed that he
would never be caught. When, however, Samuel Pellew, a brother of
Lord Exmouth, became collector of customs at Falmouth, he determined to put a stop to this illicit traffic. Wellard had the
audacity to issue notices, promising a reward to any one who would
kill the collector. Captain Pellew was not to be daunted, and sent
out his cruisers in every direction to look for the smugglers. At
length two of the king's vessels, early one morning, found the Happy-
go-Lucky at anchor, not far from St. Michael's Mount. On seeing the
royal cruisers, the outlaws cut their cables, and making sail, stood
out to sea. Undaunted by the vastly superior odds against them, the
daring smugglers stood to their guns, and fought with a bravery
worthy of a better cause. For a whole hour—entertaining to the last
the hope of escape—they maintained the unequal contest. They knew,
indeed, that if taken alive, they would to a certainty be hanged.
At last Wellard fell, mortally wounded; but he held out as long as
life lasted. His mate was then killed, and twelve of his crew wounded,
when the survivors were compelled to surrender, and the smuggling
craft was carried in triumph into Falmouth Harbour. Here the
prisoners were shut up in Pendennis Castle; but their friends outside
were not idle. A large body of armed smugglers soon collected, and
breaking into the castle, rescued the imprisoned outlaws, and at the
same time carried off some of the wounded who were lodged in the

town. One man was too much hurt to be moved, so he was left behind, and eventually sent to London, tried, and—having been captured red-handed—was hanged. This happened only at the end of the last century.

We walked as far as the curious hollow in the earth called 'The Devil's Frying-pan.' It is like a vast crater, two acres in extent, two hundred feet deep, and converging to an orifice at the bottom, some sixty feet in diameter. Round the upper edge we observed furze, gorse, and a variety of grasses growing in great profusion, but below was the bare rock. Carefully creeping down, we noticed through the hole the shine of the water in the cavern beneath. We were wondering how this curious aperture could have been formed, when papa explained that the ground was once level, but that there had been a cavern below it, which was gradually increased by the roof crumbling away, and the *débris* being washed out by the sea, until the rock became too thin to bear the superincumbent weight of earth, when the centre gave way, and sinking down, the surrounding earth followed, until it was formed into its present shape. The sea continually rushing in, again cleared out the cavern. As we were anxious to look up it, we hurried back to the boat, and the tide being suitable, we pulled in, and were able to look up through the hole down which we had before gazed.

We afterwards visited two other extraordinary caverns, known as 'Dolor Hugo,' and 'Raven's Hugo,' up one of which we pulled for a considerable distance. Grand and picturesque in the extreme were the cliffs above us, which in every variety of shape extend along the whole of the Lizard peninsula.

The curing establishment we found was much more extensive than we had expected it to be. It consists of a circular court, called a cellar, inside which the fish are piled up on the slabs running round the court. First, a layer of salt is spread, then a layer of pilchards, and so on—layers of pilchards and salt alternating until a vast mound is raised. Below the slabs are gutters which convey the brine and oil oozing out of the fish into a large pit in the centre of the court. Upwards of three hundred-weight of salt are used for each hogshead. After the pilchards have remained about a month, they are cleansed from the salt, and packed in hogsheads, each of which contains two thousand four hundred fish, weighing four hundred and seventy-six pounds. Pilchards when thus cured are called 'fair maids'—a corruption of *fumado*—the Spanish for smoked. Originally they were cured by smoking, but salt preserves them much better.

The fish are not always caught near the shore, for the school frequently keep out at sea, where the fishermen go in search of them. For this purpose two descriptions of boats are employed; the largest measures about thirty tons, the other is much smaller. The fishermen use a number of nets—about twenty in all—called a set, which are then joined together ; each is about forty feet deep, and one hundred and seventy feet long. When united they form a wall three quarters of a mile in length, though sometimes they are much longer. The fish are not caught by being encircled, but by running their heads through the meshes, where they are held by the gills, which open in the water like the barbs of an arrow, and consequently cannot be withdrawn ; their bodies being larger than the meshes, they thus remain hanging, unable to extricate themselves.

At one end of this wall of nets a boat is secured, and drifts with the tide. Here she remains until it is supposed that all the fish coming in that direction have either passed by or been caught. The fishermen then begin hauling in the net. The operation of hauling in nearly a mile of net, perhaps full of fish, is no easy task, especially when there is a 'loppy' sea and the night is dark. This is, however, the most easy way of catching pilchards, which can be pursued at nearly all times of the year, for the fish swim about in small schools away from the shore, from May until winter is well advanced, when the water becoming cool, they return westwards to a warmer climate in the depths of the Atlantic. The fishermen told us that the most propitious time for fishing is when there is a loppy sea during a thick fog at night, as the pilchards do not then perceive the nets in their way, and swimming against them, are caught. When the water is transparent, the fish, perceiving the luminous meshes, swim aside and escape. This appearance is called brimming. As it rarely occurs during twilight, the fishermen choose that time for shooting their nets, and wait until dawn before hauling them again into their boats.

We could learn nothing about the natural history of pilchards; the fishermen did not appear to trouble their heads on the matter. Some said that they went away to far-off regions during February, March, and April, to deposit their spawn; others, that they went in search of food; but where they went to, none of them could venture to suggest.

As we wished to get to Penzance before dark, should a breeze spring up, we returned on board. Sailing along very close to the coast, we came off Helston, situated on the inner side of a curious lagoon, separated from the sea by a narrow spit of sand. Occasionally, in rainy seasons, when the streams which run into the lagoon cause the water to rise to an inconvenient height, so as to flood the shores, a narrow channel is cut in the spit; and' the water rushing through it at tremendous speed forms a broad and deep passage, until the lake speedily sinks to its usual level.

The breeze now freshening, we ran across the bay past Marazion, until we sighted Mousehole, on the western side. Near it was a large cavern in the side of the cliff, from which the village is said by some to take its name. Mousehole, though a small place, contained some gallant men, who, in the time of Queen Elizabeth, defended it bravely, under Sir Francis Godolphin, against an attack of four hundred Spaniards, who came in four galleys, and landing, did considerable damage to the neighbouring places. In its harbour we now saw a large fleet of boats, engaged in the pilchard and mackerel fishery. Not far off, on the summit of a cliff, we observed two batteries, with guns mounted, to keep any enemy who might venture near at bay.

Mackerel are caught much in the same manner as pilchards; but as they will not keep, and are not so suitable for pickling, they are sent off immediately to market.

All along this coast are caverns, which we much wished to explore. In this neighbourhood also, up a valley which extends from a pretty little place called Lamorna Cove, is a place where a large amount of the finest granite is quarried.

Tacking when off Mousehole, we stood directly for Penzance. Approaching the north shore, we had a fine view of St. Michael's Mount, rising out of the blue water washing its base, crowned by its far-famed and ancient monastery.

Sailing on, we passed the white lighthouse at the end of the pier, and dropped our anchor in the sheltered harbour, where, to our great delight, we found the Dolphin.

Uncle Tom, and Jack, and Oliver at once came on board, very thankful to find that we had escaped all dangers. Uncle Tom said that he was on the point of sailing to look for us. We had just time to see the outline of the tower, its domed hall rising in its midst, with pretty villas surrounded by woods beyond, before the fast-gathering darkness shut them out of our view, while the twinkling lights from the old town and a number of stone-vessels and other coasters and fishing-boats cast their glimmer on the surface of the water.

Penzance is a pretty and picturesque place, and is now an important fishing-town. It is also celebrated as being the birthplace of Sir Humphrey Davy. It has greatly improved since the last century, when it is said that the people refused to allow a mail coach road to be extended to their town, that they possessed but one carpet and one cart, and had not heard of silver forks; while the *Sherborne Mercury* was the only newspaper which circulated among them. When a stranger approached, the boys in the town invariably armed themselves with stones to fling at him, shouting out, 'Whar do you come from? Be off, now!' John Wesley did much to introduce the pure gospel among the inhabitants; and we saw several fine churches, in addition to a number of houses in which the floors were undoubtedly carpeted.

Next morning we put off in our two boats to visit St. Michael's Mount, on which we landed on a stone pier, with a few houses near it. As we gazed upwards at the pile of buildings which crowns the summit of the mount, we expected to find much interest in exploring its ancient halls and passages. We were somewhat disappointed

ST. MICHAEL'S MOUNT, CORNWALL.

when, having made our way up to the top, we found that it had been so greatly renovated as to be deprived of much of its antique look. But it is a grand old pile,—the tower, which rises in the centre, and is the most ancient portion, having been built in the fifteenth century. Although used as a monastery, it was strongly fortified; and guns round the walls still remain, notwithstanding that they would be of little use in the present day. We saw, just above the edge of a cliff, a curious and ancient cross, richly carved. The monks' refectory was, after the Reformation, turned into a banqueting hall; and the cornice which runs round it represents hunting scenes of boars, stags, wolves, and bulls. Obtaining a light, we descended by a flight of stairs, through a small door in the side of the wall, down to a low, dark vault, in which it was said the bones of a man were discovered when the vault was found, some years ago. Whether he had been shut up there by the monks, or had been a prisoner of war, it was difficult to determine. The vault was evidently used for the purpose of concealing the treasure of the monastery.

We afterwards climbed up by a narrow spiral staircase to the top of the tower, from whence we had a fine view over the whole of the bay and the surrounding shores. On the summit are the remnants of a lantern which was formerly used as a beacon for the benefit of mariners entering the bay. This monastic castle, for such it should be called, has frequently been besieged. On the last occasion it was held by Sir Francis Bassett, for Charles the First, when it was besieged by the Parliamentary forces; but he was at last compelled to capitulate, though as a reward for his bravery he and his followers were allowed to retire to the Scilly Islands. Altogether, we agreed that it was one of the most interesting spots we had hitherto visited during our voyage.

As we were anxious to see the Land's End, and could not approach the point in the yachts without risk, we determined to visit the famous promontory by land. Engaging a carriage, we set off, making a circuit to see several curiosities on our way. First we stopped at a cave, apparently part of a fortification. Near it are two upright granite rocks, fifty yards apart, said to form the head and foot-stones of a Cornish giant.

'He must have been a tall fellow!' exclaimed Oliver, as he paced the distance between the two stones. The site is called the Giant's Grave; and a countryman who met us declared that 'Once upon a time, two giants fought here,—for I don't know how many days,—until one had his skull knocked in by a club formed out of an enormous oak.'

Another legend assigns the name of 'The Pipers' to them, because not far off is a circle of nineteen stones, said to be the petrified bodies of a number of damsels who spent the Sabbath in dancing instead of going to church. These stones were therefore called the Dancing Stones, or the 'Merry Maidens.' Some time ago a farmer, to whom the field on which they stand belongs, wishing to get rid of them, commenced operations by harnessing a yoke of oxen to one of the damsels; but he was warned to desist, in consequence of one of the animals falling down dead. Since then they have remained unmolested, except by the hammers of amateur geologists.

Farther on we reached a fine headland called Castle Treryn, an ancient entrenchment having occupied the whole area. On the summit stands the famous Logan rocking-stone, which is said to weigh eighty tons. Putting our shoulders under it, by some exertion we made it rock or move. Once upon a time a Lieutenant Goldsmith of the Royal Navy—a nephew of the author of the *Vicar of Wakefield*—happening to land here, took it into his head to try to dislodge the stone; and, somewhat to his dismay, probably, he succeeded in doing so completely. Over it fell, but did not go rattling down the cliffs, as I had heard asserted, for it would then have inevitably been broken to pieces. Still, as the stone was on the ground, and could no longer rock, the people in the neighbourhood were highly incensed against the lieutenant, especially as visitors were not likely to come as heretofore to the spot. They accordingly memorialized the Admiralty, complaining of what had happened, and Lieutenant Goldsmith was ordered to replace it. He thereupon erected over it some vast shears, and by means of tackles ingeniously contrived, lifted back the stone on to the pivot on which it had before rested. He, however, found it impossible to poise it as nicely as before, and consequently it is necessary to exert more strength to make it move than was required before it had been tumbled over. To make some amends to the people, the gallant lieutenant replaced another stone of a similar character which had fallen from its position.

We passed numerous very small cottages built with enormous stones. They have diminutive windows, which will not open —this style of architecture being necessary to resist cold and the fierce gales which blow across the narrow peninsula. As we proceeded, trees grew

FIRST AND LAST HOUSE, LAND'S END.

scarcer and scarcer. At last we came to a tavern with a sign-board, on the east side of which was painted 'The last refreshment house in England;' and on the other, facing the Atlantic, 'The first refreshment house in England.'

Among the many pretty coves we saw was one called Vellan Dreath, or the Mill in the Sand; but not a vestige of the mill remains. Once upon a time it was inhabited by a bold miller and his stout son. One morning, as he was looking seawards, just as he was about to turn on the water to move his mill, he observed above the sea-mists the masts of a tall ship. What object she had in coming so near the coast he could not divine; but it was as well to be cautious, lest she should prove an enemy. Going down to the edge of the water, he listened, when he heard the sound of oars, indicating the approach of a boat, and voices which sounded strange to his ears. Calling to his son, he summoned him back into the mill, the door of which he closed. A hole formed for lifting the latch enabled him to look out, when he saw a party of Spaniards with long guns coming towards the mill. On this. running the muzzle of his piece through the hole, he ordered the enemy to keep off; but as they—regardless of his warning—still came on, he fired, and knocked one of them over. After he had fired, the Dons retired to a distance; but it was pretty evident that they intended to attack the mill. On this. being certain that the small garrison could not hold out, and seeing the enemy again approaching. he set fire to a rick of furze, and while the wind blew the smoke in the faces of the Spaniards, he and his son, each taking a sack of flour on their shoulders, issued out through a back door and made their way up the hill. They had got some distance up the steep ascent before they were discovered by the Spaniards, who then began firing at them. The gallant millers made their escape, but the old man received a wound of which he ultimately died. The son declared that his sack, from the number of bullets in it, was far heavier than when he set out.

Near it is Sennen Cove, where there is a fishing village and a Coastguard station. Some way off the shore, rising from amid the foaming waves, is a high rock, denominated 'The Irish Lady,' from the peculiarity of its form, which is that of a female figure, with a long robe, advancing into the sea. We were told that many years ago an Irish vessel was driven on the rocks; but that one female alone was seen clinging to the wreck until the waves washed her away, and that it is her figure which now appears still surrounded by the foaming billows.

'I wonder she hasn't got tired of standing out there all by herself!' exclaimed Dick.

Another rock in the same neighbourhood, far out in the sea, is called 'The Armed Knight.' It is a magnificent pile, two hundred feet in height. The summit, from the point we saw it, assumes the profile of a man's head, while the regular way in which the blocks of granite join each other has much the appearance of armour. As Dick observed, he must have been related to the giant whose grave we had visited.

Later in the day we reached what we were assured was the Land's End, although other rocks appeared to project as far westward into the ocean. It was a grand scene. In all directions were headlands, crowned by what appeared to be ruined castles and towers, rocks scattered around, piled up into a variety of fantastic shapes; while afar off we could distinguish the faint outline of the Scilly Islands. Imagination might picture them as some fairy land, likely at any moment to vanish, though we had little doubt that they would remain to let us pay them a visit. A few hundred yards off is a headland called 'Doctor Johnson's Head,' because the rocks at the extremity present somewhat the appearance of a human face with massive features, like those of the great lexicographer. The point is surmounted by an oval boulder, which is so easily poised on one point that it rocks far more easily than the better known Logan Rock.

Land's End itself consists of a mass of granite which extends in a lofty ridge far into the sea, the summit crowned by rocks which have the appearance of some vast castle. Indeed, so curiously shaped are the rocks in this neighbourhood, that they have generally an artificial appearance.

Many years ago, a party of officers had come to Land's End on a visit of inspection. Two of them proposed riding down the slope towards the extreme point, which has perpendicular precipices on both sides. A third officer—Captain, afterwards General, Arbuthnot

—dismounted, and led his horse after his companions, considering that the place was too dangerous to ride down. After enjoying the view for some time, the party proposed returning, when Captain Arbuthnot, believing that there would be no danger in riding up, mounted to follow his companions. Scarcely, however, was he in his saddle, than his horse, a spirited animal, became restive, and began to kick and plunge, inclining to the precipice on the right side. In vain its rider tried to show the animal her danger; to his horror, he found that her feet were close to the precipice. He had just time to throw himself off, and clear his feet from the stirrups, when over she went down the cliff, and was dashed to pieces, leaving him on the slippery sward close to the edge of the precipice. The spot where the accident occurred is still shown.

Two miles off Land's End, on a mass of rocks which rise some seventy feet above the surface at low water, stands the Longships Lighthouse, the summit of which is fifty-six feet above the rock. The tower is divided into three stories. In the lower is kept provisions, with water and coal; the second is a cooking-room and oil-store: while the third is a sleeping-room. The lantern consists of a brilliant catoptric fixed light, produced by nineteen Argand lamps. It was built in 1793 by a Mr. Smith. Before the granite blocks of which it is composed were brought to the rock, they were hewn out and put together at Sennen Cove. The stones are dovetailed one into the other, and are secured by oak trennels strongly cemented. Often, when a storm is raging, the waves beat completely over the structure; indeed, when any wind is blowing, it is surrounded by masses of foam. Four men belong to the lighthouse, three always remain in it, and one goes on leave every twenty-eight days, when the weather permits; but this, during the winter season, is very often impossible; and sometimes for weeks together the man on shore cannot get off.

During a storm, some years ago, so furious were the waves, that the lantern was broken in, and the keepers fully believed that the whole structure would be washed away. We heard of an inspector who had visited the rock during fine weather, and who had begun to find great fault with the large stock of provisions kept in the store-house. Before the cutter which brought him could return, a heavy

LONGSHIPS LIGHTHOUSE.

gale sprang up, and he himself was kept a prisoner for nine weeks, after which the lighthouse-keepers heard no more complaints as to the quantity of food kept in store.

The bright light, which burst forth from the top of the white tower, warned us to beat a retreat

Not far from Land's End we found another inn, which looked much out of place in that wild region. Dick declared that it should be called 'The firster and laster inn in England,' it having been built some time after the one we had previously passed. As it was too late to return to Penzance that evening, we took advantage of it, and put up there for the night, that we might visit some mines and other interesting spots in the neighbourhood.

The first thing in the morning we set off to visit the Botallack mine, the machinery of which we could see perched among crags that looked almost inaccessible. We had not time to go into the mine, which is carried far under the ocean. In some places there is not more than six or eight feet between the roof of the galleries and the water. Once the sea broke into it; but the hole was plugged and the water pumped out. On another occasion, a party of miners discovered a magnificent piece of ore little more than three feet below the ocean. The treasure tempted them to risk their lives to obtain it. They cut it out, and successfully filled up the hole. It is said that so terrific is the noise during heavy weather, when the waves dash in on the shore, and roll the pebbles backwards and forwards, that even the bold miners are compelled to rush out, unable to endure the uproar. The scene was most extraordinary. Vast pumps appeared amid the cliffs, unceasingly drawing up water, which rushed in a red torrent into the sea. Steam and smoke were spitting out in all directions; and men, women, and boys were employed in sorting the ore as the kibble brought it to the surface. This was only one of many similar mines along the coast. Having satisfied our curiosity, we drove back to Penzance; and at once repaired on board the yachts, as papa and Uncle Tom were unwilling to lose more of the fine weather.

Without a moment's delay, the anchors were got up, and we made sail out of Mount's Bay.

BOTALLACK MINE, CORNWALL.

CHAPTER VI.

N passing Rundlestone, a hidden rock upwards of a mile from the southern shore of the Land's End peninsula, we came in sight of the Wolf Rock, about ten miles off the coast. It was one of the greatest dangers in the English Channel, for the beacon placed on it was not visible at night or during thick weather. Attempts were made to fix bells on the rock, which might be rung by the waves dashing against them; but the first gale quickly carried away the well-intentioned contrivance. Now, however, a lighthouse has been erected of great strength and massiveness, to endure the fierce battering it must encounter from the angry billows. The wind shifting against us, we had a good view of the Wolf Rock, and afterwards of the Longships Lighthouse, the white tower of which, rising above its black base, can be seen afar off. It was with difficulty that we could distinguish Land's End from the neighbouring headlands, Cape Cornwall, to the northward, apparently approaching further into the ocean.

As we looked at that fearful Wolf Rock, we thought of the number of vessels, out of their reckoning, homeward-bound, or coming round from the North Sea, intending to proceed up the Irish Channel, which must have run against it in days gone by. But now the red and white 'flashes' which follow each other at half-minute intervals all through the night, enable mariners to steer clear of the danger.

Papa remarked: 'I wish that every Christian man would remember that he is bound to be a lighthouse, and to warn his fellows of the peril into which they are running. How many human beings would thus be saved from shipwreck, if all thus understood their duty and acted accordingly! Remember the text—"Let your light so shine before men, that they may see your good works, and glorify your Father which is in heaven."'

Papa told us it was the opinion of geologists that the surrounding rocks, as well as the Scilly Isles, were once connected with England. Indeed, of that there can be no doubt. Tradition declares that articles have been fished up proving that cities once stood on spots over which the tides now ebb and flow; but then tradition is the most uncertain of all uncertain things. Although an iron kettle may have been fished up from the bottom of the sea, it might only show that it had been thrown overboard, or washed out of a sunken vessel.

As we had determined not to be defeated, we continued beating backwards and forwards until we saw the coast of Cornwall, and the bright beams of St. Agnes' Lighthouse appeared on our port bow; while those from the light-vessel moored off the Seven Stones were seen on the other.

We hailed the Dolphin, which passed us on the opposite tack; and papa agreed to lead in.

'The sooner we are in the harbour the better,' he observed; 'I don't quite like the look of the weather.'

Clouds had, indeed, been thickly gathering in the south-west; and the stars, which had hitherto shone brightly, were totally obscured. The wind also, which had been steady, now began to blow in strong squalls, compelling us to shorten sail. First, two reefs were taken down in the mainsail; it was then closely reefed, while the foresail was hauled down, and the storm jib set. Still, it was as much as the cutter could do to look up to it. Heavy seas now began to roll in from the Atlantic, tumbling the cutter about. Now she rose to the summit of a foam-crested wave, now she sank down into the hollow.

'Will she ever come up again?' exclaimed Dick, who was clinging on to the companion hatch. 'Oh, dear—oh, dear! I thought the sea was always going to remain as smooth as it has been since we sailed.'

Presently, up we rose again, and Dick drew a long breath. Papa, however, advised him to go below.

'We will look after the craft in the meantime, my boy,' he said. 'There is nothing to fear, though it is possible that one of these seas may break on board, and, if you are not on the look-out, may carry you away.'

A flash of lightning which now burst forth from a dark cloud, accompanied by a heavy squall, causing the cutter to heel over until her lee bulwarks were almost under water, revealed Dick's terrified countenance. As may be supposed, he clung on the harder to the companion hatch; and papa had to repeat his advice and help him down the ladder.

'You'd better go too, Harry,' he said. 'I can't answer for a sea not coming on board; and it might tear even you from your hold. Those who remain on deck will secure themselves with lashings; and as the craft is as light as a cork, we shall weather out the gale, even should it come on to blow twice as hard as it now does.'

I begged to be allowed to remain.

'Well, it will be but a summer gale. You may stay on deck; but here, make yourself fast with this rope;' and papa secured one round my body, which he fastened to the companion hatch.

He now gave the word to set the trysail; and the mainsail being stowed, it was hoisted in its stead. Still we had as much sail as the cutter could carry. The night had become very dark, except when

the flashes of lightning dashed from the black clouds. Papa had
resolved to heave the vessel to, when we caught sight of a white sail
a short distance ahead of us.

'That must be the schooner,' shouted Truck; 'she is taking a wise
course, and is intending to run under Cape Cornwall, or maybe to get
into St. Ives Bay, in case the gale should continue.'

'We may as well do the same,' observed papa; and the helm being
put up, away we ran before the wind.

Though the cutter behaved very well, still there was a chance of
our being pooped. A strong current was setting us in the direction
of the Longships light, which now appeared broad on the starboard
bow. We ran on, following, as we supposed, the Dolphin; but she
was going faster than we were, and we soon lost sight of her. We
knew our exact position, for, although we had got beyond the gleam
of St. Agnes' Lighthouse, we could still see on our port-bow the two
lights on board the light-vessel off the Seven Stones. I own I wished
that we were safe back in port, though papa appeared so cool that I
could not suppose there was any real danger; still, as the seas came
rolling up on either quarter, high above our deck, it seemed impossible
that the vessel could escape being swamped.

At last papa peremptorily ordered me to go below, and coming to
where I was standing, lifted up the hatch and literally pushed me
down, closing it again over me. I groped my way into the cabin,
where I found Dick holding on to one of the sofas. The cabin lamp
had not been lighted, so that we were in perfect darkness.

'Oh! where are we? Where are we going? What's about to
happen?' he exclaimed, in a weak voice, which I could barely hear
amid the uproar caused by the seas dashing against the vessel's sides
and deck, the creaking of the bulk-heads, the whistling of the wind,
and other sounds.

'Papa says there is no danger; so you need not be alarmed, Dick,'
I observed. At the same time I confess that I felt far from comfortable myself. Poor Dick was dreadfully sick. I had to assist him as

best I could; but I need not enter into particulars. His sickness overcame his terror. Every now and then, however, he cried out, 'Oh, I wish I was on shore! couldn't your papa land me? If he cannot, please ask him to throw me overboard. Oh, how miserable I am! Oh dear, oh dear!' and then for certain reasons he could not utter a word.

Having to attend to him made me think perhaps less of our situation; but I know that I was not at all happy. All sorts of dreadful thoughts came into my mind. Every instant I expected to hear a tremendous sea come rushing over our deck, and perhaps to find that papa or some of the men had been washed away. I was most anxious about papa. If he was lost, I believed that the vessel would be lost too; but then I remembered what a good sailor he was; and as he had been to sea all his life, he was sure to manage the vessel properly; and, as he had often said, she was such a tight little sea-boat she would go through anything. Still, we were in a part of the ocean where the tide runs with great force, and when meeting the wind a very awkward sea is beaten up. This made the cutter tumble about in a way I had never known her do before. Everything in the cabin had been securely lashed except a few books and charts. First one came flying out as the vessel rolled over, and hit poor Dick on the head.

'What a shame of you to be heaving books at me, Harry!' he cried out.

I assured him that I was innocent of anything of the sort; and presently another flew out, and nearly knocked me over. I tried to reach the books, to secure the remainder; but the whole lot came tumbling out, and sent me sprawling on the cabin floor. I picked myself up, and crawled back to assist Dick, who just then greatly required my support.

I cannot describe more of that fearful night. Finding that Dick was tolerably quiet, advising him to hold fast to the sofa, I lay down at the opposite end, where I clung on like grim death; and, in spite of the tossing and tumbling the vessel was undergoing, I at length fell asleep. I cannot say I was very fast asleep, for I was conscious all the time that something very unpleasant was taking place.

Occasionally I fancied that I was being tossed in a blanket by my schoolfellows, who were jeering round me as I entreated to be let down; then that a wild bull was throwing me up in the air, and was about to catch me on his horns. Then that I was on a raft danced up and down by the foaming waters. Now, that I was on deck, and was pitched overboard, and left to struggle alone amid the raging seas. My voice—as I shouted out for help—awoke me; and to my infinite satisfaction I found that the vessel was much steadier than she had hitherto been. In a short time daylight gleamed through the bull's eyes on deck, and getting up, I made my way to the companion hatch. Just before I reached it, it was lifted up, and papa put his head down.

'All right, my lads,' he said; 'we are under the lee of the land, and the wind has greatly moderated. In a short time, if it continues to be fine, we shall be able to haul up and beat back to Scilly. How is Dick?'

'He has been very ill; but he is now fast asleep; and it would be a pity to awaken him,' I answered as I got up on deck.

I looked round, and could see the land on the starboard side bearing south and east. The Longships Lighthouse was no longer in view. I could make out a cape, which papa said was Cape Cornwall, to the southward. I looked out for the Dolphin, but she was nowhere to be seen.

'I am rather puzzled about her,' said papa; 'she could scarcely have run us out of sight. Perhaps the vessel we saw last night was a stranger bound up the Bristol Channel; still, she was closer in shore than was advisable. Possibly the Dolphin remained hove-to, or if not, perhaps she bore up before we did, and is already safe at anchor in St. Ives Bay. We must make the best of our way there. Hand me the glass.'

I took the telescope from the bracket on which it hung inside the companion 'hatch, and gave it to him. He looked earnestly for a minute towards some high rocks which were at some distance from the land.

'I feared so,' he observed; 'there's a vessel on the rocks, with her masts gone; but she's much too high for the Dolphin, or I should have supposed it was that. We will stand in closer and have a look at her; we shall find less sea there, and the wind has gone down so much and the weather is so evidently improving, that we shall run no unnecessary danger. What do you think, Truck?'

Papa had handed the glass to Truck, who was looking through it.

'If anybody is left alive, we may have a chance of taking them off,' answered Truck. 'As the wreck lies, she is not likely to be seen from the shore, and the people may perish before they can receive assistance.'

As soon as it was settled that we should do so, the trysail was lowered, and the mainsail, with a couple of reefs down, was set, with a bigger jib and foresail. We now stood in towards the rocks. As we drew nearer, we saw that the wreck was that of a large vessel, and that she so lay as to be partially sheltered from the heavier seas, which must have been raging when she struck. The depth of water, however, would prevent us anchoring. Papa proposed to heave the cutter to while the boat pulled in under the lee side of the rock, whence he hoped to be able to communicate by means of lines with the people on board, should any still remain alive.

As we drew still nearer, I took the glass, and turning it towards the wreck, I could distinguish a number of people on the fore part, which was the least battered, from having been more protected than the stern. I spied out a man who had climbed to the upper part of the bulwarks, and was waving a handkerchief or towel.

'She went on shore at high water, and the tide left her where she is. When it returns it will wellnigh cover her; and as those poor people will be washed off, there is no time to be lost,' observed Truck.

Papa agreed with him. We had a long way to beat back to where the wreck was lying. Those on board probably knew their danger. How anxiously must they have looked out for our coming!

It was a question whether we could get near the vessel. Papa ordered all the spare rope we possessed to be coiled away in the boat, and he had one of our round life-buoys, slung by four ropes, fastened to a block—the largest we had on board. This formed a cradle, by which, if necessary, we could haul the people from the wreck to the boat, could we once get close enough to pass a rope on board.

At length, getting sufficiently near to leeward of the rock, we hove to, when, greatly to my satisfaction, papa allowed me to go and steer, while he, with two hands, went in the boat, leaving Truck and Dick to manage the vessel. We first pulled round to where the wreck lay; but papa was soon convinced that we could not approach her on the weather side without great risk of being swamped. Papa hailed, and made signs that we were going round on the lee side of the rock; we there found a little cove, or bay, into which we could pull and remain without risk by securing the boat with a grapnel.

Carrying the line and the cradle, we made our way over the rock until we got abreast of where the vessel lay. The distance was considerable, and the water whirled and surged round and round in a way which would make swimming difficult; still I had often swum much further.

'Let me carry a line,' I said to papa. 'I think I can do it, if no one on board will undertake to swim to the rock.'

We shouted to the people, who, strange to say, did not hear us; nor had they seen us come over the rock, for they had all been looking seaward. Two or three of the men at length appeared on the side nearest us; but when we called on them to swim on shore, they shook their heads, evidently not liking to make the attempt. The tide was now flowing fast, and their position was every instant becoming more perilous. It, however, made the passage less dangerous, as even in a few minutes the water became smoother than it had hitherto been.

The people on board threw an oar, with a line fastened to it, into the water; but it was carried sometimes on one side, sometimes on the other, and did not approach the rock.

'I am sure I can do it, papa,' I said, at length. 'Just fasten a line round me, and I shall be able to get hold of that oar. You can soon haul me back.'

Papa no longer refused my request, and having stripped, and fastened a rope round my waist, I plunged in, and struggled hard to make way through the hissing water. Sometimes I found myself carried onwards towards the stern of the vessel, but another sea brought me back again; and in a few minutes, greatly to my satisfaction, I clutched hold of the oar, when, securing the end of the rope which held me round it, I sung out to papa and the men to haul away. In a short time I was brought back close to the rock. My chief danger was in landing, as the sea at times beat violently against it; but papa, quickly seizing me, hauled me up.

'You have acted bravely, Harry,' he said. 'Now put on your clothes, and we shall soon have a communication with the vessel.'

While I was dressing, the rope with the cradle was hauled up to the side of the vessel, and secured to a stanchion; when the crew, getting up a stouter warp, shouted out to us to haul it in, they having secured the cradle to it. We thus had a safe communication established with the wreck, and a stout line to draw the cradle backwards and forwards.

Greatly to our surprise, a female was the first person we drew ashore; she burst into tears as we lifted her out of the cradle. Another and another followed; two had infants in their arms; and then came two little boys secured to the cradle. Three men followed, each with a child.

'Have all the women and children landed?' asked papa.

'All who have escaped,' was the answer. 'Several were washed away with the master and two mates.'

Six more men now came, the sole survivors of the crew.

'Are all hands out of the ship?' asked papa.

'Every soul, sir,' answered one of the men.

There was no time to make inquiries as to how the vessel was wrecked. We heard that she was a homeward-bound barque from the United States, and that the passengers on board were returning to see their friends. We hurried over to the leeside of the rock, and at once embarked the two women with the infant, who seemed to be totally exhausted.

As soon as we got alongside, we lifted them on board, where papa and I remained, he sending the boat back with our two men. Truck had lighted the galley fire, and we soon had some hot broth for the poor creatures, who, having taken off their wet clothes, got into our beds. Papa then looked out all the blankets, and we made up as many beds as we could on the sofa and cabin deck.

By this time the boat had returned with the remaining women and children. She made no less than seven trips before all were brought off; and, as may be supposed, our little vessel was pretty well crowded. Even the men were in a greatly exhausted state, and could not do much for themselves. Papa, however, seemed to think and act for everybody.

As soon as all were on board, we hoisted in the boat, and the wind being fair, having shaken out the reefs in the mainsail, we steered for St. Ives. Dick, who was not fit for much when we first left the vessel, had now recovered, and assisted in getting off the wet clothes from our young passengers, and in carrying round food.

The cabin presented a curious appearance, with the people stowed as thickly as herrings in a cask, all wrapped up in blankets and pea-coats. Fortunately, the water was smooth under the lee of the land; but the number of people on board brought the vessel much below her usual bearings.

'I am thankful we have not a long voyage to make, or we should soon be short of provisions,' said papa, as we got out tin after tin of soup and meat.

The soft bread and fresh beef we had taken on board at Penzance were soon consumed by the women and children, who speedily rallied from their exhaustion.

The wind, however, fell very light, and there appeared to be a prospect of our not being able to get in that night.

On inquiry, papa found that the master and first mate of the wrecked ship had been tipsy for some days, and had quarrelled desperately with each other, and the second mate, interfering, had been nearly killed. They had got completely out of their course, and none of them knew where they were. They had been bound for the Thames. The men said that when they saw the Longships they fancied that it was the Eddystone, and that when they struck they supposed that they were not far off Plymouth Breakwater, though they were wondering why they did not see the light.

'It is one of the many sad examples we have had of the effects of drinking,' observed papa. 'If I had to make a voyage, I should choose a temperance vessel. Though a master may appear sober enough in port under the eyes of his owners, unless he is a temperate man, one can never tell what he may do at sea.'

On further inquiries we found that nearly half the crew were as tipsy as their officers, and that they, with the cabin passengers who had remained aft, had been washed away. The people saved were steerage passengers, with the exception of one little boy, whose parents and friends had perished. However, the satisfaction of having been the means of saving the lives of these poor people was to us very great. We were of course greatly interested in the boy, Nat Harvey, who was about six years old. Poor little fellow, he had been so frightened that he was not fully aware of what had occurred, and did not appear fully to realise his loss. He seemed to think that his papa and mamma, and his Aunt Fanny and brother and sister, had gone off in a boat, and that he should see them again before long. He kept continually asking why they were not with us. When he heard that we were going to St. Ives, he said that he hoped we should find them there. One of the women, with a kind heart, had taken him under her charge, and she sat on the cabin floor holding him in her arms with his head resting on her lap, every now and then speaking words of comfort, and endeavouring to get him to go to sleep. Papa inquired from the passengers and crew if they knew anything of his family, or where they were going. No one could say what part of the States Mr. and Mrs. Harvey, with three children and a young lady, who was sister either to Mr. or Mrs. Harvey—these were their names—had come from.

'We can't turn the poor child adrift among strangers,' observed papa. 'We must take him with us, and try to find out his friends.'

'Oh pray do!' Dick and I exclaimed. 'I'll look after him, and keep him out of mischief,' added Dick.

At last papa agreed that the best thing he could do for the child was to keep him on board, unless some kind person of influence at St. Ives would take charge of him, and endeavour to find out his friends.

When speaking of the way the wreck occurred, papa said he was not surprised, as he had known an instance of the master of a vessel who with his mate had got drunk, and who had managed to take his vessel to the south of Jersey, while all the time he fancied that he was among the Scilly Islands.

The wind had fallen, and we feared that a calm would come on and keep us all night, which would have been a great trial to our poor passengers. It was therefore with much satisfaction that, the wind holding fair, we came in sight of the peninsula on which part of St. Ives is situated, the remainder being on the mainland on the south side of St. Ives Bay.

The water was smooth, the sky bright, and as papa looked at the town he exclaimed—'Why, I could almost fancy myself among the Greek islands, so exactly does the place, in its form and picturesque beauty, remind me of a Greek village.'

We stood on until, running under a battery which defends the town on the sea side, we anchored off a pier. The view was indeed highly picturesque. The town has an ancient appearance, the houses being built without any regard to order, many of them looking as if destined ere long to tumble down. Then our eyes wandered round the deep bay, on the surrounding broken ground, and the commanding cliffs, lighted up by the rays of the setting sun, which cast a dark shadow over the town itself on the western side.

Papa, hastening on shore, immediately applied to the authorities, who received the shipwrecked crew. The poor people expressed their gratitude for the service we had rendered them; and papa, to assist them still further, headed a subscription which was raised in the town for their relief.

We were very thankful when we got them all on shore. We looked out on entering the bay for the Dolphin; but among the various vessels which had brought up there, she was not to be seen; and on inquiring on shore we could gain no tidings of her. Papa now thought, or hoped, as he had at first supposed, that she had got safely into St. Mary's.

Of course our cabins had not been improved by being occupied by so many passengers. We therefore slept on shore, that our bedclothes might be washed and the cabin cleaned; and we had also to replenish our stock of provisions, which had been almost exhausted. Papa's first care was to arrange an outfit for little Nat, as he had only the garments he wore. We soon had him rigged out in a regular sailor's suit, with a piece of crape round his arm, for we could find no black clothes ready. He frequently asked for his papa and mamma, as well as for his Aunt Fanny.

'You must not expect to see them, my boy,' answered papa; 'but we will take care of you; and Harry here will give you your lessons, as I dare say you do not wish to be idle.'

'Oh yes, I like lessons. Aunt Fanny used to teach me,' answered Nat; 'but if she doesn't come back soon I should like to learn of Harry.'

I gladly promised to be his tutor while he remained on board, and felt not a little proud of the position. I at times fancied that he had a suspicion of what had happened to his friends. The first time we were alone together he looked up into my face, while the tears sprang into his eyes, as he said, 'Do you know, Harry, that I am afraid that the sea washed papa and mamma and Aunt Fanny and dear Reuben and Mary away? I don't like to ask, because I am afraid of anybody telling me that I shall never see them again.'

I had not the heart to say that his suspicions were correct, so I at once got out a book and said, 'Come, Nat, you shall read to me, then I will read to you, and then we will talk about what we have read.' I did the same whenever he again mentioned the subject.

St. Ives itself was soon seen. There is a church standing so close to the sea, that when there is a strong wind it is almost covered with spray. Most of the inhabitants are engaged in the pilchard and herring fishery.

We made an excursion along the coast to visit the ruins of the church of Perranzabuloe, supposed to be the most ancient in Britain. It had for centuries been covered up by the sand. We had left Nat under the charge of the landlady, and engaged a boat to carry us round to visit these interesting ruins. After a long pull we landed up a little creek, near which stand two rocks, known as 'The Old Man and his Wife.' Near at hand was a small fishing-village, in the neighbourhood of which we visited an ancient amphitheatre, still wonderfully perfect. We here obtained a guide to conduct us to the church. It must be understood that the whole shore is covered with fine sand, which is moved in a wonderful manner by northerly winds. It has gradually swept over the country, destroying vegetation and covering up buildings as effectually as has been done by ashes from burning mountains. The progress of the sand is sometimes gradual and almost imperceptible; at other times, in the course of a gale, whole villages have been overwhelmed, allowing the inhabitants scarcely time to escape. Such was the case with this ancient church and the surrounding habitations. So completely had the sand swept over it, that it had quite disappeared; and it was only, after the lapse of centuries, discovered about forty years ago, though a tradition existed in the neighbourhood that a church had once stood there. It was discovered by a Mr. Mitchell, who, undeterred by difficulties, succeeded in removing a mass of sand and exposing the building

RUINS OF PERRANZABULOE CHURCH.

which had so long been covered up. The masonry is rude, but the walls are solid and complete. The interior was perfectly free from the modern accompaniments of Roman Catholic places of worship. There was no roodloft, no confessional, no pictures of the Virgin and saints, nothing to indicate the unscriptural adoration of the wafer, or masses for the dead. The most diligent search was made for beads and pyxes, censers and crucifixes; not a fragment of either could be discovered. At the eastern end we saw a plain, unornamental chancel; in the nave are stone seats attached to the walls.

Near the church were discovered three skeletons, one of gigantic dimensions, the second of moderate size, and the third apparently that of a female; and the wind blowing off the sand, the ground around was found covered with human bones.

We were deeply interested with our visit to this ancient church, which tends to prove that our ancestors worshipped God in simplicity and truth, and that they knew nothing of the forms and ceremonies of Rome.

With regard to these sand-dunes we heard a curious circumstance, that even a narrow stream will stop the advance of the sand, which will accumulate on its banks, but has not the power to cross to the opposite side.

On returning on board, we found that our stock of provisions had arrived, that our blankets were dried, and the cabin cleaned out. We therefore immediately got under weigh, and stood out for the bay.

'What!' exclaimed Dick, 'is this the St. Ives I've heard of all my life?' and he repeated—

> 'As I was going to St. Ives
> I met a man with seven wives;
> Seven wives had seven sacks,
> Seven sacks had seven cats,
> Seven cats had seven kits,—
> Kits, cats, sacks, and wives,
> How many were going to St. Ives?'

Papa laughed, and said he believed that the honour was also claimed by a little town in Huntingdonshire of the same name. 'The two,' he said, 'may fight it out. It is not very important.'

The wind now blew from the northward, and in a short time we opened the Longships, bearing due south-west. It had hitherto been hidden by the land, so that we knew perfectly well where we were. We then kept away until we came in sight of the two lights of the Seven Stones Lightship, until we brought them on our starboard beam, when we were within the radius of St. Agnes Lighthouse just before daybreak.

We were hoping to get in or off St. Mary's in the morning, when it fell calm; and there we lay, with our sails flapping idly, and rolling in the swell of the Atlantic, which came in from the southward. We could see through our glasses the Longships Lighthouse on one side and the light-vessel on the other, while the Scilly Islands rose blue and indistinct out of the ocean. One tide carried us to the north-ward; but in the next we regained our lost ground. It was, however, very tantalising, as we were anxious to ascertain what had become of the Dolphin.

Though papa always hoped for the best, he could not help acknow-ledging that he feared that she might have met with some accident. At length a breeze sprang up, but it was against us; still, that was better than a calm, as we could gain ground by tacking. Dick and Nat asked more than once why we were sailing away from the land when we wanted to get there.

At last we came in sight of a lofty tower on the top of a hill in St. Martin's Island, with the long low outline of St. Mary's beyond. Still, we had several tacks more to make before we gained the entrance to Crow Sound, between St. Mary's and St. Martin's. By this time it was dark. A bright look-out was kept for rocks and shoals in the channel. Suddenly rounding a point, the light from St. Agnes shone brilliantly down on us, and further to our right we saw the little twinkling lights from the windows of the houses in Hugh Town, the capital of the Scilly Islands.

Having come safely to an anchor among several other vessels, we shouted out, 'Dolphin, ahoy!' hoping that she was among them, though in the dark night we could not distinguish her. We had shouted out several times, and papa was on the point of putting off in the boat to make inquiries on shore, when a hail came down from the other side of the harbour, ' Is that the Lively ? '

'Ay—ay!' we answered. ' Is that the Dolphin ? '

'Ay —ay!' was the reply. ' I'll be aboard you presently.'

HUGH TOWN, ST. MARY'S, SCILLY.

In a short time we heard the splash of oars, and, much to our relief, Uncle Tom, followed by Oliver and Jack, sprang on deck.

Our first inquiries were as to how they had weathered the gale.

'Famously,' answered Uncle Tom. ' We kept hove to till the

morning, when, as the wind moderated, we stood in here, a pilot having boarded us and showed us the way.'

'Who have you got here?' exclaimed Oliver, as he looked into Nat's little berth.

Great was the astonishment of all the party when we described the adventures we had met with. We talked over various plans for finding out Nat's relatives, and what should be done with him, should we not succeed.

Next morning we went on shore to inspect the town and to make the tour of the island, which is easily done, as it is only two and a half miles long and one and a half broad. The town had a somewhat sombre look until we got on shore when the neat gardens full of flowers, and the clean appearance of the streets, made us think better of the place. Most of the houses are low, few of them having more than two stories.

On the hill, about one hundred feet above the town, is the castle, which has seen a good many stirring events in its time; but its only garrison now consists of a single individual, who, I suppose, is placed there to prevent the rats from taking possession. It was built in the time of Queen Elizabeth, by Sir Francis Godolphin; but its chief interest arises from its being the last spot on British soil which held out for the Royalists in the days of Cromwell, when Sir John Grenville was governor. Prince Charles fled here, and remained until he took his departure for Jersey. For six years the stout Sir John retained his post, and having collected a number of vessels, fitted them out as cruisers, for the purpose of crippling the forces of the Parliamentary party. These cruisers had, in truth, very much the character of pirates, and were not particular what vessels they robbed. Having plundered some Dutchmen, they were very nearly being severely punished by old Van Tromp, who appeared with a squadron. When summoned to surrender, Sir John refused, and Van Tromp sailed away. At length, so urgent became the representations of the merchants whose vessels had been captured, that Parliament sent an expedition, under Admiral Blake and Sir George Askew, when Sir John was compelled to surrender; and he, with the eight hundred men forming his garrison, received honourable terms.

Though at one time the inhabitants of the Scilly Islands were noted for their barbarous customs, they have now become as peaceably disposed and civilised as any of Her Majesty's subjects.

St. Mary's is divided into two parts by a narrow neck of land, on which Hugh Town stands. It is very possible that some day it will be washed away. We passed over a well-laid-out piece of ground covered with soft turf, on which sheep and deer were feeding, called the Park; and from it we could see the tall lighthouse and the few cottages on St. Agnes Island.

We then proceeded to Buzza Hill, whence we could look down on the harbour, which had the appearance of a large lake. Sometimes, we were told, several hundred vessels take shelter within it. Opposite to Hugh Town was Tresco, the residence of Mr. Smith, the lord proprietor, surrounded by gardens containing avenues of geraniums and plantations of the rarest exotics.

Some of the heights we reached were grand and picturesque in the extreme—one of them, Penninis, especially so. Rocks seemed piled on rocks; beneath, vaults and caverns, abounding with lichens and ferns, with crystal pools in the hollows of granite. Climbing to the summit, our eyes ranged over the ocean, rolling in sublime magnificence, its voice never silent.

On Tolmen Point is a Druidical monument—a perforated stone, which we examined. Papa said that no one knew for what purpose this monument, and others like it, were intended. He told us of one especially, which he had seen at Constantine Penryn, of which he had a photograph. It had lately, he said, been thrown down for the sake of getting at the granite underneath. I think such destruction of old monuments ought to be forbidden by law!

Then we went to Porthhellick Cove, with wild rocks seen beyond it, on which, in the year 1707, Sir Cloudesley Shovel, with four of his ships and two thousand men, were cast away. The body of the admiral, known by a valuable ring on his finger, was buried on the shore of the cove. It was afterwards removed to Westminster Abbey.

Papa remarked that the strong current produced by the indraught of the Irish Channel drifted these ships out of their course, and was the cause of the catastrophe.

The inhabitants of the islands were once known for their smuggling

CONSTANTINE TOLMEN STONE, CORNWALL.

and wrecking propensities. A fisherman whom we fell in with—a venerable-looking man, with white hair streaming under his cap—pointed out several spots on which ships with rich cargoes had run on shore, and assured us that coin was still to be picked up in the sand, if people would but take the trouble to look for it. In former days everybody was engaged in smuggling, or trusting to salvage from wrecks. There was but little farming. No potatoes were grown, and there were no gardens, while their huts were as low and damp as

those in the Hebrides. But when Mr. Smith came he changed all
that; and now the people live in comfortable houses, have gardens
full of flowers, and the productions of the islands afford them ample
support. Wheat and rye, and every description of vegetable, are grown;
scarlet geraniums flourish, while fuchsias, and a variety of other
magnificent flowers, not only grow in the gardens, but form hedges
several feet in height.

Next morning we got under weigh to take a cruise among the
islands. Passing round on the other side of Hugh Town, we perceived
the narrowness of the strip on which it stands, and sincerely hoped
that the sea would not again—as it once did—break across and
inundate the place. I cannot attempt to describe the numerous rocks
and islands we sighted in our course, there being altogether upwards
of three hundred, large and small. Steering to the south-west, we
passed Gorregan and Rosevean, where our pilot told us that many a
stout ship had been lost; some, striking on the rocks, having gone
down and left no sign of their fate, except some articles thrown up on
the shore. Coming to an anchor, we pulled off in the boat to catch fish,
with which the sea literally swarmed. We could see them swimming
about through the clear water. We were amused by the way in
which our pilot, who was a great fisherman, caught them. Throwing
the bait always before their noses, and singing out, ' Come along, Dick,
come along, Tom ; bite, my boy;' and, sure enough, the fish bit, and
were caught.

We afterwards passed several ruins of ancient chapels, when we
arrived off St. Agnes, on which the magnificent lighthouse stands.
On the island were a few cottages ; and here the scarlet geranium was
almost a tree.

From this point we steered for the Bishop's Lighthouse, the most
western part of Scilly. It is a magnificent stone tower, one hundred
and forty-seven feet high, with one fixed bright light. This can be
distinguished from that of St. Agnes, which revolves every minute.

Passing up Broad Sound we came off a fine headland, the proper name of which is the 'Menavawr'; but our pilot called it the 'Man o' war.'

In our cruise we passed Bryher and Sampson, the two largest islands in the group. The latter island is called after a saint of that name. It consists of two hills, the outlines of which present the form of the back of a camel. Landing on the shore, we made a collection of beautiful shells, which accumulate in large quantities on the beach. Our pilot told us that, until lately, the isle of Sampson was thickly peopled; but the inhabitants, being addicted to certain illegal practices, such as wrecking and smuggling, and illicit distillation of spirits, it was found necessary, as the only means of weaning them from their bad habits, to disperse them, either on the mainland, or through the other islands, where they could be better watched.

We again got out our fishing-lines, which we baited with flies formed out of untwisted pieces of rope. In a short time we had caught a dozen fine whiting-pollock. We, however, had a still greater catch shortly afterwards.

As we were sailing along through the Sound, a herd of porpoises came gambolling by, their black bodies and fins now appearing, now sinking beneath the surface. Captain Truck had a harpoon ready, and he placed himself in the forechains, with a rope round his waist. He stood with his weapon high poised in the air, ready to strike. We were all on the watch. In a few moments his harpoon flew from his hand.

'Pay away, lads!' he shouted out; 'the fellow's fast.'

The porpoise dived, and the line ran out at a rapid rate. Truck sprang in board, and quickly checked it. We then got two running bowlines ready, one in the fore part of the vessel, and the other aft. There was great excitement.

'Now haul away,' he sang out; and the porpoise was dragged, in spite of its struggles, close alongside, when the running bowlines were passed one over its head, and the other round its tail; and all hands joining, including Nat, who took the end of a rope—although, as may be supposed, he was not of much use—we hoisted the huge fish on board. It was at once killed and scientifically cut up by Truck and the pilot. So eager was the latter, that he very nearly let us strike on a rock. We had some pieces of the porpoise beef for dinner, which were pronounced very good. We supplied the Dolphin with a portion of our catch, and our united crews lived on it for the next two days.

Next day we had another similar cruise, during which we visited the beautiful Sound called New Grimsby. On one side stands the tower, known as Cromwell's Castle—not that he was ever in the island, but he ordered it to be built. On the opposite side are the ruins of another fort. It was here that the forces under Blake and Askew landed, and attacked the fortifications, though they met with a stout resistance from the Royalists, who at length took to flight.

Farther on we came off vast masses of rock piled one upon another. The two yachts having hove-to, we pulled on shore, and, under the guidance of the pilot, managed to land; when, climbing up some distance, we reached a cone, from the bottom of which we could hear the sea roaring fearfully. We then arrived lower down at a small opening, when a guide, who had joined us, lighted some candles, that we might find our way into a celebrated cavern, called 'Piper's Hole.' For some distance we had to crawl along on our hands and knees. At length we reached a narrow but high vault; this we followed until we arrived at the head of a ladder. 'You will find a boat at the bottom, gentlemen,' said the guide.

Jack and I, with Uncle Tom, descended, as we were told that the boat could not carry a larger fare. After looking down for a few seconds, we distinguished a light; and going down the ladder, we stepped into a boat, in which a man, whom we of course denominated Charon, was seated. Instead of oars, he used a long pole to urge on the boat. We noticed the dark appearance of the water as we made our way through the vaulted chambers. We now found ourselves floating on a lake, the water black as ink, but perfectly smooth.

Above our heads was a lofty and extensive dome; but the sides were invisible. Charon ferried us across, and landed us on a smooth sandy shore, along which we proceeded for a considerable distance through a succession of caverns, until we arrived at a small circular chamber where they appeared to terminate.

On putting my hand into the water on my return, to my surprise I found it perfectly fresh, although so close to the sea. Here any number of outlaws might take refuge, with small chance of being discovered, or defend themselves against any force sent in pursuit, provided they had food to hold out until their enemies had grown weary of looking for them. Charon—unlike his namesake—had no objection to ferry us back across the Styx; and having made our way into the upper air, we regained the boat.

Our next visit was to Rock Island, the resort of countless numbers of sea-birds. It is at the extreme northern end of the group, and consists of a high table-land, surrounded by precipitous cliffs. As we approached, the gulls rose in masses so thick as positively to darken the air, while all around the sea was speckled with the white feathers of innumerable puffins. On the cliffs were ranged numerous clusters of black cormorants, who seemed to be watching us eagerly. Their plumage was very fine, being of a lustrous invisible green, while their eyes were of the brightest emerald hue. The boats which went in pursuit brought back a number of gulls and puffins and cormorants, some of which Oliver begged might be preserved for stuffing.

We paid a visit on the last day of our stay to the residence of Mr. Smith, in the island of Tresco. On landing, we proceeded across a park, and approached the large, many-gabled house, in front of which the rocky ground was completely concealed by masses of blooming creepers. We passed between beautiful flower-beds, among which grew magnificent aloes, twenty feet in height, covered with bloom. We wellnigh lost ourselves in the labyrinth of walks, literally shaded by scarlet geraniums of giant growth, and shrubs, such as grow nowhere in the open air on the mainland, many of them of extreme beauty, brought from all parts of the world. In the midst of the gardens we came upon the ivy-mantled arches of the ruined abbey of Tresco, which has reared its head in these far-off islands for the last eight centuries. We all of us agreed that we had never before been in so perfect a garden, so rich with a profusion of flowers. Mr. Smith, in making this 'Paradise,' had an object in view—to set an example to the inhabitants of these lonely islands, to show them what

REMNANT OF TRESCO ABBEY.

Nature will do for them, when they put their shoulder to the wheel; and in few parts of the world are the climate and soil so suited to the production of floral wonders.

I must not venture to give a further description of the place, but I must say that Scilly is well worth a visit; and I am sure that any of my friends who may go there will not be disappointed. We were quite sorry when papa and Uncle Tom determined to sail, reminding us that, if we remained longer, we should have no time to see the other places of interest it was our intention to visit on our voyage round England.

CHAPTER VII.

NCE more we were steering to the north-east, intending to visit several places on the Cornish and Devonshire coast, before standing across the Bristol Channel. The sea was calm, and the wind, coming off shore, was light, as we slowly sailed past the Cow-and-Calf Rocks.

'Dear me, what a strange creature! Why, there's a black calf!' exclaimed little Nat, who was looking over the side of the vessel as we glided on.

Captain Truck turned his eyes in the direction of the rocks, where, sure enough, there was a strange-looking creature lying perfectly still, and gazing up at us with large lustrous orbs.

'That's a seal, Master Nat. If you could just look into one of the caverns on this coast, you'd find lots of them creatures. Though they are without feet or hands, they can manage to make their way along the beach at a pretty fast rate with their flappers and tails. If you were to see one, you would laugh.'

'Couldn't we catch it?' asked Nat.

'Maybe if he was to come near enough I might with my harpoon; but he is too big to be a passenger on board our small craft.'

Truck got his harpoon in readiness, but, fortunately for itself, the seal did not come within reach of his deadly weapon.

Rounding Stepper Point, we stood up the broad estuary which forms the mouth of the river Camel, on the southern shore of which stands Padstow. The town is situated in a valley, with pretty gardens on every side, while in front is a lake-like expanse of water apparently surrounded by granite cliffs, the entrance being completely shut out from view. Vessels of considerable size were at anchor, showing that the water was deep. We observed many ancient-looking buildings in the old part of the town near the quays, from which a fine pier projected. Higher up were more modern-looking buildings.

Having replenished our stores, which was our chief object in coming in, though the place itself was well worth seeing, we again sailed, and the same evening came off Tintagel Head.

Here both yachts were hove to. We all pulled on shore in the boats, taking Nat with us. The place where we landed was near the village of Trevena. Over an inn door was painted the name of ' Charity Bray,' which we found to be the appellation of the landlady. As we promised to take tea at her hostelry before returning on board, she undertook to procure us a guide, who would lead us by the shortest cut to the far-famed ancient castle of Tintagel. Hurrying on, for we had no time to spare, we descended by a steep path along the side of the cliff until we reached a lofty rock, on which one part of the castle stands, while on the mainland another portion is built. We were now standing at the bottom of a chasm looking up two hundred feet or more to the castle walls, which were originally joined by a drawbridge. The castle was anciently called Dunchine, or the Fort of the Chasm. A zigzag path enabled us to gain the summit of the cliffs. The entrance to the castle was through a gateway, a ruined archway which still stands. Passing through it, we entered a court, called King Arthur's Garden, immediately beyond which rose a precipitous rock, crowned by a tower and wall—evidently the keep. At the further side the cliff descends perpendicularly to the sea, while on the other is the chasm I have mentioned as dividing the two

TINTAGEL CASTLE.

portions of the castle. The walls altogether encircled the larger part of the promontory, and in some places can hardly be distinguished from the cliffs, out of which they seem, as it were, to grow. The headland, I was told, contains about forty acres. We remarked that the walls were pierced with a number of small square orifices, probably intended for the use of bowmen. In the rock overlooking the ocean is a recess, which our guide told us was called 'King Arthur's Chair'; and in another part is a subterranean passage called 'King Arthur's Hiding-place.' It is undoubtedly one of the most ancient castles in the kingdom, though it was greatly enlarged in later years, and was kept up until the reign of Elizabeth, when it was abandoned as a stronghold, and allowed to fall into decay. As it was King Arthur's birth-place, so it was the spot where he lost his life. I found some lines by the poet Wharton, describing the battle:

> 'O'er Cornwall's cliffs the tempest roared;
> High the screaming sea-mew soared;
> On Tintagel's topmost tower
> Darksome fell the sleety shower,
> When Arthur ranged his red-cross ranks
> On conscious Camlan's crimson banks,
> By Modred's faithless guile decreed
> Beneath a Saxon spear to bleed.'

Once upon a time the Cornish men were noted for being heartless wreckers. There is a story current of a wicked man, who, having tied up a donkey by the leg, fastened a lantern round its neck and drove it along the summit of the cliffs; the halting movement of the creature, resembling the plunging of a ship, being calculated to tempt vessels to their destruction, from the belief that there was ample sea room. Happily, at the present time the Cornish men are as prompt to save as they were in their savage days to lure hapless barques on shore. This part of the coast is indeed a fearful one for any unfortunate ship driven upon it, though, by means of the rocket apparatus and the lifeboats, the crew have a better chance of escape than formerly.

Soon after leaving Tintagel we came in sight of the higher light, which beamed forth from Lundy Island, revolving every two minutes. We stood on across Bude Bay, steering for Hartland Point, at the southern side of Barnstaple Bay. The wind heading us, we stood off the shore until we caught sight of the lower fixed light on Lundy Island, where, from the distance we were from it, papa calculated that the next tack would carry us into the bay.

I always enjoy sailing at night when finding our way by the lights, with the chart spread out on the cabin table. The lighthouse of Lundy Island—which is at the very entrance of the Bristol Channel —is a great blessing to mariners; while the island itself, which runs north and south, and is long and narrow, affords shelter in a westerly gale to the storm-tossed vessels bound along the coasts.

I was quite sorry when papa ordered me to turn in; but I was on deck again before daybreak, and found that we were standing towards the two bright fixed lights at the entrance of Bideford Harbour, while we could still see the lights of Lundy Island astern; so that we knew where we were as well as we should have done in broad daylight. By keeping the two lights in one, we knew that we were standing for the passage over the bar into the harbour.

It was just daylight as we entered the broad estuary where the rivers Taw and Torridge flow into the ocean. We came off Apple-dore, at the mouth of the Torridge, on which Bideford is situated. Bideford has an ancient school-house, where many a naval hero acquired such education as was considered necessary to prepare him for a life on the ocean. Another interesting object is its bridge, six hundred and seventy-seven feet in length, supported by twenty-four small arches, and carrying iron buttresses on its side to widen the roadway; very ugly, I thought.

From Bideford also sailed many an exploring expedition; while its gallant mariners were well known on the Spanish main, where they filled their pockets with doubloons, won at the point of their swords from the haughty Dons. A new school has lately been established in

BIDEFORD.

this neighbourhood for the sons of naval and military officers; and Dick and I agreed that we should like to go there.

Returning down the river, we pulled up the northern arm of the estuary. Barnstaple is a place of considerable importance, which has existed since the reign of the Saxon kings : Athelstan having built a castle here, made the town into a borough. It is a handsome-looking place, but the harbour is much blocked up, so that only small vessels can enter. The river is spanned by an ancient stone bridge, the width of which is increased, as at Bideford, by iron projections for foot passengers ; there is also a railway on either side. We saw a number of vessels building, and passed some large woollen and lace manufactories.

As we had all read *Westward Ho!* we were anxious to see Clovelly, which lies at the south side of the bay. So, early the next morning, getting under weigh, the tide being favourable, we ran out of the harbour, and stood across to that most picturesque of villages. Bringing up, we went on shore. We might almost have fancied ourselves in some Chinese place, as we climbed up the High Street, which is built in a hollow, with cliffs on either side, a rapid stream rushing down it towards the sea. The streets are very narrow, running in a zigzag fashion; but the little gardens full of flowers at the side of each doorway give it a most attractive appearance. It is also clean and neat in the extreme; while the romantic scenery around, and the views over Bideford Bay, covered as it was then by the dark red sails of numberless trawling-boats, made us very glad that we had landed.

As we had not much time to spare, we again put off, and sailed to Ilfracombe. We passed on our way Morte Point, a dangerous headland, so called on account of the number of vessels that have been shipwrecked there. There is a lighthouse on the cliff, to show the position of this dangerous place, and a red buoy also floats over the sunken rocks.

We had with us a chart, showing the position of the wrecks round the English coasts. There were a considerable number around this headland; but many more up the Bristol Channel, especially at the mouth of the Severn, where the river appears crowded with black dots. Off Plymouth, long rows of dots show where vessels have gone

CLOVELLY.

down. Between Lundy Island and the Welsh coast they are numerous; while they are equally dense between the Eddystone and Falmouth.

ILFRACOMBE.

They cluster thickly in the neighbourhood of all the headlands round Cornwall. Though more sprinkled, they are almost within hail of each other across St. George's Channel,—from the entrance, to the north of the Isle of Anglesea,—and still thicker at the mouth of the Mersey. There are not a few off Portland. Between that and Beachy Head they lie very close; but from Dungeness to the North Foreland they almost touch each other, every part of the Goodwin Sands being covered by them. All along the shore at the mouth of the Severn they can be counted by dozens; but the sandbanks off Great Yarmouth have proved the destruction of more vessels than the rocks of any other part of the coast. There is scarcely twenty miles of shore anywhere which could be passed over without those dark spots which show that some vessel has been wrecked.

It was gratifying, however. to see painted on the map a number of little red dots, which mark the lifeboat stations. Where wrecks have more frequently occurred in past years, there they appear thickest. On the Norfolk coast there are close upon thirty lifeboats, so that they are in most places not more than five miles apart.

We got into the snug little harbour of Ilfracombe, and the next morning enjoyed a ramble among the picturesque rocks of that romantic watering-place. In winter people come from a distance to it, for it is one of the most attractive sea-side places on the English coast, with rocks and sands, and comfortable lodging-houses.

As the wind was from the southward and the tide favourable, we did not stay long, but stood across to Lundy Island, a rock at the southern end of which is called Rat Island. We had seen the revolving light of the island before entering Barnstaple Bay. The east coast is bold and precipitous, with numerous deep ravines running into the cliffs. The south end is even more rugged than the northern. Near the landing-place is a cave hollowed out of a black rock, called the Devil's Kitchen; and beyond it is a narrow opening filled with dangerous rocks, known as Hell's Gate. Indeed, from their character many spots hereabouts are called after Satan or his imps. As papa observed, people are ready enough to give Satan credit for the physical ills they suffer, but too often forget the fearful moral power he exerts, and yield themselves his willing slaves. Curiously enough, the chief proprietor of the island, who lives in a substantial house, rejoices in the name of ' Heaven.'

So narrow is the landing-place, that we had to follow each other in single file. We had a glorious scramble among the rocks. On the top of a height appeared Marisco's Castle, with low walls and four towers, reminding us of the Tower of London.

Lundy Island has been the refuge of persons of high and low degree. No small number of smugglers have made it their abode, as from thence formerly they could carry on their lawless trade with impunity. The most noted of them was a man named Benson, at one time a member of Parliament, who had ultimately to escape to 'foreign lands' to avoid punishment. The pirates also in days of yore used to make it their head-quarters; indeed, Marisco, who built the castle, may be included in the category of outlaws. He, with a daring band of followers, long carried on their depredations on foreign and mercantile shipping, until they were all captured and hanged.

We met with vast numbers of puffins, cormorants, and sea-gulls, which inhabit the cliffs of the island; and we obtained some good specimens of their eggs. The most curious were those of the guillemot, which, though little larger than the puffin, have eggs as large as those of geese. They are white, chocolate, or verdigris green, covered with curious figures and dashes; and it is said that, notwithstanding the number collected, no two have ever been found exactly alike. We took on board a number of eggs to eat. The yolk is a deep red, and the white transparent. The egg of the cormorant is but little larger than that of a pigeon. All these eggs are laid on ledges of the rocks. Being small at one end and large at the other, the wind rolls them round, but does not blow them over the edge.

It did not take us long to inspect Lundy Island, for it is only about two and a half miles long, and less than a mile wide. It consists of a mass of granite rising about two hundred feet above the sea.

We regretted being unable to visit Swansea, away to the north-east, and Carmarthen; but the coast between them is dangerous, and the passage would have occupied a considerable time. We should also have liked to look into the very pretty little seaside place of Tenby, on the west of Carmarthen Bay.

Swansea is a town of very considerable importance. It has a large foreign and home trade, and contains a number of furnaces for the smelting of copper, the ore being imported from Cornwall and Devonshire, and even from Australia and other foreign places. Five or six thousand ships visit it every year. Several canals and railways connect it with other parts of the country. It is not surprising that the wreck chart should show a number of black dots off its harbour.

A fresh breeze from the south-east soon brought us in sight of St. Ann's lights, forming the south-west entrance of Milford Haven; and guided by them we stood on towards the mouth of that magnificent estuary, which we entered by the first dawn of day. Running up it, we steered due east until we came off the town of Milford, where we brought-up, and sent on shore for fresh provisions.

Milford Haven is a wide estuary, in some places four and five miles across. We went on shore, but there was not much to see in the town. A naval dockyard, which once existed here, was removed in 1814 to Pembroke, on the southern side of the estuary. Having obtained what we wanted, we stood across to the latter place. We anchored off the dockyard, which is even larger than that of Portsmouth. We went through it, visiting several ships of various sizes. We saw also buildings and manufactories similar to those at Portsmouth. Everything is on a large scale. We were much interested in all we saw; but as I have already described Portsmouth,

I need not give an account of Pembroke. From the width of Milford Haven, and being open to the south-west gales, it does not. when

THE MUMBLES, SWANSEA.

they are blowing, afford secure anchorage ; and the wreck chart shows that a number of vessels have been lost within it.

Papa and Uncle Tom had a consultation on board the Lively, and agreed that they would stand on up the Irish Channel, and touch at no other place until we arrived at Caernarvon, at the entrance of the Menai Straits, through which they intended to pass on our way to Liverpool.

We accordingly sailed early in the morning, and steered across for the Smalls Lighthouse, to the westward of which they intended to keep before standing up St. George's Channel. Though we had a brisk breeze, it took us nearly three hours after we passed St. Ann's Lighthouse, the distance being eighteen miles, to reach the Smalls rocks. Before the lighthouse was erected many vessels were lost on them, or on others between them and the coast of Wales. To the northward are the Tuskar rocks, on the Irish coast, on which also stands a fine lighthouse; and the two may be considered the guardian angels of the Channel. Those keeping to the east can see the Smalls light, while those a short distance off more to the west are in sight of the Tuskar light, which revolves every two minutes.

The tides run with great fierceness between the Smalls and the mainland, amid the dangerous reefs which extend out from the island of Skomer. As it was nearly slack tide when we got up to the lighthouse, and as the water was smooth, papa and Uncle Tom agreed to land. The yachts were hove-to, the boats lowered, and we pulled in on the northern side, where we had no difficulty in landing.

Two of the light-keepers, seeing us coming, descended to our assistance,—for, as may be supposed, they are ever happy to receive visitors, especially those bringing newspapers and periodicals. Before ascending, our guides took us to the site of the old tower, and a curious store-room, which was cut into the rock to serve as a coal-cellar to the former edifice, of which one of them gave us an interesting account.

Centuries had passed by, and numberless wrecks had occurred on the Smalls and neighbouring rocks, when, about a hundred years ago, a ship belonging to Liverpool was lost on them. She was commanded by a Captain Phillips, who, with his crew, escaped; and from a feeling of gratitude for his providential deliverance he determined that he would do his utmost to get a lighthouse built on the rock. He shortly afterwards became a shipowner and merchant in Liverpool; and, being successful in business, he forthwith put his intention into execution. His first plan was to fit long cast-iron pillars deep into the rock, and to place upon them a circular room, as the habitation of the light-keepers, with a lantern at the top. He had already raised the pillars to a considerable height, when a heavy gale came on, and they were overthrown. Undaunted by his failure, Captain Phillips again set to work, and engaged a Mr. Whiteside—an ingenious mechanic and a native of Liverpool. Curiously enough, Mr. Whiteside, who was about twenty-six years of age, had hitherto employed his talents in making musical instruments, though, having means of his own, he did not depend upon his labour for his subsistence. He had never been to sea, and was ignorant of the power of the ocean. Accompanied by half-a-dozen Cornish miners, he arrived in the harbour of Solva, a small town near St. David's Head, on the north side of St. Bride's Bay, about twenty-two miles from the Smalls rock. He began the work by again using iron pillars, the task of the miners being to bore holes in the rock in which to fix them. Before they had been long at work a gale arose, which compelled their vessel to seek for safety in harbour, while they were left clinging to one of the iron pillars. During that fearful night several of them were nearly carried away. The gale abating on the third day, they were rescued in a very exhausted state by the crew of their vessel. Still Mr. Whiteside continued the work. After the iron pillars were fixed, and already carried to some height, another gale so bent them as to convince him that another material must be used. He accordingly obtained the longest and stoutest oak trees to be procured in the kingdom. After undergoing many hardships, dangers, and disappointments, he ultimately erected five wooden and three iron pillars.

On the summit an octagonal room was formed, with a lamp above. Afterwards the three iron pillars were removed, and oak placed in their stead, with another in the centre, the whole supported by diagonal stays, the lower ends of which were fixed in the rock.

A rope ladder leading from the rock to a trap in the floor of the room enabled the light-keepers to ascend; and in this room was stored oil, coal, provisions, and other necessities, with spare bunks for any mechanics employed on the work or shipwrecked mariners who might reach the rock. Thus but little space was left for the regular inhabitants, two of whom, however, generally remained at a time in the lighthouse.

During a severe gale, which lasted for many weeks, one of the men died; and the other, fearing that he might be accused of murdering his companion, kept the body, placed in a coffin hanging under the floor of the room, until he was relieved. In consequence of this event, three keepers were always stationed at the lighthouse. The room was only just of sufficient height for a man of ordinary stature to stand upright; indeed, one of the keepers, measuring six feet, was unable to do so, and had to bend his head, lest he should strike it against the beams.

Often, during even ordinary gales of wind, the whole structure was completely covered by the water, so that when the waves rose the light could not be seen. Having inspected the holes in which the towers stood, we examined the cellar. It was cut out of the solid rock, and is twenty feet long by eight wide, and four feet deep, and has a covering of granite eight inches thick, the entrance being by two gun-metal doors, or rather man-holes, perfectly impervious to water when closed; it was formed to hold the tools and stores of the labourers. The rock itself is twelve feet above the level of the sea at high water, and the lantern of the old lighthouse stood seventy feet above the water.

For eighty years this curious pigeon-hole of a dwelling-house towered in mid air, surrounded by the furious waves which dashed wildly against it, until at length the Trinity Corporation, who had purchased it from the heirs of the original possessor, resolved on building a stone lighthouse, similar to that of the Eddystone; and Mr. James Douglas was entrusted with its construction. The first stone was laid in 1857; and the light on the new tower was exhibited on the 1st of August, 1861, the old structure being immediately afterwards removed.

We made our way to the new lighthouse, which is of granite. Twenty-nine feet above high-water mark, it is of solid masonry; in the next eighteen feet there is a well-staircase seven feet in diameter, all the courses being secured in the most perfect manner. Having climbed up by thirteen gun-metal steps, wedged into the solid granite, we reached the entrance port. As may be supposed, we had to stretch our legs to get up to it. We ascended the staircase by twenty-eight steps to a room containing three iron water-tanks, holding a thousand gallons, with a coal-cellar below it. Here a crane is fixed for hoisting in stores. Seventeen more steps led us to the oil room. The arched granite floors are composed of twelve radiating blocks of granite, dovetailed to a centre stone nine inches thick in the centre, and one foot seven inches in circumference. A slated floor is cemented on to the surface of the granite. Another seventeen steps took us up to the store-room, in which the meat and bread casks are kept. Ascending a third series of seventeen steps, we arrived at the living room, the walls of which are two feet six inches thick. Here is a cooking-range with an oven, a bookcase, tables, &c. A fourth series took us to the bedroom, in which there are five berths; and by a fifth staircase of seventeen steps we reach the watch-room, immediately below the lantern; but there is no seat, as the keeper is not allowed to sit down during his watch. Sixteen more steps we mounted, making altogether one hundred and twenty-nine, when we arrived at the lantern. The apparatus is of the first catadioptric order, lighted by a first-class pressure lamp. By it stands the machine for striking the fog-bell, which weighs three hundredweight, and sounds about every two seconds by means of a double clapper. There is also a flagstaff, by means of which the light-keepers can hoist signals to passing vessels. The total height of masonry above high-water mark is one hundred and fifteen feet six inches; and the diameter of the tower over the outside of the cornice is twenty-one feet. Although not so lofty, this magnificent lighthouse is a far stronger structure than that of the Eddystone.

There are four light-keepers belonging to the lighthouse, one—as is customary—being on shore. They seemed perfectly happy and contented, liking the regularity of their lives, feeling, as they said, fully as safe as they would miles inland. They were very glad of a packet of newspapers and a couple of magazines we gave them, which we obtained at Milford; and the men begged us to give them another look in, should we come that way again. This we promised to do if we could.

The weather had hitherto been very fine, and we hoped to have a pleasant run. We were gliding smoothly on, and had got very nearly half across Cardigan Bay, when the weather gave signs of changing.

'We shall have a dirty night of it, sir, if I don't mistake,' observed Truck to papa; 'if the wind comes from the westward, it will be all we can do to weather Bardsey Island.'

'If we once round it, we shall have a clear run for Caernarvon,' said papa; 'and I should be sorry to delay by making for another port.'

'If you please, sir,' answered Truck, 'to my mind it would be as well to get into port as soon as we can.'

'We will see what the glass says,' observed papa.

He sent me below to look. It had fallen greatly within the last half-hour. As we looked westward we saw heavy clouds banking up in that direction, and rapidly approaching. Papa, on this, ordered the gaff topsail to be taken in, and the jib shifted. Presently afterwards we had two reefs down in the mainsail, and a still smaller jib set. The wind rapidly increased. We went below and examined the chart. The nearest port was Aberystwyth.

'At all times there is sufficient water over the bar for small craft like ours,' observed papa. 'We will run for it, and shall be in before dark; but if not, there are two lights to guide us into the harbour.'

On going on deck, we made a signal to the Dolphin, and Uncle Tom bore down to speak to us. Papa told him what he proposed doing, and immediately altering our course, we stood into the bay. Having a good chart, we had no difficulty in making out the land-marking. In about an hour we came in sight of the ruined walls of an ancient castle above the harbour. A number of fishing-boats were making for the harbour, to find shelter from the expected gale; and, following them, we ran over the bar—it being high water—and brought-up before the old-fashioned town.

The old town has not a very attractive appearance, as the streets are narrow, and the houses covered with black slate, which give them a sombre look, but there are also a number of large good-looking houses, inhabited by visitors, who come here to bathe and enjoy the sea-breezes, and we saw several churches and other public buildings; so that Aberystwyth may be considered a place of some importance.

We were thankful to be in harbour, for we had scarcely dropped our anchors before the gale broke with fearful violence. The sun had already set, and the rain came down in torrents. We remained on board, hoping to be able to see something of the old town and its ruins the following morning, before sailing.

All night long we could hear the wind howling and whistling, and the sea dashing against the rocks outside the harbour. When morning broke, the storm was raging as fiercely as ever; but as the rain had ceased, as soon as we had had breakfast we went on shore and walked down to the beach.

We met several people, who looked eager and excited, and inquiring of them the cause, they pointed seaward to the north-west, where, amid the spray, we made out a large vessel on shore.

Presently we saw a carriage dragged by four horses, coming along at a great rate, and as it came up we discovered that it contained the lifeboat. Reaching the shore, it was turned round, with the back of the carriage, on which the bow of the lifeboat rested, towards the sea. The horses were now made to back it nearer and nearer the water. I felt so eager to witness the proceedings that I would have given anything to go off with the gallant crew.

'Now, lads! on board!' cried the coxswain.

As he uttered the words, not only the crew but a number of other persons rushed down to the side of the boat. I found myself among them. In one instant the crew leapt on board, and, seized by a sudden impulse, I too sprang up the side, and slid down into the bottom of the boat. The coxswain was standing up, watching the seas as they rolled in. That moment was a favourable one for launching the boat, and, crying out to the men on the beach to haul away on the detaching lines, the boat, ere two seconds had passed, began to glide towards the raging billows. The crew had seized their oars, and were already giving way. Bravely the boat rolled over the first sea she encountered; and in less than a minute—before I was discovered—she was far from the beach, and pulling swiftly away out to sea. Now, for the first time, the coxswain, casting his eyes down, beheld me.

'Where do you come from, my lad?' he exclaimed; 'you have no business here.'

'I was on board before I had time to think about that,' I answered. 'I beg your pardon; but now that I am here I hope that you will let me remain.'

'Provided you are not washed out of the boat,' he replied. 'Here, take one of these cork-jackets and put it on, and then sit quiet. Whatever happens, hold fast,—or, stay, lash yourself down; remember your life depends upon it.'

I did as he directed, and had now time to reflect on the folly of my proceeding—not that I feared for myself, but I knew papa and the rest of our party would be dreadfully anxious when they missed me.

The coxswain took no further notice of me. He had enough to do to attend to the steerage of the boat. I confess that before many minutes were over I wished myself back safe on shore. Still, I kept up my spirits; my only regret was that I had got on board without papa's leave, and that he, and Oliver and Uncle Tom, and the rest, would be made unhappy on my account.

In spite of the coxswain's orders, I stood up, holding the rope with my left hand, waving my handkerchief with the other, hoping that papa would see it, and at once know what I was doing.

I quickly sat down again, for I heard the coxswain cry out, 'Hold fast, my lads!' and, turning my head for an instant over my shoulder, I saw a tremendous wave come rushing on with a crest of foam curling over it as if about to overwhelm the boat. On the crew pulled, however; when in an instant the sea broke, a large portion coming right down into the boat, wetting us through fore and aft. But the men seemed to think nothing of it, and on they pulled. Several other seas broke over us in the same way, half filling the boat; but she was so constructed that the water ran out again, and directly afterwards she was as buoyant as ever. We were pulling away to windward, to get a sufficient offing from the land to set sail. It was a long business, for although the men pulled hard, the wind was in our teeth, and the seas seemed to be sending us back as fast as we advanced. Such, however, was not the case, for on looking towards the shore I saw that we were gradually increasing our distance from it.

Thus some hours were passed; they appeared to me the longest I had ever known, and I again and again wished myself on shore. Had I been one of the crew, and felt that by my exertions I might have contributed to the saving of the shipwrecked sailors, the case would have been very different; but I had to sit quiet.

At last the coxswain shouted out, 'Make sail!' The mast was

stepped, and a double-reefed foresail and mizen were set. The boat could scarcely carry a smaller sail out; even with that she heeled over. Her head was now pointed towards the wreck, which seemed farther and farther off; indeed, we could only occasionally get a glimpse of her as we rose on the summits of the seas. How fearful must have

TO THE RESCUE!

been the anxiety of those on board the wreck! They might possibly have seen the boat; but if they did they might have feared that she would not reach them, or that they would not be able to get on board her before their ship went to pieces. At length the bank was reached which must be crossed before the wreck could be gained.   The sea here was breaking tremendously; the waves leaping and clashing together, gave the water the appearance of a huge boiling cauldron. The boat seemed literally struggling for life; now the water poured in on one side, now on the other, as she rolled to starboard or port.

'Hold on, hold on, my lads, for your lives!' cried the coxswain; and a tremendous sea broke bodily over her, threatening to sweep every man on board away.   I held on, as may be supposed, like grim death. The men, slipping from their seats, placed their breasts on the thwart, thrust their legs under them, and clasped them with both their arms, while the water rushed over their backs and heads, so completely burying us that I fully believed the boat was going down; indeed, it seemed as if we were gone.   Suddenly regaining its buoyancy, up it sprang again, throwing out most of the water through the side, while the rest sank to the bottom of the boat, and once more she floated bravely.

The men looked round, as did I, expecting that some of their number would have been washed away; but they had all instantly regained their seats, and on she sped amid the hissing foam.

The wind, instead of lessening, appeared to increase, and the clouds came down close above our heads, seeming almost to meet the dancing crests of foam.   With the masses of spray which continually broke over her and the thick clouds above us, it was almost as dark as night; and even the coxswain, with his sharp eyes, could with difficulty distinguish the wreck.   At last, the sands were crossed, and the boat was once more ploughing her way through the seas, which rolled in towards the shore with greater regularity than those we had just passed.

'I see her! I see her!' cried the coxswain, who was standing up peering ahead.   'She is little better than half a mile to leeward.'

The direction of the boat was slightly altered, and we stood down towards the wreck.   As we approached her we saw that her mainmast was gone, that her foremast and yards were still standing, with their sails fluttering wildly from them. The lifeboat crew now looked anxiously towards the wreck, to ascertain if any men were still left in the rigging or on the forepart of the hull, which alone remained above the water.

'I see one! I see *two!*' exclaimed the men, in rapid succession. 'They are waving to us.'

As we got still nearer, we could count no less than eight men in the rigging; but how to get to them was the difficulty.

'The mainmast has not been cut adrift; it will be a dangerous task,' said the coxswain. 'Lads, we shall have to board her on the weather-side, I fear.'

From the position we had gained we could now see to leeward; and there, sure enough, hung the mainmast, which the sea was tossing up and down in a way which would speedily have destroyed our boat. The coxswain's resolution was taken. Running to windward, he ordered the anchor to be let go and the sails lowered. His object was to get sufficiently near the wreck to receive the people on board without actually touching her. This was a dangerous undertaking; but it had to be performed, if any of the shipwrecked crew were to be saved. Six hands went to the bow, and gradually the cable was paid out, the huge rolling seas carrying us nearer and nearer the wreck. Several broke over us, and, rising against the side of the vessel, concealed her and the crew hanging on to the rigging from our sight. I remained seated, clinging on to the thwart, for I knew that I could do nothing. The brave coxswain, standing up, watched for an advantageous moment to approach the wreck. It seemed to me that it would never come.

'Slacken the cable,' he shouted out; 'three fathoms, a little more, a little more!'

And now the stern of the boat got close up to the wreck. With a wild cry of 'Now, lads, now!' four men sprang into the lifeboat. They were active seamen, or they could not have done it. Scarcely were they on board, than, looking forward, I saw a tremendous sea come rushing down on the boat. The coxswain shouted, 'Haul in, lads! haul in!' The crew, with two of the men who had just joined us, hauled away from the wreck, only just in time; for the sea would otherwise have carried us right up on her deck, and either have dashed the boat to pieces or upset her, and sent us all struggling into the water. The huge wave having broken, again the boat was allowed to approach, and six more of the crew, having unlashed themselves, sprang into her one after the other. Neither they nor we were in safety. 'Are there any more of you?' asked the coxswain, who was compelled to keep his eye to windward to watch the approaching waves.

'Yes, five more,' was the answer.

'Haul away! haul away, lads!' shouted the coxswain, for at that instant he saw another huge wave rolling in.

The lifeboat crew saw it too, and knew full well that it would prove our destruction, should we not get to a safe distance. Still, the remainder of the crew were not to be deserted. Three were men, the other two boys. I could see the poor fellows, as I looked back, lashed to the rigging, holding up their hands in dumb show, imploring us not to desert them. Neither the coxswain nor his crew were men to do that; but already the boat was crowded, and should the sea break on board, some of those saved might be washed out of her. Sea after sea rolled in on the wreck; every moment I expected to see the masts go, with the helpless men clinging to the shrouds, when all must be lost.

'Pay out, pay out, my lads!' exclaimed the coxswain, just as a huge sea was breaking astern of us, and three or four smaller ones of less consequence were approaching.

Again the boat got close up to the wreck. Two more men sprang into her. Another made the attempt, but his foot slipped, or he let go his hold of the rope too soon, and, falling between the boat and the vessel's side, disappeared. One shriek only escaped him; it reached the ears of the two poor boys, who seemed paralyzed with fear and unable to help themselves.

The coxswain shouted to them to let go, and spring towards him. One did as directed, and was caught by the strong arm of one of the crew. The other appeared to be entangled in the rigging. The brave man who had saved the other lad, seeing that the boy would be lost, regardless of the danger he himself was incurring, sprang on board, cutting the lashings with his knife, which he then threw from him. He seized the boy round the waist. At that instant I heard the cry, 'Haul off, haul off!'

'Hold fast for a moment!' shouted the gallant man who had gone to rescue the boy.

By the delay of that moment the lives of all of us were fearfully imperilled. The man sprang with the rescued boy on board; but scarcely had his feet touched the boat when the sea which had just before been observed surrounded her and carried her right up high above the deck of the wreck. The crew forward were hauling away with all their might, although the bow of the boat was pointed downwards, and must, I thought, be dragged under water. Every instant I expected to hear the fatal crash. Had our mizenmast been caught in any of the rigging, our destruction would have been certain; but ere the boat actually struck the wreck she was hauled off; and now the crew, labouring with all their strength, drew her up to her anchor. To weigh the anchor with the sea that was running was impossible. Should the boat drift down on the wreck before sail could be made she must be dashed to pieces.

'Hoist away!' cried the coxswain.

A few strokes with an axe severed the cable, the foresail filled, and away we dashed through the foaming seas, passing so close to the wreck that I thought our mast-head must have struck her bowsprit.

Fourteen human beings had been saved; and with our rescued freight on board we stood towards the harbour. Scarcely had we got clear of the wreck than the remaining mast and the bowsprit went. Had any delay occurred, all those fourteen of our fellow creatures would have lost their lives. How long we had been away

I could not tell, but it appeared like a lifetime to me. I saw that the day was waning, and it would be long still before we could get back safe to land. The gale blew as fiercely as at first, and the seas which occasionally washed over us seemed to threaten our destruction. We could dimly see the land; but the lifeboat crew knew well where they were going; and they now did what they could to relieve the sufferings of the shipwrecked seamen by handing them the flasks of restoratives, with which they had come provided.

Had I gone out with papa's leave, I should have been delighted to see the gallant deed I had witnessed. As it was, I could not help being secretly pleased, though now, strange to say, as the danger decreased, and I had time to think again of my friends, I earnestly longed to be safe on shore.

At last we caught sight of the lights at the mouth of the river, towards which the boat was making her way, although we had to go a long distance round to reach it. I was, of course, wet through, and cold and faint from want of food, though I felt no hunger. The light grew higher and nearer. The wind was at last brought on the quarter, and on the lifeboat flew. I felt her lifted by a monster sea, then down she came, and was the next instant in comparatively quiet water.

Loud cheers greeted us from the shore, which were heartily answered by our crew.

We rushed on, the sails were lowered, and we were alongside the wharf. I was so numbed and cold that I could not stand or spring out of the boat; but I heard a voice, which I knew to be that of papa, shouting out:

'Did you take off a boy with you?'

'Yes, sir; all right; here he is;' and the coxswain, lifting me up in his arms, handed me to papa and Uncle Tom.

They neither of them said anything, but carried me to the boat, which pulled off at once to the yacht. My teeth chattered with cold, so that I could scarcely speak. I was very thankful that they did not ask me questions. I was immediately put into my berth, and Truck soon brought a basin of hot soup, while a stone bottle of hot water was placed at my feet. In ten minutes I felt wonderfully better. Hearing papa in the cabin, I at once acknowledged that I had acted very wrongly.

'The impulse seized me, and I could not resist it,' I said.

'You should not allow yourself to be influenced by a sudden impulse; but I am too thankful that you escaped destruction to be angry with you. Let us thank God that you are preserved.'

After offering our sincere thanks to God for His merciful deliverance, papa said no more; and a very short time afterwards I fell asleep. The next morning, when I awoke we were at sea with the wind off shore, the sun shining brightly, and the water comparatively smooth. There was still a swell from the westward, the only signs of the recent storm.

CHAPTER VIII.

FTER passing Aberdovey and Barmouth, in Cardigan Bay, we sighted St. Tudwell's Island; and then rounding Bardsey Island, on which stands a square white tower, ninety-nine feet in height, with one bright fixed light shining far out over St. George's Channel, we ran north past Porthdinlleyn, steering for Caernarvon, at the southern entrance of the Menai Straits.

As we sailed along we had a great deal of conversation about life-boats. They have been in existence since 1789, when the first boat built expressly for saving life was launched by Mr. H. Greathead, a boat-builder at South Shields; but some years before that a London coach-builder—Mr. Lionel Lukin—designed a boat which he called 'an unimmergible boat;' and, for the purpose of carrying out his experiments, he purchased a Norway yawl, which he tried in the Thames. His plans were entirely successful. He soon afterwards fitted a coble, sent from Bamborough, in Northumberland. The Duke of Northumberland, approving of Mr. Greathead's invention, ordered him to build a boat, which was afterwards stationed at North Shields. For a long time his plan was considered the best, and there are several of his lifeboats, which are impelled exclusively by oars, still in existence.

For years after their invention, the greater part of the coast was without lifeboats, until Sir William Hillary, who, while residing in the Isle of Man, had seen numerous vessels cast away, and lives lost, expressed his wishes to Mr. Thomas Wilson, M.P. for the City of London ; and the two gentlemen called a meeting in 1824, the result of which was the establishment of the 'Royal National Institution for the Preservation of Life from Shipwreck.' From that time forward great encouragement was given to the building of lifeboats ; and there are few parts of the coast now without them. Of course, a lifeboat must differ greatly from a common open boat, for even the best of them is easily filled with water, or upset.

A lifeboat must be buoyant, and firmly ballasted, self-righting, containing plenty of space for the rescued, strength to battle with the heavy seas, and power to resist the many strikings against rocks and wrecks. The buoyancy is obtained by having air chambers formed along the sides of the boat, and a water-tight deck, the space between which and the boat's floor is filled by air chambers. Beside this, at each end there are air cases built across, and reaching to the high gunwales of the bow and stern. The power of discharging water is obtained by forming a watertight deck at the load-water line. In this deck there are several large open tubes, having their upper openings on the surface of the deck, and the lower ones in the boat's floor, thus passing through the space between the deck and the floor, and, of course, hermetically closed to it. In some boats the tubes are kept open, but in the self-righting boats they are fitted with self-acting valves, which open downwards only, so that they will allow any water shipped to pass through them, whilst none can pass upwards. Papa explained that, as the deck is placed above the water-line, any water resting on it will be above the outside level of the sea, and will run out through the valves and tubes into the sea. As fluids always gain their level by specific gravity, the water passes through the valves until none remains above the surface of the deck. In the smaller lifeboats, which have no decks, the only way to relieve the boat is by bailing. It is important that a lifeboat should be well ballasted, especially the larger sailing-boats. These are now ballasted with water, which is let in after the boat is off the beach, and is allowed to fill every available space to a certain height. By being thus heavily ballasted, they can make their way through the most tremendous seas, which would drive back any ordinary boat. Only once has a boat of this description been upset.

A very important feature is that of self-righting. This is obtained by having air chambers of large size, both at the bow and stern, placed high above the centre of gravity. As the boat must be well ballasted, she must have limited breadth of beam, as also limited side buoyancy. By being properly ballasted, a boat can pass either through or over a sea without being driven astern. The raised air chambers prevent the sea breaking over her at the bow or stern; while, if she dips into the sea, she instantly rises again. By having a limited beam, she gains in speed, although she loses in stability; but, at the same time, if upset, she is much more speedily righted; while shorter oars are required, and fewer men to work them.

Papa was strongly in favour of the self-righting principle. The best boats are diagonally built, and copper-fastened. The planks are of mahogany, two thicknesses of half-inch board, with painted calico between them. The keel is of American elm, and the false keel is one piece of cast iron, two and a half inches in width, by four and a half in depth, weighing nine hundredweight. The stem is of English oak, and the gunwale of American elm. The floors are of ash or oak. The deck is of mahogany, well caulked, and seven-eighths of an inch in thickness. These boats are about thirty-three feet in length over all, eight feet in breadth, four feet in depth. They pull, when double-banked, ten oars, which are made of ash, or sometimes fir; and they carry five or six pairs of spare oars, to replace any which may be broken. They are fitted with life-lines outside, by which the men, if thrown out of the boat, can hold on to her, or people swimming can haul themselves on board. No other boats are built so strongly. The principle adopted for planking—that of placing the planks diagonally—gives the greatest possible strength and elasticity, while the mahogany used is of the best.

The lifeboats themselves are liable to disaster. They may be crushed by falling masts, or driven right on board a wreck, or against rocks, where, in spite of the efforts of their crews, they may be dashed to pieces. It is now very rarely the case that lifeboats are lost. In some places steamers are used to tow the lifeboat out to sea; but in most instances she alone can approach a wreck sufficiently near to take off the crew. The cost of establishing a lifeboat on a station is estimated at eight hundred pounds, five hundred and fifty being the price of the boat, her stores, and carriage, and two hundred and fifty pounds that of a substantial boat-house, while the annual cost is about seventy pounds.

The weather was remarkably fine, and the sea smooth, as the wind was off shore. We were generally in sight of the cliffs, which extend along the coast, and had occasional glimpses of blue mountains beyond, Snowdon towering above them all, with the Isle of Anglesea on our port side, and the county of Caernarvon on the starboard. After passing the entrance, the Straits widen out into a lake-like expanse; but the shores again close in where the town of Caernarvon is situated.

Except its far-famed castle, there is nothing very particular to see in the town itself, which is not so picturesque as many we have visited. A small river, the Seiont, passes close to it. The whole town is surrounded by walks united to the castle. The streets, though rather narrow, are laid out at right angles to each other, and are well paved and lighted. We landed, and traversed the town. We presently made our way to the castle. The external walls are ten feet thick, are nearly entire, and enclose a space of three acres. Within them is a gallery running right round, with loop-holes for the discharge of arrows. We clambered up two or three of the towers, which had turrets on their summits; the most important of them is called the Eagle Tower. We were shown a dark chamber, twelve feet by eight; and our guide declared that it was the room in which the first Prince of Wales was born; but, as papa observed, that could not have been the case, as the tower was not built at the

CAERNARVON CASTLE.

time; besides, it was not at all the sort of place the queen would have selected as her bed-chamber; it was far more likely to have been a prison or guard-room. The castle was built by Edward the First, soon after his conquest of Wales; and it was finished about the year 1293. We all considered it the finest ruin we had yet seen. About the time it was finished, the Welsh, led by Prince Madoc, attacked and captured the castle; when, according to the customs of the times, they put its garrison to death, and burnt the town.

Rather more than a century after, Owen Glendower attempted to take the castle, which was so gallantly defended by the governor placed in it by Henry the Fourth, that he was compelled to raise the siege. During the Civil Wars it was captured by the Parliamentary forces, under General Mytton. Such are the chief historical events I recollect connected with the fine old ruin.

A considerable number of trading vessels were alongside the quays, taking in slate and copper ore, the chief products of the district. Enormous quantities of slate are exported from Wales.

We remained a night here, as it was too late to run through the Straits to Bangor. Early the following morning, however, the wind was fair, and we continued on the same course. The tide also favoured us. Had it been against us, as it runs at the rate of between five and six miles an hour, we should have made but little progress. The shores are high and picturesque, with villages here and there, and some handsome residences, the finest belonging to the Marquis of Anglesea.

We soon came in sight of the tubular bridge carrying the railway across the Straits. The distance between the cliffs on either shore is eleven hundred feet. It was curious, as we sailed under it, to look up to a height of one hundred and four feet, and to see these two enormous tubes above our heads. Their total length is one thousand eight hundred and thirty-three feet, which includes two hundred and thirty feet at either end resting on the land. The tubes are composed of wrought-iron plates, three quarters of an inch thick, tightly riveted together, the one carrying the up, and the other the down line. The bridge is supported by three vast piers, measuring sixty-two feet by fifty-three feet at their base. This wonderful work is considered to surpass that of the Menai Bridge. It may be asked how these tubes could ever have been got up to their present positions. This was accomplished by means of hydraulic presses of the most powerful description; indeed, it is asserted that one of them could throw a stream of water twenty thousand feet into the air,— above five times higher than Snowdon, and five thousand feet higher

TUBULAR BRIDGE OVER THE MENAI STRAITS.

than the summit of Mont Blanc. The bridge was commenced in 1846 by Robert Stephenson, and the first train passed through it on the 1st of March, 1850; since which time no accident has happened to it.

A little further on we saw above us the celebrated Menai Bridge. The piers are each one hundred and fifty three feet high, and five hundred and fifty three feet apart. Sixteen iron chains, one thousand seven hundred and fifteen feet in length, pass from pier to pier, and support the bridge. The chains have a dip in the centre of forty-four feet, thus allowing the roadway to have a clear elevation of a hundred feet above high water at spring tide. These sixteen chains are carried through sixty feet of solid rock. The whole length of the bridge is about one-third of a mile, including four arches at one end, and three at the other, which carry the road out to the two suspending piers. The bridge was opened in January, 1826. It was designed by Thomas Telford, the engineer. The work occupied six years, and cost £120,000, —much less than an ironclad, and infinitely more useful and durable. Before it was built people had to cross by a dangerous ferry. We were surprised to hear that the compensation given to the owners of the ferry for the surrender of their right amounted to £26,577—the annual income of the ferry being computed at £815 18s.

We sailed on to Bangor, before which we brought-up in the Bay of Beaumaris. There is not much to see in the town itself, except that it is pleasantly situated. By climbing the hill above it we obtained a fine view over the island of Anglesea.

Our chief object in coming here was to see the slate quarries at Penrhyn. They are of enormous extent, and not less than three thousand men and boys are employed in them, whose wages amount to upwards of £2000 per week; and it is calculated that upwards of 11,000 people, including wives and children, find subsistence from working these quarries. A railway conveys the slate about six miles, to the shores of the Menai Straits; and upwards of 70,000 tons of slate are annually exported, the income derived from them being £250,000 per annum. They are the property of the noble owner of the magnificent Penrhyn Castle.

We passed through the village of Llandegai—a model of beauty and neatness—situated at the chief entrance of the castle grounds. We crossed over by the ferry to Beaumaris, in the island of Anglesea. It is a very picturesque place, on the north-western side of the bay called after it. The distance across the bay is about eight miles. From the shore we could distinguish Penmaenmawr, Puffin Island, Great Orme's Head, Conway Bay, and other interesting spots. The distance round the whole island is about eighty miles. On the western shore lies the island of Holyhead, joined to Anglesea by a bridge. This little island is made the chief port of departure for the Irish coast.

The appearance of Anglesea is not picturesque, as the country is level, and there are few trees; but it is surrounded by rocks on the northern shore. The most rugged portion is Moelfre Bay, where the unfortunate Royal Charter was wrecked, when so many people lost their lives.

Anglesea was the last part of England in which the Druids practised their rites. Many of the Druidical remains still exist, the most remarkable of which are called cromlechs—flat stones resting upon others, probably serving as altars. Anglesea was governed by its native princes until the reign of Edward the First, when it became subject to England. We made our way to the ivy-covered castle, which stands a short distance from the town. It is nearly square, has a round tower at each angle, and another at each side, and is surrounded by low massive walls. The inner court is about one hundred and ninety feet square. To the north-west of it stands the banqueting hall, seventy feet long. On the east side is a chapel, in the Early English style of architecture. The castle was built by Edward the First, soon after those of Conway and Caernarvon. It was surrounded by a deep fosse, which could be filled by water from the sea. It held out like that of Caernarvon, but was captured by the Parliamentary forces under General Mytton.

We got back late, and did not sail until next morning, when we stood for the entrance of Conway harbour, but had to pull up to the town in a boat.

We have seen many interesting places; but as we gazed up at the great walls of the ancient castle of Conway, we agreed it is the most beautiful and picturesque of them all.

I can give only a brief description of the town. It is surrounded by a wall twelve feet thick, and a mile and a quarter in length, having twenty-seven towers and battlements. One of them is called Llewellyn's. It is entered by five gates, three principal, and one postern; and another has been formed to admit a suspension-bridge across the river, similar to that constructed by Mr. Telford across the Menai Straits. Mr. Stephenson also designed the tubular bridge through which the Holyhead railway passes. The town contains some very picturesque houses, built in the time of Elizabeth.

The castle stands on the verge of a precipitous rock on the south-east corner of the town. Its walls are triangular in shape, being said to resemble a Welsh harp; they are fifteen feet thick, and are strengthened by twenty-one towers. The most striking portion is Queen Eleanor's Tower; the most curious is the Fragment Tower. Two centuries ago some of the inhabitants, searching for slate, undermined it, when a portion fell, leaving a perfect arch, since which period not a stone has fallen away, and it is still as firm as ever. We wandered round and round the castle, wondering at the massiveness of the masonry. It would have still been perfect—for it was spared by the Parliamentary forces who captured it—had not a Lord Conway, in Charles the Second's reign, stripped off the timber, lead, and other materials to sell. The vessels, however, conveying the materials to Ireland, were lost, and the greedy baron gained nothing by the barbarous proceeding.

Pulling down the river, we returned on board, and immediately getting under weigh, beat out of Beaumaris Bay. Having taken a look at Puffin's Island, and rounded the lofty promontory of Great Orme's Head, with a fair wind, we stood for the mouth of the Mersey.

By keeping very close in shore for some distance we got a view of Llandudno, now become a fashionable watering-place, and sighted Abergele, where the fearful railway accident happened some years ago, when so many people were crushed or burnt to death. We also passed over the spot where the Ocean Monarch was burnt, almost close to the land; yet out of nearly four hundred passengers, nearly half were lost.   The ship was so near the beach that good swimmers could easily have reached the shore.   The survivors were rescued by the boats of various vessels which came to their assistance.

CONWAY CASTLE.

It was getting dusk when we sighted the bright light on Ayr Point. at the mouth of the river Dee.   As the navigation of the Mersey is difficult during the dark, we ran up the river a short distance, and came to an anchor off the town of Mostyn.

The Dee is a most picturesque river, from its source in Merionethshire to Chester; but its navigation at the mouth is somewhat difficult, owing to the large deposits of sand, which have to a great extent blocked up the channel. Between Chester and the mouth are two flourishing towns, Holywell and Flint. The chief wealth of Flintshire consists in its lead mines, which are very productive; and not only is lead dug up, but silver, of which about ten ounces is found in every ton of ore. Flint has a castle; but it is not equal in picturesque beauty, we are told, to those we had already seen.

Before daylight we were again under weigh, as we had numerous lighthouses and light-ships to guide us; indeed, no river is more perfectly lighted than the Mersey, for numerous shoals lie at its entrance, and few rivers have so many vessels standing in and out at all hours. We counted no less than eight lights as we sailed along.

Daylight broke as we came off the mouth of the river; and the wind being fair and moderate, we stood up without fear of getting on shore. We followed a homeward-bound clipper fruit vessel, passing the entrance to numerous fine docks, and shipping of all descriptions. We picked up a tolerably safe berth among several other yachts. It was well we got up when we did, for soon afterwards the whole river seemed covered with spluttering, hissing, smoking, panting, busy little steam vessels, crossing to Birkenhead, on the Chester shore, or running up the river or down the river, or visiting vessels at anchor in the stream. The tide also had just turned. The wind being light and fair, numbers of outward-bound ships got under weigh, carried on their course by steamers lashed alongside. As soon as we had dressed and breakfasted, we pulled to a landing-stage outside the docks.

Giving a description of Liverpool is out of the question. We made our way over bridges until we reached the quays, and then through streets with enormously high warehouses, many of them constructed entirely of iron. We passed the Custom House, which stands on the very site of Lyrpul, the old pool from which Liverpool derives its name having been long since filled up. It is said to be one of the most magnificent pieces of architecture that our age has produced. Near the Custom House is the Exchange, with a wide square in front ; and further to the left the parish church of St. Nicholas, interesting from its antiquity. Passing along a fine street, we reached St. George's Hall, a sumptuous Corinthian building, upwards of four hundred feet in length. As within it the judicial proceedings of Liverpool are conducted, it is known as the Assize Court. The most interesting place we visited near the water was the Sailors' Home, a fine building, opened in 1850. At each corner is a square tower, surmounted by a dome, the summit of which is one hundred feet from the ground. Passing through the Canning Place entrance, we entered a lofty hall, surrounded by galleries communicating with rooms on the several floors. The building contains a large dining-hall, a lecture-room, reading-room, savings bank, and nautical school. Both officers and men are received, and a seaman may lodge there a day, or for as long a time as he remains in port, during which time he is provided with board and medical attendance at a very moderate rate.

After walking through the streets of Liverpool, we crossed by a ferry to Birkenhead, and made our way to a spot of high ground, from whence we could obtain a complete panoramic view of the town and river. Looking to our right, we saw the Mersey flowing from the south in a northerly direction towards the Irish Sea. Below us, in the midst of the stream, we could distinguish, extending in a long line from right to left, some of the largest merchant ships in the world. There were also smaller craft of every description, with the flags of nearly all nations flying from their mast-heads, either ready to sail, waiting for orders, or preparing to go into dock ; while others, with wide-spread canvas, or with steam tugs alongside, were coming up or down the river. Before us we made out a huge tobacco ware-house, and behind it, dock beyond dock, far away to the south, and

still further towards the sea and the north.   On one side was the
King's Dock, the Queen's Basin and Dock, the Coburg Dock, the

SAILOR'S HOME, LIVERPOOL.

Union Dock, and the Brunswick Dock—'their names showing,' as
papa observed, 'the periods at which they were formed.'   To the

O 2

north of King's Dock we saw the Albert Dock, with the Marine Parade
in front of it; also Salthouse Dock, Canning Dock, George's Dock, with
its landing-stage towards the river; and the enormous Prince's Dock
still further to the south, and a line of basins and docks beyond.   These
docks are not small pools, but large rectangular lakes, crowded thickly
with magnificent shipping loaded with the produce of numberless
countries, their tall masts rising towards the sky in dense groves, their

STRAND STREET, LIVERPOOL.

yards so interlocked that it seemed impossible that they could ever be
extricated.   The sight gave us some idea of the number of vessels
which belong to Liverpool, or annually visit this port.

Beyond this double row of docks we saw the vast city rising gradually from the water, with winding streets extending from the Custom House in all directions, the larger running eastward, with numerous churches and other public buildings scattered amid them ; and far beyond, squares and parks, with streets of handsome private residences.

Little more than a century ago Liverpool possessed only three small docks, and the shipping belonging to the port amounted to only 236 vessels. At present upwards of 10,000 vessels belong to the port; while the ships entered outwards and inwards number upwards of 30,000, with a burden of more than four million tons. We went on board a training-ship for poor boys taken from the streets, to fit them for becoming seamen in the merchant service. There is also another ship to prepare officers, conducted on the same principle as that of the Worcester in the Thames. We then pulled on board a large Australian emigrant ship about to sail. She carried three classes of passengers. The first had very handsome cabins surrounding the saloon, which was fitted up in a luxurious style. On the deck below there were the second-class passengers, whose cabins were comfortable, but confined, and their mess-cabin was rather small for the number of people to occupy it. The larger part of the lower deck was fitted with rough wooden berths, partitioned off for each family, one sleeping-place being above the other, and a small space in front for the people to dress in. There was an after division occupied by the single women, who had a matron to superintend them; while the single men were also in a division by themselves. They were all under the care of a surgeon. There was a schoolmaster, to teach those who wished to learn during the voyage, and to act as chaplain. Constables were selected from amongst the most respectable of the married men, whose duty it was to keep order, and to see that the rules and regulations were properly observed. Of course, with so many people crowded together, it is highly necessary that cleanliness should be attended to. The ship was getting under weigh, and the people who had come to see their relatives and friends off were ordered into their boats. We witnessed many pathetic scenes. There was much fluttering of handkerchiefs as the boats pulled away, while the women crowded the sides, and the men climbed up into the shrouds and waved their hats. The moorings were slipped, the tug began puffing and snorting, and the stout ship commenced her voyage half round the world, bearing away many who were never again to see their native shores. Many thousands of people thus leave Liverpool for Australia, New Zealand, or the Cape, as well as for Canada, the United States, and South America, every year.

It took us four days to obtain even a cursory view of Liverpool and Birkenhead. We were very glad to be at sea again. The weather was hot, and running about all day was tiring work. Leaving the river, we steered along the Lancashire coast, but did not put into any of its numerous harbours, contenting ourselves with looking at the chart and reading a description of each place as we came off it. Our course was for the Mull of Galloway, the most southern point of Scotland; but we could not steer directly for it, as we should have run down the Isle of Man, 'and sunk it, for what we could tell,' as Dick observed. We had therefore to keep to the eastward of that island. Among the places we passed were Lytham, Blackpool, and Fleetwood; and then, crossing Morecambe Bay, we passed Walney, to the south of the river Duddon. From Fleetwood a number of vessels run across to the Isle of Man. We were much amused on coming on deck in the morning to hear Dick Pepper remark:

'Hullo! what's become of the land?'

It was the first time that we had been actually out of sight of land.

'How shall we manage to find our way now?' he asked.

I pointed to the compass.

'That will take us there,' I answered.

‘Oh, yes ; but suppose it made a mistake ? We should be running on to some coast or other before we knew where we were.’

‘We crossed the big sea,’ observed Nat, ‘and for days and days together we did not see any land.’

I got out the chart, and showed Dick the point of Ayr, the most northern part of the Isle of Man, towards which we were now directing our course.

‘We shall see it in the course of the morning. If you were to go to the mast-head, you would probably make out the land to the south of it.’

‘Are we to touch at the Isle of Man ?’ asked Dick. ‘I should very much like to see some of the places described by Sir Walter Scott.’

‘Papa says that we have no time,’ I replied. ‘If we don’t make more speed than we have hitherto done, we shall not get round England before the summer is over ; and the east coast is not to be trifled with. Although he says that we shall be unable to see many of the places he would like to visit, we shall nevertheless obtain a general view of the country.’

I have not said much about Nat. Poor little fellow! He was quite reconciled to his lot, and had become completely one of us. We had as much affection for him as if he had been our brother. I took a special interest in him, as he was my pupil ; and I devoted a part of every day to teaching him. He was very obedient, and always did his best to learn his lessons ; so that it was quite a pleasure for me to instruct him.

Dick was greatly astonished when papa came on deck with the sextant in his hand, and ‘shot’ the sun, as it is called ; that is to say, he ascertained our exact latitude by observing through the instrument the height of the sun at noon. Placing it to his eye, he watched it until it ceased to rise, the indicator showing the number of degrees it was above the horizon. The *Nautical Almanack* gives the height it would be at noon on that day along every parallel so that a few figures enabled him to ascertain how far north we had sailed. The way to find the longitude, he explained to us, was by means of the chronometer. An observation is then taken of the sun, moon, or a star, which would appear at a certain height above the horizon at that particular hour.

AILSA CRAG.

The wind fell before we reached the Isle of Man. In the evening we saw several bright lights burst forth—some on the Isle of Man, others on the mainland. On the right we saw a fixed light, which the chart showed us was St. Bees' Head; while another shone from the point of Ayr. Leaving St. Bees' Head astern, with the light on the point of Ayr on our port beam, we came in sight of the intermittent light of the Mull of Galloway. Most of these lights were visible at the same time; and as we sailed up the channel we could see those on the Irish coast, as well as those on the coast of Scotland.

When we came on deck the next morning, we were passing along the coast of Ayrshire, within sight of Ailsa Crag, a fine rock, which stands out of the sea to a great height. It is a mass of columnar trap of a grey colour. We steered so as to pass it on our starboard side. We had come in sight of the southern face, where we could distinguish a square tower, perched on a terrace, about two hundred feet above the sea. The ascent to the summit must be no easy matter. As we sailed on, we came off the north-west side, which is almost perpendicular, and composed of successive tiers of enormous columns. Here we made out a cave, above which was a grassy declivity sloping upwards towards the summit. Though it is at the very mouth of the Clyde, its great height causes it to be seen at a distance, preventing it being dangerous to vessels bound to Glasgow. Any person inclined to solitude might take up his abode there, and live without leaving it, as it is inhabited by numerous flocks of sea-fowl, with goats and rabbits; while nettles, and a variety of hardy plants, grow in the interstices of the rocks. I asked Dick if he would like to remain there, saying that I would get papa to put him on shore, if he wished it; but he declined the offer, preferring rather to go back to school at the end of the holidays.

Passing Ayr and Troon, we came off Ardrossan, then stood on to Port-in-cross, close to Fairlie Head, which forms the south-eastern point at the entrance of the Firth of Clyde. Opposite, in the distance, rose the Isle of Arran, with its lofty picturesque hills. We brought up off Port-in-cross for the night, as we wished to have daylight for ascending the Clyde, so as to enjoy the scenery.

Next morning, the wind being fair, we made good progress. The country on our right, though very smiling and pretty, was not so grand as we expected; but we saw, far away over the port bow, blue mountains rising one beyond the other. Directly after getting under weigh, we passed two islands, the Lesser Cumbrae, at the entrance of the Firth, and the Greater Cumbrae, a little higher up.

To our right we saw the village of Largs, celebrated as the scene of a great battle, won by the Scottish army, under Alexander the Third, over Haco, King of Norway. To our left was the Island of Bute. We sailed on nearly due north, until the channel gave a sudden bend, just after we had passed the town of Greenock, a busy-looking place, with ship-building yards, and smoking chimneys, interesting to us because Watt was born here; near it we had seen on the opposite shore the village of Dunoon, a pretty watering-place. The wind being from the southward, we were able, close-hauled, to stand up the Clyde. We passed Port Glasgow, which was at one time really the port of Glasgow; but the river having been deepened by dredges, vessels of large size can now run up to Glasgow itself.

We appeared to be in quite a labyrinth of lochs, Holy Loch running up in one direction, Loch Long in another, and Gare Loch in a third, all joining the Clyde on the north. We were eagerly looking out for Dumbarton, which stands on a lofty projecting point of rock where the river Leven runs into the Clyde. The scenery round us was the finest we had yet beheld. The summit is crowned by bristling batteries pointing down the Firth. Bringing up, that we might pay it a visit, we at once pulled towards the Governor's house, which stands on a platform at the base of the rock. We ascended a flight of steep steps to a space between two summits, where are erected some barracks and the armoury. The most interesting object we saw was Wallace's great double-handed sword, which he wielded with such terrific power against his southern foes. Of course, as we looked at it, we sang—

'Scots wa' hae wi' Wallace bled.'

When the unfortunate Mary was Queen of Scots, in the year 1571, and the place was in possession of her partisans, it was captured in an extraordinary manner by Crawford, of Jordan Hill, an officer of the Lennox. He and a few followers, landing there during the night with ladders, climbed the cliffs. During the ascent one of the party was seized with a paralytic fit. As any sound would have aroused the garrison, the man was lashed by his companions to the ladder. It was then turned round, and they all ascended, leaving him hanging there until they had gained the fortress, when he was released.

From this eminence we obtained a magnificent view over the Vale of Leven, with lofty Ben Lomond in the distance; while the views down and up the Clyde were such as we had never seen surpassed in beauty.

As papa and Uncle Tom did not wish to take the yachts further, we got on board one of the steamers running up to Glasgow. During the passage we passed numbers of steamers, large and small, rushing up and down the stream at a rapid rate; and sailing vessels of all sizes outward-bound, or returning home; the former laden with the cotton and woollen manufactures produced in Glasgow and the neighbourhood, giving us some idea of the vast amount of trade carried on in the city. Curious-looking steam dredges were also at work, with wheels ever revolving, ladling up the mud from the bottom of the river—an endless task, for fresh mud is constantly being washed down from the upper parts of the stream. Clouds of smoke and increasing signs of activity showed us that we were approaching Glasgow.

We took a hurried view of that famed city, wandered through its broad streets, with stone-built houses and fine edifices, people bustling about, and numberless tall factory chimneys smoking; drays and carts carrying merchandise from the quays, and everything wearing an air of prosperity. We looked into the ancient sombre Cathedral, with its beautiful modern stained-glass windows, and visited the University, with its museum and library,—the museum bequeathed by William Hunter, the great surgeon, who gave at the same time £8,000 to erect a building for its reception.

Uncle Tom told us a story of Hunter's first lecture. Being unknown to fame, no one had come to hear him. On entering the hall, he found only Sandy M'Tavish, the old custos. He was not daunted, however. Bidding the old man sit down, he brought a skeleton from a cupboard, and having placed it in front of him, he began to lecture to it and Sandy. First one student by chance looked in, and, seeing what was going forward, beckoned to another. In the course of a few

GLASGOW UNIVERSITY.

minutes another dropped in, and soon discovered that no ordinary lecturer was speaking. The whole audience could not have amounted to a dozen; but they soon made a noise about what they had heard, and the next day the hall was crowded.

Our next visit was to a fine cemetery across a valley above the town; and Dick declared that it would be quite a pleasure to be buried there. It was crowded with fine monuments to celebrated persons.

Glasgow owes much of its prosperity to its situation in the midst of a country producing coal and minerals, and having water communication down the Clyde towards the west into the Atlantic, and through the great canal which connects that river with the Forth and German Ocean. We got back to Dumbarton, where the Dolphin's boat was on the look-out for us, just at nightfall.

It being moonlight, we sailed down the Clyde, and enjoyed the beautiful scenery under a different aspect. Had we possessed steam, we could have run through the channel of Bute, and then up Loch Fyne, passing through the Crinan Canal into Loch Linnhe; but as that could not be done, we had to sail round Arran and the Mull of Cantyre, and then up the Sound of Jura. We thus lost the enjoyment of much magnificent scenery; but the shorter route would probably have taken us a far longer time to perform, as in those narrow waters we could only sail during daylight, and might be detained by a contrary wind.

OLD LIVERPOOL.

CHAPTER IX.

THE day after leaving the Clyde, we were coasting along the not very attractive-looking island of Islay, inhabited by the Macdonalds. It was often the scene of forays, which one clan was wont to make on another, in the good old days, as people delight to call them, when the ancestors of the present race were scarcely more civilised than the South Sea islanders. Though rock-girt, Islay is fertile, and a large portion has been brought under a state of cultivation.

A fair breeze, with the tide in our favour, carried us through the sound between the islands of Islay and Jura, the broadest part of which is about a mile in width, and is lined by abrupt but not very high cliffs. More than a century ago, Islay received a visit from the French Admiral Thurot; and a few years later Paul Jones made a descent on the island, and captured a packet which had on board a Major Campbell, a native gentleman, who had just returned with an independence from India, the larger portion of which he unfortunately had with him in gold and jewels, of which, as may be supposed, the American privateer relieved him. In later years another American privateer, 'the true-blooded Yankee,' captured a considerable number of merchant vessels at anchor in Port Charlotte.

We anchored at nightfall in a deep bay at the southern end of Colonsay, called Toulgoram. A narrow strait divides that little island from the still smaller one of Oronsay.

Next morning. before sailing, we pulled across the strait, which is dry at low water, and visited a ruined priory of considerable extent and tolerably entire. We saw also many other ruins of abbeys or monasteries; indeed, the monks must have been almost as numerous as the rabbits, which we saw running about in all directions. The wind still favouring us, we steered for the western end of Mull, and in a short time came in sight of its lofty cliffs; while we could see in the distance astern the peaked mountains of Jura and the island of Scarba, between which lies the whirlpool of Corryvrechan, a place we had no desire to visit. In stormy weather, when the tides rush through the passage, a regular whirlpool is formed, which would prove the destruction of any vessels attempting to pass that way. Standing on a height above it, the waters are seen to leap, and bound, and tumble, then whirling along as over a precipice, then dashed together with inconceivable impetuosity, sometimes rising in a foaming mass to a prodigious height, and then opening and forming a vast abyss, while the roar of troubled waters as they strike against the rocky shore is heard far and wide.

We reached Iona in ample time to take a walk around the island. This was the island on which the so-called St. Columba lived. It is about three miles long, and one wide, and the most lofty hill is not more than four hundred feet in height. The remains show that the nunneries and monasteries Columba established were of a very rude kind. It was looked upon as a holy island, and many kings and chiefs were buried there. Macbeth was the last king of Scotland who had that honour paid him. Opposite the cathedral we saw a beautiful cross, carved in high relief. It had fallen down, but had been replaced on a basement of granite.

The next place of interest before which we brought-up was the island of Staffa. We could see in the distance the islands of Coll and

Tiree. The latter, only about a mile and a half in circumference, rises out of the ocean to the height of about one hundred and forty-four feet. Before landing we sailed along the eastern shore, examining the

IONA.

wonderful caves and the fine colonnades which form its sides. One might suppose that it was rather a work of art than thrown up by Nature. The yachts were hove-to, and we pulled off to examine the caves in the boats. One is known as the Clam Shell Cave, another as the Herdsman's Cave, and a third is denominated the Great Colonnade and Causeway. Then there comes the Boat Cave, and Mackinnon's Cave, and lastly, the most magnificent of all, Fingal's Cave. Into this we at once rowed. I scarcely know how to describe it. On either side are lofty columns, mostly perpendicular, and remarkably

FINGAL'S CAVE.

regular, varying from two to four feet in diameter. The height of this wonderful cavern is sixty-six feet near the entrance, but it decreases to twenty-two feet at the further end; it is two hundred and

P

twenty-seven feet long, and forty-two wide. At one side is a causeway formed of the remains of broken columns, upon which people can walk to the very end. We next pulled into what is called the Boat Cave, where columns are even more regular than in Fingal's Cave, but it is much smaller. Our last visit was to Mackinnon's Cave ; its sides are perfectly smooth, it is about fifty feet high, and forty-eight broad, the roof being almost flat. We pulled on for two hundred and twenty-four feet, until we reached a beach of pebbles at the further end, when we appeared to be in a vast hall. Several places, where the tops of the columns crop up, have the appearance of a tesselated pavement.

A steady breeze carried us in sight of Ardnamurchan, when, steering to the east, standing close to the sea-coast, we passed Castle Mingary, the battlemented walls of which presented no opening. A few miles further on we came to an anchor in the snug harbour of Tobermory. It is a very picturesque village, situated at the foot of hills which run round the bay. We were told that one of the ships of the Invincible Armada, the Florida, was sunk in the bay by something resembling a torpedo, manufactured by a renowned witch who lived in those days on Mull. She was instigated to the deed by the wife of MacLean of Duart. The lady had become jealous of a fair princess, who was voyaging on board the Florida, and had fallen in love with her lord. It is asserted that the Spanish damsel was a daughter of the King of Spain ; and having dreamed that a young gentleman of engaging appearance had invited her to become his bride, was sailing round the world in search of him, when, on seeing MacLean, he seemed to be the creature of her fancy.

Sailing from Tobermory, bound for the western coast of Skye, we passed the island of Muck, an unpleasant-sounding name. To the north is the curious island of Eig, the southern side of which is perfectly flat, but in the north rises a lofty perpendicular rock, called the Scuir of Eig. Within it is a large cavern, which was the scene of one of those atrocious acts in 'the good old days' when might made right. Two hundred Macdonalds, fugitives from a superior number of Macleods, had taken refuge in the cavern, when, unfortunately for them, one of their party, having left the mark of his footsteps in the snow, their place of concealment was betrayed. The Macleods filled up the mouth of the cavern with wood and dried sea-weed, and setting it on fire, literally smoked them to death. One of the Macdonalds being connected by marriage with the Macleods, was offered permission to crawl out on his hands and knees, and to bring out four others along with him in safety; but having selected a friend hated by the Macleods, who refused to spare the man's life, he preferred to suffer death with his clansmen than to live on without them. Until quite a late period, the bones of the ill-fated Macdonalds were still to be seen lying near the entrance. Say what we will in favour of the Highlanders, they were a fearfully savage people in those days.

The part of the Highlands amid which we were sailing was the scene of many of the Pretender's adventures. Had not Prince Charles been an excellent climber, he would not have escaped his enemies, when they were hunting him like a hare. They nearly entrapped him in one of the many rock fastnesses in which he took shelter.

We passed along these coasts a continual succession of caves and wild rocks, presenting the appearance of ruined castles, Gothic arches, buttresses, towers, and gateways; others again having a curious resemblance to faces, profiles, even ships under sail.

Passing the Point of Sleat, at the southern end of Skye, we sailed up the wild and grand Loch Scavaig. Rising up abruptly from the water are rugged mountains of a dark and gloomy aspect,—the bare rocks alone are seen without a particle of vegetation. Their metallic appearance arises from their being composed of a mineral called hypersthene. On either side rose sharp peaks, one called the Shouting Mountain, another the Notched Peak; while a small island at the foot of another height, called the Hill of Dispute, goes by the name of the Island of the Slippery-Step. From its appearance no one would wish to land there. Not a tree was to be seen.

'The essence of savagedom!' cried Uncle Tom.

'Well, grand; yes, very grand!' exclaimed Oliver; 'but I'd rather not live here.'

'I shouldn't like to be on shore there during an earthquake!' cried Dick. 'A fellow would chance to have his head broken if those mountains should begin to tumble about.'

An artist who came here is said to have thrown away his pencil in despair; but it is still more difficult to give a description of the place in words. Having selected a spot for anchoring, with the help of a fisherman who acted as our pilot, we pulled on shore, and making our way over about four hundred yards of rock by the side of a small stream, we reached the dark fresh-water Loch Coruisk, round which rose a circle of gigantic barren mountains of purple hue. On this side the sun was shining brightly, lighting up the pointed crags, while the other was thrown into the deepest shade.

'I shouldn't like to find myself here in the evening, without knowing my way out!' exclaimed Dick. 'I wonder how the clouds manage to get over those tall peaks.'

Dick might have wondered, for several of them are nearly three thousand feet in height; and on the topmost, called the Black Peak, probably no human foot has ever trod.

'Just give a shout, sir,' said the fisherman, who, having been on board a man-of-war in his youth, spoke English. As he uttered the words he gave a loud hail, the echo coming back with wonderful distinctness. We all followed his example, and it seemed as if a thousand people were all shouting together in chorus,—the sound at length dying away, apparently many a mile off. Dick then began to laugh, and immediately a laugh came back, which set us all laughing, and a curious chorus we had, till our jaws began to ache from over-exertion.

We then made our way out of this wild region, not sorry to get on board, and to dive down into the comfortable cabin of the Dolphin, where dinner was waiting us. Still, although everything was familiar round us in the confined space of the yacht's cabin, so deeply impressed on my vision was the grand wild scene outside, that I could not help viewing it over the sides and back of the vessel, and I never for one moment lost the consciousness of where we were.

We remembered that it was at Coruisk that Bruce encountered Cormack Doil. Sir Walter Scott makes him say:

'A scene so wild, so rude as this,
Yet so sublime in barrenness,
Ne'er did my wandering footsteps press,
Where'er I happ'd to roam.'

At dawn next morning we left this wild bay, not without regret, though Dick declared that he felt much happier when he was once more on the open sea. We then sailed along the western coast of Skye, looking into many other places (which, if not so wild and grand, were highly picturesque), until we reached Dunvegan Loch; and making our way amid several small islands, we came to an anchor a short distance from the castle, and took to the boat. The castle stands on a rock projecting into the water, protected by a stream on one side and a moat on the other, and before conical shot were invented must have been a very strong place. Though it retains much of its ancient and imposing appearance, it is still in perfect repair, and is of great extent. It belongs to Macleod of Macleod, whose father and grandfather expended large sums in making it one of the most comfortable residences in the Western Highlands. On the side next the sea is a low wall, pierced with embrasures, while a handsome centre building is also surmounted by battlements. There are two towers, one of which the steward, who politely showed us over the castle, said was built in the ninth century, and the other was added in the thirteenth. Doctor Johnson paid this castle a visit, and was hospitably received by the laird.

We were shown the drinking-horn of Sir Roderick Macleod, an ancestor of the family, and the remains of a 'fairy flag,' made of stout yellow silk, which used to be unfurled when the tide of battle was turning against the Macleods, and which always had the effect of again turning it in their favour.

Again getting under weigh, we sailed round the northern end of Skye, up the Sound of Raasay, between the small island of that name and Skye, to Portree. It stands on the end of a point of land, far up a deep harbour, and is a picturesque-looking place.

DUNVEGAN CASTLE.

Here we had a long discussion as to our future proceedings. It was finally settled that Uncle Tom should sail round the north of Scotland in the Dolphin, while we were to go south again, and through the Caledonian Canal, waiting for him off Fort George, at the mouth of the Moray Firth.

Early in the morning we sailed with the Dolphin, to accompany her as far as the Island of Rona, to the north of Raasay, where we looked into a curious little loch, at the head of which is a farm-house. The owner—as is the case with most people residing on that shore—had been a seafaring man. He had gone away to Skye, and was expected back by his loving wife, when a furious gale arose. To light him on his way, she had been accustomed to place a large lamp in the window of the cottage, which looked down on the loch. On that night she trimmed it with double care. In vain, however, she sat and watched; hour after hour passed by as she waited, expecting to hear her husband's cheerful voice as he came on shore, calling out to her amid the howling storm; but in vain she watched. Day dawned, and the little vessel had not reached her accustomed moorings. The next night her lamp was lighted as usual. When the storm abated, tidings came that portions of a wrecked vessel had been picked up on the shore; but she hoped against hope that it might not be her husband's craft. Still, though he came not, she lighted the lamp. Night after night, and month after month, that bright light streamed forth from the solitary cottage on the beach; and many a storm-tossed vessel owed its safety to that unpretending beacon. At length the Scottish Commissioners of Lighthouses heard of this volunteer lighthouse. An annual sum of money was voted for its support, and the widow received a lamp with reflectors, with a supply of oil to keep her lamp burning. The commissioners paid her and her family a visit; and, though years have passed, that lamp burns as brightly as ever.

As papa wished Oliver to see the Caledonian Canal, he had returned on board the Lively. We now parted from the Dolphin, saluting each other with loud cheers; and while she sailed northward, with the wind on the beam, we steered south through the broad passage which separates Raasay from the mainland.

'I'll tell you all about the northern coast and John o' Groat's House; and you shall give me an account of the canal, though I don't envy you,' shouted Jack, as we parted.

The wind sometimes headed us, but we saw more of the coast until, passing Applecross, we reached the Island of Scalpa. We then had a fair wind past Loch Carron to Loch Alsh, which lies between one end of Skye and the mainland. Steering due east, we ran through it, and then again had to haul up to pass through the narrow channel which separates the south end of Skye from the main.

Hauling our wind, we stood through a very narrow passage, and entered Sleat Sound, a broad expanse, when once more we had Eig in sight on our starboard bow, and passed the entrance to numerous lochs, many of them, like Loch Hourn and Loch Nevish, between lofty mountains. Passing Muck and then Ardnamurchan on our port side, we entered Loch Sunart. Running by Tobermory with the wind nearly aft, we entered the Sound of Mull, which carried us into Loch Linnhe, opposite the Island of Lismore. Just opposite to us, on the south end of the island, we saw Auchindown Castle, a lofty square building on the top of a rock rising out of the sea, which was once in possession of the Bishops of Argyle and the Isles, but which is much more like a castle than an episcopal residence.

Standing on, with the wind on our port beam, we ran up Loch Linnhe, passing the entrance to Loch Leven, near to which is the Pass of Glencoe, where, as every one knows, Mac Ian, the chief of the Macdonalds of Glencoe, with a number of his family and followers, was treacherously murdered by Campbell of Glen Lyon, and a party of military under his command.

It was dark when we reached Fort William, at the head of Loch Linnhe, though the water still ran a long way, turning to the left and forming Loch Eil. This loch gives its name to a branch of the Camerons, to which belonged one of the most redoubtable opponents of Cromwell in the Highlands—Sir Ewan Cameron. In consequence, the Protector built a fort at Inverloch, which in King William's reign was greatly enlarged, receiving the name of Fort William.

Beyond the fort to the eastward we saw Ben Nevis, while to the north was the entrance to the Caledonian Canal. Not far off from

Loch Eil is Loch Shiel, at the head of which is the spot where, on the 19th of August, 1745, Prince Charles Edward unfurled his standard, when he made the audacious attempt to win the crown which his

LOCH LEVEN.

ancestor had forfeited. On that occasion the then Lord of Lochiel headed seven hundred of the clan Camerons, who with three hundred of the Macdonnells formed the chief part of the hapless band. Of course, they thought themselves very fine fellows, and were so, in one sense, though terribly mistaken; and had they succeeded they would have brought ruin and misery on the country. A monument was erected on the spot, some years ago, by one of the Macdonnells, and a bronze tablet on it records what took place.

As soon as daylight broke we went on shore, and walked to the old castle of Inverlochy. It stands above the river, and consists of four large round towers connected by high walls, forming an extensive quadrangle. The greater part is entire; indeed, the walls being ten feet thick are calculated to stand for ages. A moat surrounds the walls. The principal entrance is on the south-east side, and directly opposite it is a sally-port. Above the gateway was a guard-room, defended by iron gates and a heavy portcullis.

Below its frowning towers, the Marquis of Montrose defeated the Duke of Argyle, in the year 1645. It was just when the first rays of the sun shot athwart Ben Nevis, that, having led his men across pathless wilds covered deep with snow, he pounced down on the astonished Campbells, who were driven back in confusion, when numbers were slaughtered or drowned in the waters of Loch Eil. Of the latter, fifteen hundred men fell; while only three of Montrose's soldiers were killed, and one officer wounded.

As soon as we got back we made sail; and no other vessel impeding us, we entered the basin of Bannavie, from which a series of eight locks, called Neptune's Staircase, raised us to the level of Loch Lochy. It was rather tiresome, though at the same time interesting work, to see the yacht lifted gradually up step by step, while the water rushed down from the lock above to raise that on which we floated to its own level. Whoever first thought of such a contrivance deserves great credit.

As the wind was perfectly fair, we sailed along the canal for about eight miles without any impediment. It is deep and broad, and would allow a very much larger vessel than our little yacht to pass through it. It was on the banks of the river Lochy that a body of King George's soldiers first encountered the Macdonnells of Glengarry, who were up in arms for Charles Edward, when the former, being greatly overpowered, had to yield themselves prisoners.

Soon after entering the lake, we came off the house of Achnacarry, the mansion of Lochiel, on the northern side. The mountains on the south side extended nearly the whole distance of the lake without any break, while those on the other are rent by numerous gullies. The ground, though covered with heather, had few trees to ornament it. We were quite sorry when, in about an hour and a half, we had again to enter the canal, which quickly carried us into the small, pretty Loch Oich. We passed two or three islets decked with trees, which greatly embellish them. On the north side the mountains of Glengarry shot up in a succession of high and bold peaks. Below them is the castle of Invergarry, standing on a rock overlooking the waters of the loch.

The last Glengarry who claimed to be the Lord of the Isles, instead of Lord Macdonald of Sleat, resided here, and did his utmost to keep up the recollection of former days by his mode of life. On his death his property was bought by Lord Ward.

We passed a curious monument raised by the last Glengarry over what is known as the ' Well of the Seven Heads.' It consists of a pyramid, with seven human heads carved in stone placed on the summit. The story is that two sons of Keppoch, a branch of the Macdonalds, having been sent to be educated in France, their affairs were managed by seven brothers, who, on the return of the young men, murdered them, in order that they might continue in possession of their property. The old family bard, discovering the bloody act, applied to the Glengarry of those days for assistance; and having been furnished with a body of men, caught the assassins, and cut off their heads, which, after having washed in the spring, he presented to the noble chief in Glengarry Castle.

Just before leaving Loch Oich we passed Aberchalder, an un-pretending-looking house, where the forces of Prince Charles assembled before crossing Corryarrick. We soon reached Fort Augustus, when we descended by some locks into Loch Ness, where, on account of the depth of water, we had to anchor close to the shore, with warps made fast to some trees, to prevent our drifting away. As there was nothing to see at Fort Augustus, the garrison having been removed, we did not go on shore.

At an early hour the next morning we got under weigh, and glided down Loch Ness, which is twenty-four miles long, and about a mile and a quarter broad, although it is narrower in some places. The depth is very great, in some parts one hundred and thirty fathoms. In consequence of this the water seldom freezes in the loch. The rugged and heath-covered mountains rise on either side to the height of about a thousand feet; and frequently we saw growing on them forests of oak, ash, elm, and other trees, with a thick underwood of hazel and holly intermingled with a profusion of wild roses.

About midway we passed the lofty dome of Mealfourvournie, rising in solitary grandeur to the height of upwards of four thousand feet. Here there were tracts of cultivated ground; and in the openings of Glen Urquhart and Glenmoriston we came in sight of fields and substantial-looking houses. A few miles further we passed under a magnificent precipice crowned by pines. Not far distant we came to the House of Foyers, where we landed and hurried up the glen to the falls. We got down to the bottom of the perpendicular cliffs, over which we could see a large volume of water rushing with headlong force and speed, bubbling, foaming, and roaring into the channel which leads to the loch. Above us was a bridge thrown across the chasm, while the mountain sides were clothed with graceful birch and other trees. We had brought a copy of Burns, whose lines on the subject begin:

> 'Among the heathy hills and ragged woods
> The roaring Foyers pours his mossy floods;
> Till full he dashes on the rocky mounds,
> Where through a shapeless breach his stream resounds,'

which describe the falls far better than I can do.

Hurrying back, we continued our voyage. We passed the mouth of the deep defiled Inverfarigaig, with the black rock resembling a ruin above it, and further on Urquhart Castle, built on a detached rock overlooking the loch, the most conspicuous object being a strong square keep, surmounted by four turrets. The banks of the loch now appeared far more cultivated than at the other end. Sailing through little Loch Dochfour, we again entered the canal, which runs down into Loch Beauly; while the river Ness, which we had on our right side, falls into the Moray Firth, close to Inverness, which stands on a plain about a mile off.

It was curious to be looking from the deck of our yacht down on the loch so far below us, while we could see on either side of the town the far-famed battlefield of Culloden, where Prince Charles and his hapless followers were so signally defeated by the Duke of Cumberland.

Descending the locks at Muirtown, we could see in the far distance, guarding the entrance to the upper part of the mouth of the Moray Firth, the walls of Fort George extending out into the blue water. On reaching the ocean level, we at once made sail, standing for Inverness. By the time we dropped our anchor it was dark, so that we did not go on shore until the following morning. We then took a ramble round the town.

It stands on both sides of the river, across which a handsome stone bridge is thrown, but the finer portion is on the east side. The monasteries and churches were mostly knocked to pieces by Oliver Cromwell; but a good many fine buildings have been erected of late years, one of the most important of which is the Academy.

Inverness has always been a place of importance, and from its situation has a considerable trade. It was looked upon also as the capital of the north of Scotland. The inhabitants were staunch Jacobites, and very much inclined to be lawless, though at the present day they are as peaceably disposed as any in the country. Expecting to encounter stalwart Highlanders in kilts, with dirks by their sides, we were disappointed to meet only staid-looking burghers and labouring men, in the ordinary dress of the present day.

There was a castle, built by Cromwell to overawe the turbulent inhabitants, but it was pulled down, and the inhabitants had erected many of their houses with the materials. We, however, took a walk over the ramparts, which still remain. Here Queen Mary had her quarters for some time, protected by the clansmen of Frazer, Mackenzie, Munroe, and others, who kept the garrison of the castle in awe.

Far more interesting is an account we obtained of the Caledonian Canal, which may truly be said to make an island of Sutherland, Caithness, Cromarty, Rosshire, and a part of Inverness. The canal was designed by Watt, as far back as 1773; but the present work was not commenced until the year 1804, when Telford was directed to make a report on the subject. By his plan the canal was to be one hundred and ten feet wide at the surface and fifty feet at the bottom, and the depth of water twenty feet; so that a thirty-two gun frigate of that day, fully equipped and laden with stores, could pass through it. The works, however, were carried out on more moderate proportions. There are twenty-eight locks, each one hundred and seventy feet long and forty feet wide, with an average lift of eight feet. Some of the lock gates are of timber, and others are of cast-iron, sheathed with pine planking. The summit level is in Loch Oich, into which pour a number of streams, supplying an abundance of water for both sides. It stands exactly one hundred feet above high-water mark at Inverness. The extreme length from sea to sea is sixty and a half miles; and so direct is the continuity of the lakes that a line drawn across from point to point would only exceed the distance by rather more than three miles. There are twenty-two miles of canal cutting, and thirty-eight and a half miles of lake water is made available for the canal.

We found passing through the lakes the pleasantest part of the voyage. We might have been many days doing the distance, had we not had a favourable breeze. The wind changed directly after we reached Inverness, of which we were very glad, as it gave us some hopes of soon meeting the Dolphin, which we feared must have been detained off John o'Groat's House.

We made several trips down to Fort George, to look out for the Dolphin. At length one evening, having stood further down the Firth and looking into Cromarty, made classic by having been the scene of many of Hugh Miller's rambles, we caught sight of a small white sail, shining brightly in the rays of the setting sun. Papa, taking the glass, looked steadily at her, and then, to our great satisfaction, declared his belief that she was the Dolphin. We immediately tacked towards her, and in a short time heard Uncle Tom's cheerful hail across the water. We immediately hove to, and the Dolphin doing the same, papa and I pulled on board her. They were in good spirits, although they had begun to think that they should never get round Duncansby Head, which is close to John o'Groat's House, until the wind drawing once more from the westward, they had reached Wick, the great resort of fishing vessels. After this they had a dead beat until they sighted Tarbet-ness Lighthouse, on the northern side of the Moray Firth. Their further adventures they kept for another day.

'I am glad to get back again to you,' exclaimed Dick; 'it's dull work sailing all alone. I confess that I sometimes thought you would never get through overland; for by no other way, it seems to me, could you have come, except along those little trout ponds I saw marked on the map.'

Dick was not a little astonished when we told him the size of the canal and its locks, and that a vessel very much larger than the Dolphin could have got through with equal ease.

We had brought an abundance of fresh provisions for both yachts, and were glad to find that Uncle Tom did not wish to go to Inverness; and we accordingly shaped our course for Kinnaird's Head, not intending to touch at any place on the Scotch coast until we reached Aberdeen.

CHAPTER X.

ANOTHER WRECK.

S we sailed down the Moray Firth with a northerly wind, which enabled us to stand close in shore, the water being perfectly smooth, we passed numerous headlands, the names of which we learned from the chart. After the mountainous scenery amid which we had been sailing, the shore looked flat and uninteresting.

I had thus plenty of time to attend to little Nat, who was fast becoming very dear to all of us. We looked forward with regret to the time when he might be sent away to join his friends, should they be found. He had learned to walk the deck in true nautical style; and in his sailor's suit, with his broad-brimmed straw hat, he looked every inch a young seaman. He was generally in capital spirits, apparently forgetting his loss; but if any allusion brought back to his remembrance his father, mother, or Aunt Fanny, his brothers and sisters, the tears sprang to his eyes, and he looked grave and sad. Happily, however, a cheerful word brought him back to his usual mood, and he became as merry as ever.

'Do you know, Harry,' he said to me one day, 'I intend to be a sailor. I should like to have just such a vessel as this, and cruise about the world that you tell me is round, though I cannot make it out; still, as you say so, I am sure it is.'

I pointed to the top-gallant sails of a vessel on which the sun was shining brightly,—'Now, watch that sail, and in a short time you will see her topsails, and then her courses, and then the hull. If the world was not round, we should see them all at once, just as clearly as we now see the top-gallant sails.'

As I spoke I took up a large ball of spun yarn, and placing a splinter on it, I advanced the piece of wood gradually until he saw the whole of it. 'Now, this splinter represents that ship,' I said, pointing to it. 'As we also are moving towards her, we shall soon see all her sails and her hull.'

Nat kept watching the ship with intense interest; and although summoned to luncheon, he begged that he might have something brought up to him, so that he could watch her hull come in sight. This in a short time happened, when he clapped his hands and shouted,—

Now I know that the world is round; but I thought it was so very big it could make no difference.'

'Well,' exclaimed Dick, who had been listening to my remark, 'I never knew before how it was people guessed that the world was round. I saw ships' sails popping up out of the ocean, but had not any idea how it was, and did not like to ask.'

'There you showed your want of wisdom,' observed papa; 'you should have tried to think the matter out, or inquired.'

The wind continued to favour us, drawing gradually to the westward. We sighted a red light on Kinnaird's Head, which, as we got more to the eastward, changed to a bright colour. Beyond it was Fraserburgh. By hauling our wind we were able to steer for Rathay Head. Near it we caught sight of Inverugie Castle. We gave a wide berth to the head, from which a dangerous reef of rocks run out; for though the ocean was tolerably calm, we could see the water breaking over them.

We were now hoping, as the wind was off shore, to stand due south for Aberdeen, which we were all anxious to see. We had

sighted Slaines Castle, standing out solitary and grand on the very
edge of the crag, when the wind suddenly backed round to the
southward, and in a short time began to blow very hard. Dark
clouds, which had been gathering thickly in the horizon to the
south-east, came careering on over the blue sky. In spite of the
heavy sea which was getting up, we held our course, standing away
from the land, intending to tack again when we could to fetch
Aberdeen. By the way the Dolphin was tumbling about I could
readily understand how we must have appeared to her. Dick began
to show signs of being far from happy, and Nat's cheerfulness
entirely left him. Papa sent him down below, and told him to
turn in. Dick, however, braved it out, but grew more and more
yellow and woebegone.

'This won't do,' observed papa; 'it's fortunate that we have a port
under our lee. Up helm, ease away the main sheet. We'll let the
Dolphin know that we are running for Peterhead.'

The Dolphin followed our example; and away we went, careering
on before the fast-rising seas. Very glad we were that we had so
fine a harbour to run for. The gale blew harder and harder, and
the waves looked as if every instant they would engulf us; for we
were now exposed to the whole roll of the German Ocean. On sailing
in we were struck by the remarkable appearance of the flesh-coloured
pinkish rocks, whose needle-shaped points rose up out of the water.
We had, however, little time to notice them, ere rushing by we
brought up in the harbour of Peterhead. Most thankfully we
dropped our anchor and furled our sails.

Peterhead appeared to be a bustling place. A number of merchant
vessels, coasters, and fishing-boats were at anchor. As the days were
long, we hoped the gale would blow itself out before the next morning.
Directly we had dined we set off on foot to visit a curious cavern
called the 'Bullers of Buchan.' After walking for about two hours
we found ourselves on the top of a cliff, from whence we looked down
into an immense cauldron some fifty feet in diameter, open at the

bottom to the sea, which was rushing in, and whirling round and round in foaming masses. We went round it, between the cauldron and the sea, where the ledge, with the foaming whirlpool on one side and the perpendicular cliffs on the other, was sufficiently narrow to make us feel the necessity of keeping our eyes open. On the west side, or the furthest from the ocean, we observed that the water rushed under an arch. A person told us that in fine weather a boat could pass under this arch, though at present one would have been immediately dashed to pieces. The whole cliff was completely perforated by caverns. 'Buller,' I should have said, means the 'boiler.' Having watched it until our ears were wellnigh deafened by the roar, and our eyes dizzy from gazing at the seething whirlpool, we hastened on to get a sight of Slaines Castle, which we had seen from the sea. As we viewed it from a distance, the walls appeared to be a continuation of the cliff on the summit of which it stands. It is a large quadrangular building, without a tree in the neighbourhood. It had a somewhat gloomy aspect under the dark sky when we saw it. The property belonged, till lately, to the Earl of Errol, whose nearest neighbour to the eastward was, as Dick said, 'Hamlet's Ghost,' or the Castle of Elsinore, which stands on the shores of the Skagerack.

We had spent a longer time in visiting the castle than we had intended, and had only got a short distance back when we were overtaken by the gloom of evening. The wind was blowing dead on shore, and a tremendous sea running. We were casting our eyes over the German Ocean, when we saw what we took to be a brig, with her mainmast gone, and several of her sails blown away, evidently steering for Peterhead. Unable to keep close to the wind, she was drifting every instant nearer and nearer the shore.

'I fear she'll not weather that point,' observed papa; 'and if she comes on shore, there'll be little chance for any of her people, as no lifeboat could get near her.'

We had passed a Coastguard station a little way to the northward. Uncle Tom volunteered to hurry on, and I accompanied him—in case the people there should not have observed the brig—to give them notice of the danger she was in; that, should she strike, they might be ready to render assistance with their rocket apparatus.

It was now quite dark, and we had great difficulty in making our way; there was a risk of finding ourselves at the edge of some chasm, down which we might fall. The distance seemed very long, and I thought we must have missed the Coastguard station, which was situated at the edge of the cliffs. At length, however, we saw a light gleaming from a window, and arrived at the wall which enclosed the house where the lieutenant and his men lived. We found them on the alert. Two had just gone off for some horses to drag the waggon in which the rocket apparatus was to be carried, as one of the men stationed to the southward had seen the brig and reported her danger.

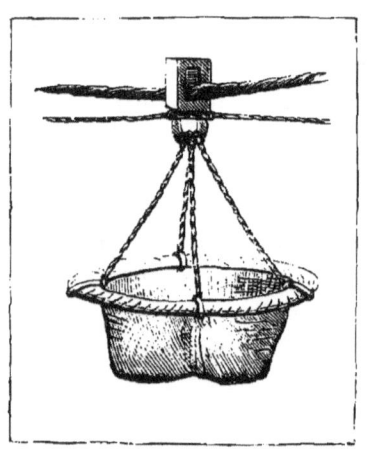

THE BREECHES BUOY.

In the waggon were already placed the rocket tube, with three rocket lines, several rockets, three spars to form a triangle, an anchor, lantern, spades, and pickaxes, some signal rockets, a rope ladder, and a sling life-buoy, with what are called 'petticoat breeches' fastened to it, in which a person can be placed. There were also a strong hawser and a whip or fine rope, by which the sling life-buoy was to be drawn backwards and forwards from the wreck to the shore. By the time these were got into the waggon a couple of horses had arrived, and a party of men immediately set off with the waggon. The lieutenant conducted us back by the way we had come; as he knew every inch of the ground, we had no fear now of falling over the cliff. We had not gone far before we saw a rocket thrown up about a mile to the southward.

'It is as I feared,' said the lieutenant; 'the brig has gone ashore, and that rocket, fired by one of my men, shows the spot where she has struck. There is no time to lose, for in all probability she will not hold together long.'

The signal made us hasten on even faster than before.

'There she is! there she is!' cried the lieutenant, just as we reached the summit of a cliff.

We could see the brig about a hundred fathoms off on the rocks, the sea making a fearful breach over her. There was light sufficient to enable us to see that the foremast was still standing.

We found that papa and the rest of our party had arrived at the spot, and were watching her, but of course utterly unable to afford any assistance. It would have been a sad thing to watch her, had we not known that we should soon have the means of saving the poor people. Scarcely a minute had passed when a shout gave us notice that the waggon had arrived. We all instantly hurried to her to assist. While the men handled the heavier articles, we carried the lighter ones. Each man knew exactly what he was to do. The lines, I should have said, were in boxes, two of which were carried to the cliff; the tube was then fixed, and the line fastened to it. It was an anxious moment. Would the line pass over the vessel? would the crew be able to secure it? I could not help fearing that the rocket might strike the vessel, and perhaps kill some one on board; but the lieutenant took very good care to avoid that, by giving the tube sufficient elevation.

'Now, lads, stand by!' he sang out.

The men tilted the box in which the line was secured, so that it might run out freely. The officer now fired; and the rocket, rising in the air, made a grand curve of light, which we watched with intense interest until we saw it fall completely over the vessel. We had now to ascertain whether the men on board had secured it. No signal came, and of course we could not venture to haul in on the line, lest we might draw it back.

'They probably have no blue light or gun on board, or any other means of making a signal,' observed the lieutenant.

Scarcely, however, had he spoken, before a faint light from a lantern was shown in the rigging.

'All right,' he exclaimed: 'they have secured the line; make it fast to the warp.'

Upon this, one of the Coastguards, going a short distance from the rest of us, exhibited a lantern with a red light, and presently we found that the ⋅whip—or double line—with a tailed block was being hauled off by the men on the wreck.

We had now to wait again until once more the lantern was shown on board. This was a signal to the Coastguard to secure the end of the hawser to one part of the double line or whip, when all hands taking hold of the latter, we hauled off the hawser to the wreck. The tailed block had probably been secured to the mast; and as long as that held we had every hope of establishing a communication.

If we felt anxious, how much more so must the poor fellows on the brig, which might at any moment be knocked to pieces, and they be sent struggling hopelessly in the foaming seas! We knew from the length of the whip that we must haul out the hawser almost to its end. Soon after we had done so another signal was made, which implied that the men had secured it round the mast. We then immediately hauled away on the hawser until we had got it stretched and secured to the anchor, which had been imbedded in the earth some way back from the cliff. It was necessary, however, not to get it too taut, as the vessel was moved by the seas, and might either break it, or tear the anchor out of the ground. This done, the 'buoy with the breeches' was secured to a block, adjusted to the hawser, and was immediately hauled off.

I should have said that a triangle, formed of three small spars, over which the hawser passed, was fixed in the ground nearest to the edge of the cliff; and now, to our infinite satisfaction, we had a perfect communication with the wreck. Still we had to watch for another signal, to give us notice that a person had been placed in it. Again the light appeared. We hauled away on the warp.

'Handsomely, handsomely!' sung out the lieutenant, as the men were hauling in rather fast on the line.

We eagerly watched; when at last through the gloom we saw the life-buoy appear, and discovered that a person was in it. With anxious haste the lieutenant and two of his men stepped forward, and grasping the buoy and its burden, gently lifted out the occupant.

'My arm is broken, sir; take care, please.'

We found that it was the mate of the vessel who spoke; he was the first sent on shore. We carried him up to the waggon, where he could be sheltered from the wind by the awning which covered it. While Uncle Tom remained with him, we hastened back to the cliff.

By this time another person had arrived—a young boy—who was also somewhat hurt. He was almost fainting from pain and terror; his state was such that he could only utter the words, 'Make haste! make haste!'

There was good reason for this, for we could judge by the way the hawser was moved that the vessel was rolling more and more; and the men were compelled to slacken it out every now and then. It may be supposed no time was lost. Three men were now successfully brought on shore.

We were going to carry the boy to the waggon, but he intreated to remain. The first of the men who arrived told us the reason. He was the captain's son. The captain himself would not leave the vessel until the last. Two of their number had been washed overboard, the captain alone now remained. We could hear the boy crying out every now and then, 'Make haste! make haste!'

Once more the life-buoy was hauled off; every possible speed was made. I don't think I ever before felt so intensely anxious; for I could sympathise with the poor boy whose father was still in fearful danger. Each moment it seemed as if the hawser would be carried away. Again the light was shown, and seemed to be advancing towards us. The Coastguard hauled away with all their might, helped by two of the rescued crew, while the lieutenant and the rest stood by ready to take hold of the captain. The light drew nearer and nearer. 'Make haste! make haste!' again cried the boy. When at length he saw his father safe, in spite of his hurts, rising up from the ground, he rushed forward and threw his arms round his neck.

Scarcely had the captain's feet touched the ground than the hawser slackened, a loud rending sound was borne to our ears by the wind, and we knew that some huge billow had dashed the brig to pieces. Indeed, I fancied I saw fragments tossing about in the seething waves which dashed up against the cliffs.

All felt that they had done their duty, and that the lives of their fellow-creatures had been saved by their promptitude, and the skill with which the operations had been carried out. The Coastguard men, having hauled in the hawser until the mast was brought close under the cliff, the rocket apparatus was returned to the waggon, in which also the mate and the captain's son were placed, and we then all set off to the Coastguard station.

The lieutenant invited us to remain at his cottage until the morning. We gladly accepted his offer; and his wife, who was a very nice person, treated us in the kindest manner, and produced a variety of garments, which we put on while our wet clothes were drying. Uncle Tom had a lady's cloak over his shoulders. Dick was dressed in an old uniform coat, and papa got into a pea-jacket.

The shipwrecked crew were looked after by the Coastguard men, and the lieutenant and his wife attended to the mate and the boy; while the master of the vessel had a room to himself, being completely knocked up, and as soon as he had had some supper went to bed, and happily was soon fast asleep.

Papa and the lieutenant found that they had many mutual acquaintances, and they sat spinning yarns before the fire—for, although summer, a fire was very pleasant—until late in the night. The lieutenant described to us the gallant way in which the lifeboats of two neighbouring stations had gone out on several occasions to rescue the crews of vessels either on the rocks or sand-banks at the mouth of the Moray Frith.

One hears but little of the wreck of coasters; but were it not for the assistance of lifeboats, in most instances the crews, consisting of three to six men, would be lost; as the vessels, being often old and rotten, quickly break up, and being low, the seas wash completely over them. Not long ago a boat was discovered by one of the Coast-guard men on the beach; and on hurrying towards her, he found a poor fellow lying on the sand almost exhausted. On carrying him to a neighbouring fisherman's cottage, he recovered; and he then stated that he belonged to a large barque which had gone on the sands; that he and twelve other men had taken to their boat, but that she had capsized, and that all hands, with the exception of himself, had been drowned; that he had swum on shore, though he could scarcely tell how he had managed to reach it. He said that there were four men still on board. On this the Coastguard men hastened to the nearest lifeboat station, when the boat was immediately manned and pushed off for the wreck, the position of which the seaman had described, though as it was night she could not be seen. Away the gallant crew pulled through tremendous seas, which were rolling in on the coast. Having gained an offing, they made sail, and steered for the wreck, which at length was discovered with two of her masts gone, while the crew were clinging to the rigging of the remaining mast, which threatened every instant to follow the others. The lifeboat, showing a light, indicated to the poor fellows on the wreck that help was near. After considerable difficulty they got up under her lee, and were able to heave a rope on board. Getting a stronger warp, they hauled up near enough to enable two of the men to jump on board. The third slipped, and fell into the water, running a fearful risk of being crushed; but, happily, he also was got into the boat. As is often the case, the cabin-boy was the last left. It was a trying thing to see the poor little fellow clinging to the rigging, but unable to help himself.

'We can't let him perish!' cried one of the lifeboat men; and at the risk of his own life, the boat being hauled up to the wreck, he sprang into the rigging, and with his knife cut the lashings by which the poor boy was held. A crashing sound was heard, the weather shrouds and stays were giving way. In another instant the mast would fall, and not only the gallant fellow and his charge, but all in the lifeboat, would perish.

'Leap, man! leap!' shouted the crew, ready to shove off, and watching the tottering mast with anxious gaze: but even though they all knew the fearful risk they incurred by remaining, they would not desert their companion or the lad he had gone to save. The gallant boatman, seizing the boy in his arms, slid down the rigging and sprang from the chains into the boat, where he was caught by the outstretched arms of his companions. The next moment the boat was many fathoms from the wreck, when down came the mast on the very spot where she had been floating, the cap of her topmast almost striking her bow. Still the crew had a heavy struggle to reach the shore, for the gale came down with greater force than ever, and the hungry seas seemed ready to engulf her; but the shipwrecked men were landed in safety. Not until they met their companion did they learn that he and they were the sole survivors of the crew.

The lieutenant told the tale so graphically that I have tried to put it down in his own words. He related many other similar anecdotes; and it was not until the night was far spent that we dropped off to sleep in our chairs.

At daybreak, as the rain had ceased, and the wind had somewhat gone down, we started for Peterhead, papa promising to send a conveyance for the mate and the boy, that they might be carried to the hospital.

Peterhead is a substantial-looking seaport town, the houses being mostly built of granite from quarries near. It stands on the south side of the mouth of the river Ugie, and has two harbours, one on

KING'S COLLEGE, ABERDEEN.

the north and the other on the south side of the peninsula. The latter, which is the oldest, was formed in the year 1773, from plans by Mr. Smeaton, the great engineer of those days; and the north harbour in 1818, from those by Mr. Telford. Piers run out from the shore, which is lined by fine quays.

We had to wait the whole day before proceeding on our voyage, so we had time to see a great deal of the town, and something of the neighbourhood. We paid a visit to the hospital, and were glad to find that the poor mate and the captain's son were going on very well.

Next morning broke bright and beautiful, with a fine northerly breeze, which raised our spirits; and sailing out of the harbour, we stood towards Buchan Ness, on the summit of which stands a stone tower, with a light flashing from it at night, to show the approach to Peterhead. We sighted Slaines Castle, from which we steered a direct course for Aberdeen. About ten o'clock, the distance run being about thirty miles, we sighted the Girdlestone Lighthouse, on the southern side of the river Don, on which Aberdeen stands. Crossing the bar, we found ourselves in a wide bay. Several vessels and a number of boats were standing towards the spacious quays, backed by the fine granite-built houses of New Aberdeen.

On landing, we noticed the massive appearance imparted to the houses by the granite of which they are composed.

Our first visit was to Marischal College, the great seat of learning in the north, where Captain Dalgetty, that redoubted soldier of fortune, according to Scott, obtained his education. We went through the museum, library, and observatory, saw a good collection of paintings, and were especially struck by the handsome way in which the whole building is furnished.

Hurrying on, however, to the old town, on the south bank of the Don, we visited the parish church of Old Machar, a grand and venerable building. The pillars in the transept have their capitals beautifully carved in oak. We then went to King's College, a large quadrangular edifice, including the chapel, built of granite. The examination hall contains a collection of the portraits of the old Scottish kings and the early principals of the college,—a Bishop Elphinstone, the founder, being among them. We were amused by seeing the students, of whom there were between two and three hundred, walking about dressed in red gowns. They belong to all ranks of society, many labouring during the summer to obtain the means of educating themselves in the winter. We heard a pleasant anecdote of the late Duke of Gordon, who used to send out a carriage when he knew that the young men were on their way to college, in order to give them a lift for a stage or two. Many, we were told, had worked at the Caledonian Canal before thus arriving in the ducal carriage.

We saw many evidences of the prosperity of Aberdeen; and while we lay in the harbour two or three steamers came in and out; one on its way to the islands of Orkney and Shetland, and others to Leith and the Thames. Our few hours at Aberdeen were among the most interesting we spent on shore during our voyage.

Sailing again in the afternoon, with a fine northerly breeze, we passed the neat town of Stonehaven, about fifteen miles to the south, and soon afterwards the grand ruins of Dunnottar Castle, a large square tower rising from amid the ruins of other buildings on the very edge of the cliff. We could judge of its size by the extent of the remaining walls. It was here that the crown and sceptre of King Charles were kept during the Civil Wars. The castle was besieged, and the garrison was about to capitulate, when Mrs. Ogilvie, the governor's wife, put them in charge of Mrs. Grainger, the wife of the minister of Kinneff, who had paid her a visit by permission of the Republican General Lambert. Mrs. Ogilvie managed, with wonderful boldness, to smuggle out the crown, fastened under her cloak, while her servant hid the sceptre and sword in a bag of flax which she carried on her back. It was here, also, that many of the Covenanters

BELL ROCK LIGHTHOUSE.

were imprisoned, and, according to an ancient chronicler, Wallace put to death four thousand Englishmen, who had fled for safety into the church. The approaching night hid the gloomy walls from our view.

As we passed the towns of Montrose and Arbroath during the night, we saw nothing of them. The wind fell light when off the latter place, and then blew from the south-west, bringing up a thick fog, which shrouded the whole surface of the water. Papa being told of it, he went on deck, and Dick and I followed him; when he at once hauled the yacht on the wind, and stood off the coast. After running on for about an hour, the peculiar mournful sound of a bell reached us. As we stood on, it sounded every half-minute, louder and louder.

'Where does that come from?' inquired Dick.

'From the Bell Rock.' answered Truck. 'If it wasn't for the fog we should see a light from the tall tower which now stands on the rock, bright and red alternately. Once upon a time there was no tower there; but there was a bell fixed on a buoy, and as the waves beat against it, it tolled without ceasing; but I have heard say that there was a pirate, who used to cruise in those seas, who cut the bell off; but not long after, when making for Dundee, during a dark night and a heavy gale, he ran his ship on it, and was lost with all his men—a judgment on him for his evil deeds.'

The wind dropping altogether, we lay becalmed, within the sound of the bell, until morning broke and the fog lifted, when we saw the tower just ahead of us. The centre part of the building was coloured white, and could scarcely be seen against the sky; but the lower part, which was dark, and the lantern, which was in shadow, were perfectly visible. We pulled towards it; and as we approached we saw the rocks on which the lighthouse stands rising ten feet or more above the water. Iron ladders were fixed for landing, and by a gun-metal ladder we were able to reach the entrance port. The head keeper came down and received us cordially. As in other lighthouses, the first story is used for storing coal; the second for water;

the next for oil; and the next for bedrooms, with berths for six persons. Above it is the kitchen, and above that the sitting-room, in which we saw a bust of Stevenson, the engineer. The light is revolving, and has five reflectors, on each of which are two faces, one red and one white. The red colour is produced by chimneys of red glass. The keeper told us that four men belonged to the lighthouse, that they are all married, but that three only were on duty. As at the other lighthouses, birds are occasionally killed by flying against the glasses.

Soon after we left the Bell Rock, the wind freshening from the southward, we stood on for Dundee, from which it is about five and twenty miles distant. We passed through the narrow entrance of the Firth of Tay, with Broughty Castle on our right, beyond which we came off Dundee, standing on the northern shore, and rising on a gentle declivity from the water's edge, towards a high hill called the Law. The estuary here is nearly two miles wide. A number of vessels were at anchor, while the docks seen beyond the quays were full of shipping. Dundee has a handsome appearance, with its broad streets and fine stone houses. About the centre of the town, we passed what looked like one enormous church, with a lofty tower at the western end; but we found that it consisted of four parish churches, which are built side by side, so as to form one edifice.

'I wish that all Christian communities could thus live in unity,' observed papa.

These churches were, as may be supposed, all Presbyterian. There are several others in the town. We were told that there were nearly ninety schools in Dundee, at which upwards of four thousand children are educated. One of the most interesting places which claimed our attention was the Watt Institution, established in honour of James Watt, for the instruction of young men in science. There are also nearly forty mills for spinning flax, weaving linen, sail-cloth, sacking, and cordage. On the quay stands a handsome arch, built after a Flemish model. Besides the patent slip and graving dock,

DUNDEE.

R 2

there are three wet docks and two tidal harbours, while other improvements are being carried on; so that Dundee is a most flourishing place.

Not far off is Camperdown, once the residence of Lord Duncan, who called it after the famous victory he won over the Dutch; and a little distance further is Rossie Priory, belonging to the Kinnaird family.

As we were anxious to look into St. Andrews, we sailed again next morning, in the hope that the wind would continue in the north, or at all events that we should be able to beat down thus far. It is situated on the south shore of St. Andrew's Bay, some little way outside the entrance to the Firth of Tay. The wind favoured us more than we expected; and a pilot-boat showing us the way, we stood into the harbour, passing close under the peninsula on which the town stands. Above us were the ruins of the cathedral and the chapel of St. Rule, who was supposed to have founded the place, with several other buildings. St. Andrews presented a very quiet aspect, forming a great contrast to the bustling town of Dundee: but I must say it is a far more picturesque place. Of course we visited the university, the most ancient in Scotland. It consists of the colleges of St. Salvator, St. Leonard, and St. Mary. There is also a school called the Madras College, founded by Dr. Bell, the originator of the Madras system of education. By means of these colleges, at which an almost free education can be obtained, young Scotchmen without means are able to enjoy advantages which they could not do in England. The town is certainly more alive than it was when Dr. Johnson visited it in the last century; he declared that one of the streets was lost, and that in those that remained there was 'the silence and solitude of inactive indigence and gloomy depopulation.' We thought it a very picturesque-looking place, and should have remained there longer had the wind not changed and induced us to put to sea.

Having passed round Fifeness, the eastern point of the peninsula, and opened the Isle of May lights—for there are two on the summit of the island—we stood across the Firth of Forth, intending to visit Edinburgh. The wind being light the whole night, we made no way.

When morning broke, we were in sight of Fenton Law, which rose beyond North Berwick, and the Bass Rock, at no great distance off, standing high up above the blue sea. We passed close to it, and got a view of the almost inaccessible castle perched on its cliffs. It is now in ruins, but at one time was used as a state prison, in which several of the most distinguished Covenanters were confined. Wild flocks of sea-fowl rose above our heads from off the rock, and among others were numbers of gannets or Solan geese.

As we had lost so much time, and had still the whole English coast to run down, papa and Uncle Tom, after a consultation, agreed to give up their visit to Edinburgh, and to continue their cruise across to the southward.

THE BASS ROCK

CHAPTER XI.

E got a view of North Berwick, which stands on the extreme northern point of Haddington; and about three miles to the eastward of it we came off the far-famed Tantallon Castle, in days of yore the stronghold of the Douglases. Of course, we got out *Marmion*, and read the description of this celebrated fortress, which by the extent of its ruins must have been of great size and strength.

'I said, Tantallon's dizzy steep
Hung o'er the margin of the deep.
Many a rude tower and rampart there
Repelled the insult of the air,
Which, when the tempest vexed the sky,
Half breeze, half spray, came whistling by. . .
A parapet's embattled row
Did seaward round the castle go.
Sometimes in dizzy steps descending,
Sometimes in narrow circuit bending,
Sometimes in platform broad extending,
Its varying circle did combine
Bulwark, and bartizan, and line,
And bastion, tower, and vantage-coign.
Above the booming ocean leant
The far-projecting battlement;
The billows burst, in ceaseless flow,
Upon the precipice below.'

We passed the mouth of the river Tyne, south of which stands Dunbar. The next place of interest we came off was Fast Castle, of which two tall towers remain close to the cliffs,—in former days the stronghold of the Homes. It is supposed to be the original of Wolf's Crag in *The Bride of Lammermoor*. We looked through our glasses at the spot where the unhappy Master of Ravenswood sank with his steed into the treacherous quicksand.

About fifteen miles farther on, we passed the bluff promontory St. Abb's Head, and soon afterwards arrived off Berwick, which, I need hardly say, stands at the mouth of the Tweed, the river dividing England from Scotland. So close does the railway run to the cliffs, that we could hear the trains passing as clearly as if we were on shore, and could see them shooting by at a speed which made us jealous. As the wind was fair, we did not put into the Tweed, but stood close enough to Berwick to have a cursory view of it. As all the world knows, Berwick is not within any county, for although really in Berwickshire, it belongs to England. It is a county in itself. A portion is still surrounded by walls erected in the time of Elizabeth ; and it is defended by several bastions, with batteries commanding the entrance to the harbour. We could see the remains of an ancient castle, which is now a heap of ruins, but above it stands the Bell Tower, still almost perfect. A number of vessels passed in and out of the harbour while we were off it, showing that the place has a good deal of trade. As we looked through our glasses, we saw a number of churches and public buildings. A long stone pier runs out on the north side of the Tweed, with a lighthouse at its end.

We now stood on towards Holy Island, a few miles south of Berwick, off the Northumbrian coast; and as we had still several hours of daylight, we hove to off the island. Here, in the early days of Christianity, was a college of evangelists, who went forth to preach the simple gospel through the northern portions of the country, to its heathen kings, as well as to the people over whom they held sway.

Ultimately, monasteries were built here, famous for the supposed piety of their inmates.

We pulled on shore to visit the ruins of the celebrated Abbey of Lindisfarne. If the pilgrim visitors arrived at low water, they could get across by following the sandbank which connects it with the mainland; but they had to make haste, to escape being caught by the flood.

Besides the monastery, there was a castle of great strength, which often resisted the invader's hostile attacks; and heathen Danes had again and again been driven back to their ships by its stalwart garrison. Its glories, however, are departed. We could find only a few low walls, over which we could leap, and the remains of a staircase of eight or ten steps in a tower but little higher than the wall. A board warning off trespassers took away what little romance we had conjured up.

Returning on board, we again stood to the southward, sighting Bamborough Castle, elevated on a green mound above the village. Off it lies the Longstone Rock and the Farne Islands. The coast looked bleak and desolate, with here and there dark rocks running into the sea. The wind was very light as we came off the Longstone Lighthouse.

While the yachts hove to, the boats were lowered, and we pulled up to it, in order to pay a visit to the scene of Grace Darling's heroism. For upwards of fifty years the lighthouse was under the charge of William Darling, the father of Grace. We understood that the present head keeper was a member of the family. The tower stands on a rock, is painted red, and the light revolves every half-minute. We were much interested with the memorials of Grace Darling which embellished the sitting-room. The light-keeper on duty pointed out the various localities connected with the wreck of the Forfarshire.

Before daylight, on the 6th of September, 1838, a furious gale blowing, Grace Darling, who acted as William Darling's assistant and was on watch, heard, as she thought, the cries of people coming from the direction of some rocks a mile away.   She awoke her father, and together they stood listening to the appeals for help; but in the dark, with the furious sea there was running, it was impossible to put off to their assistance.   When day broke, however, the old man launched his boat, and was about to shove off, when, observing the state of the tide and weather, he hesitated to make the attempt.   As the light increased, Grace, who had been anxiously watching the wreck, declared that she saw some people still clinging to it.

'We must save them!' she exclaimed; and seizing an oar, she stepped into the boat.

The old man, aroused by her example, followed her.   Through the foaming seas, which threatened every moment to overwhelm the little coble, they pulled off to the wreck.   The fore part of the vessel, to which nine people were clinging, alone remained; to reach them it was necessary to land on the lee side of the rock.   This, after considerable difficulty, William Darling succeeded in doing, when immediately Grace rowed off in the coble, to prevent it being dashed to pieces.   One by one, five of the crew and four passengers were drawn by the lighthouse-keeper off the wreck, and placed on the rock, from whence they were transferred to the boat, and conveyed, a few at a time, to the lighthouse.

Owing to the state of the weather, no communication could be held with the mainland for two days, during which time the nine ship-wrecked persons were treated with the utmost kindness by Mr. Darling and his daughter.   The calm bravery of Grace, who was at that time only twenty-two years of age, excited the admiration of all who heard it.   Testimonials and suitable presents, together with seven hundred pounds sterling raised by subscription, showed how highly the public appreciated her conduct.   The Forfarshire steamer, of three hundred tons, had sailed the previous evening from Hull, bound for Dundee; but her boilers becoming defective, the engines could no longer work, and at three o'clock the following morning she struck on the Longstone, the outermost of the Farne Islands, between which the master was endeavouring to run the vessel. The mate, with seven seamen, lowered a boat, and were escaping, when one of the passengers leaped on board, others in vain attempting to follow his example. The nine occupants of this boat were the following

MONUMENT TO GRACE DARLING.

morning picked up by a coaster and carried into Shields,—they, with those rescued by the Darlings, being the only persons who escaped out of sixty souls.

Four years after this heroic deed, Grace Darling lay upon her dying bed. The grief of the family was very great, for Grace was endeared to them all. 'Do not mourn for me,' she said; 'I am only exchanging this life for one far better. If I remained here, I should be subject to trouble and sickness; but in dying I go to be with Christ my Saviour.' Two beautiful memorials of Grace have been erected: one in Bamborough Churchyard, and the other in St. Cuthbert's Chapel, on the Farne Island. Our picture represents that in Bamborough Churchyard. Her sleeping figure lies under a Gothic canopy, backed by the blue waves, and within sight of the scene of her heroism.

> ' She is lying and sleeping now
>   Under the verdant turf.
> Ah, there were breakers she might not ride!
> And her hair grew damp in that strong, dark tide,
>   But not with the briny surf.
>
> And out of her lonely grave
>   She bids us this lesson prove,
> That the weakest may wipe some tears that flow,
> And the strongest power for good below
>   Is the might of unselfish love.'

In 1860, the Iris, of Arbroath, struck on the rocks close to where the Forfarshire was lost. The wind was so terrific, and the sea ran so high, that the crew were afraid to take to their boat. They accordingly leaped into the water, and were washed on to the rock, though it was with the greatest difficulty that they managed to reach it. Here they remained twelve hours, the sea being so rough that no boat could come to them. Towards evening, the wind having slightly fallen, William Darling, who was then seventy-five years of age, and had been watching the wreck all day, put off with several hands from the lighthouse, and rescued the poor fellows from their perilous position.

We had a scramble over a portion of the Farne Islands, on which there are two lighthouses at a considerable distance from each other. There are three keepers belonging to the two, but only one remains on watch at a time; he has to attend to both lights, and has to walk from house to house. The keeper showed us a curious contrivance by which he can at once rouse the sleeping keeper without leaving his own post. It consists of a hand-bellows attached to a tube which rings a bell at the ear of the sleeper. He told us that occasionally blackbirds and thrushes are killed by striking against the lantern. We saw a number of rabbits running in and out of their burrows. There is an old chapel which has been restored and another building, converted into a dwelling-house for the clergyman, who at times comes across from Durham.

Nat, who had landed with us, was very anxious to keep a young cormorant which he had picked up. He took it under his arm, intending to carry off his prize; but the mother bird attacked him so furiously with its long beak, that it nearly put out one of his eyes, and succeeded in severely biting his lip. On this, Nat very naturally let go the youngster, which scuttled off, determined not to be caught again, and, taking to the water, swam away at a great rate. The odour produced by the birds was anything but pleasant. We saw a number of cormorants diving in search of prey, and they came up with eels in their mouths. One had caught a big eel, which it battered against the rock until it had killed it; but others gobbled down small eels without the slightest hesitation. The young birds were the oddest-looking creatures imaginable. Their covering was a hard black skin, with here and there black woolly down upon it. The old birds' heads and necks were black, speckled with white feathers, while the upper part of the body was brown mingled with black. They had also white patches on their thighs, and yellow pouches under the throat edged with white. They were fully three feet long; so that, with their strong beaks, they were formidable antagonists.

The gulls were even more numerous than the cormorants. Though they kept out of our way, they did not appear otherwise to fear us. They looked very large on the wing, as their white feathers glanced in the rays of the setting sun; but they are not more than half the size of the cormorant. They act the useful part of scavengers on the coast, and eagerly pick up all the offal thrown on the shore.

We returned to the yachts, and once more made sail. We got a good view through our glasses of the old towers of Dunstanborough Castle. As the wind fell light, we pulled in to have a look at it, papa being anxious to do so, as he had visited it in his younger days. The weather-beaten ruin stands on the summit of a black cliff, rising sheer out of the ocean. Three towers, one square, and the others semi-circular, remain, with the greater portion of the outer wall, enclosing several acres of green turf, over which, instead of mail-clad warriors, peaceable sheep now wander. The principal tower overlooks a deep gully or gap in the rocks, up which the sea, during easterly gales, rushes with tremendous force and terrific noise, lashed into masses of foam, which leap high over the crumbling walls. This gully is known by the significant name of the Rumble Churn. This ocean-circled fortress was erected—so say the chroniclers—in the fourteenth century, by Thomas, Earl of Lancaster. Many a tale of siege and border warfare its stones could tell; for the Cheviot hills—the boundary between Scotland and England—can be seen from the summit of its battlements. Having bravely held out for Queen Margaret of Anjou, it was completely dismantled in the reign of Edward the Fourth, and has ever since remained like a lion deprived of its claws, crouching over the ocean, a sad memento of its former power. Had it remained until gunpowder was in general use, it would probably have been entirely overthrown.

Papa described to us Warkworth Castle, which stands further south, above the banks of the Coquet river, on a high wood-covered hill. The greater portion of the ruins remain; indeed, the woodwork alone has disappeared, and the masonry is in so good a state of preservation, that the late Duke of Northumberland proposed to restore it, and make it his residence, instead of Alnwick Castle. Near it a hermit dwelt in a cavern; he became a hermit in consequence of having killed the brother of his betrothed, whom he mistook for a rival, after his return from the Crusades.

We sighted Coquet Island, with its square white lighthouse, from which a light burst forth as we approached. Near it were the castellated dwellings of the keepers, painted different colours. In its neighbourhood are dangerous rocks, and over each a red ray is shown, to warn vessels which might otherwise run upon them. We were now almost constantly in sight of some light, which enabled us to

WARKWORTH CASTLE.

know our exact position. Dick and I turned in while Coquet Island light still shone brightly.

We expected the next morning to be off Hartlepool, at the mouth of the Tees; but when day broke we found ourselves in sight of a picturesque castle standing on a point of land, with a broad river flowing below it, and a town at its foot.   When we asked Truck what it was, he answered:

'That's Tynemouth, at the mouth of the Tyne ; and the captain says he intends to run in there to have a look at the place.   It's as well worth seeing as any place we have been to.   Beyond it you see North Shields, and South Shields on the southern bank ; and higher up is Newcastle, where coals come from, as you've heard tell of.'

We laughed at Truck's description.   'If they don't come from Newcastle, I don't know where else they come from,' remarked Dick.

'A good many other places, young gentleman.   There's no small quantity shipped from Sunderland and Swansea ; and also from some of the Scotch ports.   If we go up to Newcastle, we shall see the curious way they are put on board the colliers.'

'But why haven't we got further ? ' I asked.

'Because we have had light winds, and the tides have been against us most of the night,' answered Truck.

As not only the tide, but the wind also was against us, papa, on coming on deck, agreed to run up the Tyne.   Hauling our wind, we stood in for North Shields, passing close under the lighthouse, which stands amid the ruins of the castle.

North Shields was evidently an active commercial place.   Shipbuilding was going on in the yards, and vessels were loading with coals, bound to all parts of the world, each with a number of keels, or oval boats, alongside, which had brought down the coal from the upper part of the river.   On board the vessels cranes were at work lifting up tubs of coal from out of the keels, and depositing them in their holds.   Of these keels I shall have more to say by-and-by. Steamers emitting black wreaths of smoke were coming and going,— some towing vessels out to sea, others taking them up the harbour ; while several were conveying passengers.   After breakfast we went on board one of the passenger vessels, for papa and Uncle Tom did not wish to carry the yachts higher up.

We had clear evidence that we were in a region of coal. The greater number of vessels we met were colliers, their crews begrimed with coal dust. 'Everybody,' as Dick remarked, 'had a coaly look.' People were heard conversing in a broad Northumbrian accent, with a burr in most of their words. They were broad-shouldered men, capable of doing any amount of hard work. We came in sight of a fine stone bridge with nine elliptical arches, which connects Newcastle with Gateshead, on the opposite bank. Above it is another magnificent bridge; it is double, the lower roadway, ninety feet above the river, being used for carriages and foot passengers, while the upper carries the railway. It has two piers at the margin of the river, and four others in the stream itself, besides smaller piers. It was curious to walk under it, and to hear the trains rumbling by overhead.

Newcastle stands on the north bank of the river. At first we thought it a very smoky town, but on emerging from the narrow old streets we reached some fine broad thoroughfares with large houses and magnificent public buildings. At the quays were a vast number of vessels, some of considerable size. Formerly coals used to be put on board vessels from the oval boats I have before mentioned, called keels, of which a considerable number are still employed. Each keel carries about twenty tons of coal, the larger masses being piled up in the vessel, but smaller coal is carried in tubs, each keel having about eight tubs. The keels are antique-looking craft, such as were probably used in the earliest days of our history. They are propelled by large oars. The keel man, commencing at the bow, presses the oar before him, until he reaches the after part of the boat; he then hurries back to the bow, and again puts down his oar. The keel men are a fine hardy race. Formerly they were spoken of as 'bullies'; but this, among the colliers, means 'brothers,' or is derived from 'boolie,' that is, 'beloved.' Though their manners are rough, their character is good, and they are remarkably friendly to each other. Being all 'keel bullies' or 'keel brothers,' they support an extensive establishment in Newcastle called the 'Keelmen's Hospital.' We met a whole fleet of these keels as we came up, working their way down with their 'puys' or oars. A considerable quantity of coal is scattered over the sides when hoisting it on board, and this is brought back by the flood tide into shallow water, where a number of people are seen in their little cobles dredging for it.

The larger number of vessels are, however, loaded from the 'straiths.' These are platforms placed over the river and connected with tramways, joined to the various pits. The waggons, each containing two and a half tons of coal, come down for many miles until they reach the 'straith,' when they are brought to a stand. In the 'straith' is a hatchway, which opens by machinery, through which the waggon descends with a man in it, who, when it arrives over the hold, unfastens a catch which secures the bottom of the waggon; this being made to turn upon hinges, like a trap door when opened, the whole of the coal is poured into the hold. Attached to the suspending machinery are two counterpoising weights, which being less heavy than the waggon laden with coal, do not impede its descent. The moment it is discharged of its coal it is drawn up again by these weights.

As we descended the river we were much amused by seeing these coal waggons running swiftly on the 'straith, stop a moment, then go down with the descending men; and having got rid of their coal with a loud rushing noise, rise up again, as if perfectly aware of what they were about.

We returned in the afternoon to the yachts, and stood out to sea, hoping to obtain a slant of wind which might carry us further down the coast.

Having seen the largest coal-shipping place, we had no particular wish to visit Sunderland, the chief port of Durham. Beyond it is Seaham, which has of late years sprung into existence. The mines in the neighbourhood belonged to the late Marquis of Londonderry, who wisely formed a fine harbour here by constructing two piers running out from the land; and his heir has been richly rewarded by his enterprise.

Further south is the seaport of Hartlepool, jutting out into the sea, a short distance from the river Tees. It was once a place of great strength, and contained one of the most ancient monasteries in the

SCARBOROUGH CASTLE.

kingdom. A portion of the walls which defended the old haven still remains; and the new harbour has been formed by a pier run out from the south side of the town. It will not, however, hold vessels of large tonnage. The inhabitants are mostly engaged in fishing.

The next day we were in sight of the Yorkshire coast. Passing Whitby and Scarborough, after rounding Flamborough Head, opening up Bridlington Bay, we stood for Spurn Head, on the top of which are two lighthouses.

As we had still sufficient daylight, we ran up the Humber to visit Hull, which stands on its northern bank. A large number of coasters were at anchor before its extensive quays ; it has also docks of great size. Numbers of steam-vessels were gliding in and out of the harbour. It is properly called Kingston-upon-Hull. It took its name when it was purchased by Edward the First, who, seeing the great natural advantages of its position, formed here a fortified town and port. There is nothing very attractive in the appearance of the place ; but we were interested by a visit to a fine column on a square pedestal, erected to the memory of the great Wilberforce, whose statue adorns the summit. The town contains two colleges, several hospitals, and numerous other public institutions. We went on board the guardship stationed here, with some of the officers, with whom papa was acquainted, and were interested in hearing an account of the Coastguard system. Ships are stationed at different ports round the coast, and are called 'Coastguard' or district ships, for Coastguard and Royal Naval Coast Volunteer duties. The English coast is divided into six districts ; namely, the Hull district, which extends from Berwick to Cromer ; the Harwich, from North Yarmouth to Ramsgate ; the Newhaven district, from Folkestone, including Southampton Water, the Isle of Wight, and Lymington ; the Falmouth and Weymouth district, including Bournemouth, Land's End, and taking in Penzance and the Scilly Isles. The rest of the coast is divided between Milford and Liverpool. Scotland has two 'Coastguard' districts, the east and the west coasts. Ireland has also two districts. The services on which the ships are employed are numerous. First, for the protection of the revenue ; to keep up a reserve of seamen, and as a dépôt for stores and clothing. The captain of the ship takes the duties of the old inspecting commanders, and the officers—of whom there are a large number appointed to each ship for that especial purpose—have command of the different stations. Each ship has four or five tenders attached to her, employed in protecting either the revenue or the fisheries. The ships generally go to sea for a month or

WHITBY.

so in the course of the year, and are kept ready to proceed to any part of the world. They do not keep up their usual complement of men, but when required the crew are drawn from the Coastguard. Besides these ships, there are six in England and two in Scotland, called 'drill ships.' They, however, never go to sea. They are employed in receiving on board the Royal Naval Reserve Force,—seamen as well as officers,—who go through a periodical drill. The Royal Naval Coast Volunteers also drill on board these ships. These volunteers are seafaring men, and they rank with ordinary seamen, and not, like the men of the Naval Reserve, with able-bodied seamen.

Both the men of the Reserve and Coast Volunteers are expected to drill twenty-eight days in the year, either on board a district ship, a drill ship, or at the shore battery. By these means an efficient body of men is kept up, ready for immediate service in case of war. The men quarrel at times among themselves, the result frequently being a black eye; but they will never tell upon each other; and sometimes a very curious cause is assigned as the reason of having a black eye. A man once said 'that he had slipped and kicked himself,' though how he managed to kick his own eye it is difficult to say! Another reason often given is, 'that they have run up against a pump-handle.' The man-of-war hats are very unpopular, for they are particularly heavy. Good straw hats having lately been scarce, an armourer was found constructing one of tin; but that must have been not only heavier, but much hotter. The men usually make their own hats, and as usually manage to lose them. As soon as the hat is found, the man is placed before it, and compelled to look steadily at it for a certain time.

We got under weigh again in the afternoon of the next day, and stood down the Humber, until we came in sight once more of the Spurn lights. During the next night, while we were steering for the Dudgeon floating light-vessel, one of the men on the look-out shouted,—

'A light on the starboard bow! Starboard the helm! Hard a

starboard!' and I saw a screw steamer rapidly approaching us. Had the night been thick, and the look-out not been on the alert, we should certainly have been run down.

It was two hours before we sighted Dudgeon light, and from thence we steered for Cromer, which we knew by its having a bright light revolving every minute. Outside of it was the Hasborough floating-light, and beyond that another light-vessel. We came off Cromer in the forenoon, when the vessels were hove to ; and we pulled in for the shore to visit some friends of Uncle Tom.

We landed among a number of fishing boats, the place itself being a large and flourishing village, though there were a number of nice residences for people who visit it during the summer. In the middle rises a remarkably handsome church, its tower rising high above the surrounding buildings.

Along the coast are several round towers, which were built during the last war to defend the shore from invasion, though at present they would be of very little use. Papa was so pleased with the appearance of the place, that he said he should come there some summer with the rest of the family.

Leaving Cromer, we stood on for Great Yarmouth, inside a long line of sandbanks, which are known by the light-vessels stationed at their different ends.

Great Yarmouth is situated on the seashore, at the southern end of Norfolk. The river Yare follows a serpentine course, and falls into the sea at the village of Gorleston, a short distance from Yarmouth to the southward.

We waited until a pilot came on board to take us in, as the entrance is very narrow, between two long wooden piers, one projecting a considerable way into the sea. Further along the shore to the south rises a high sandy cliff, on the top of which we saw a good-sized vessel building. We asked the pilot how she could ever be launched, and he told us that she would be eased down the cliffs by ropes at| high tide, when the water, rushing close up to the base, would float her.

CROMER BEFORE THE RECENT EXTENSIONS.

We brought-up at some little distance from the entrance, opposite a line of neat-looking cottages, forming the village of Gorleston, and inhabited chiefly by pilots. As it was getting late, we settled not to go on shore until the following morning.

CHAPTER XII.

YARMOUTH.

FTER an early breakfast, we landed on the north side of the river, and made our way over a level sandy plain towards a tall column which rose in the midst of it. The plain is called the Denes, and extends from the mouth of the river to the town. It is scantily covered with grass and sea plants, round which the sand collects in little hillocks. We had to steer our way among a vast number of tanned nets spread out to dry. Here and there fishermen and their wives and daughters were employed in mending those which had received damage. There must have been acres upon acres of these nets. We soon reached the column, which we found was erected by the inhabitants of the county to the memory of Lord Nelson, who was a Norfolk man. At the top of each side of the pedestal were the names of the hero's chief victories. At the summit is a ball, on which stands the figure of Britannia holding a trident and a laurel wreath. The keeper invited us to enter; and we ascended by a flight of two hundred and seventeen steps to a gallery at the top of the column, the total height being one hundred and forty-four feet. From the platform we got a good bird's-eye view of the town below us, and the country as far as Norwich, and a wide extent of ocean.

'Have you been here long?' I asked the keeper.

'Not so long as the man who had charge before me,' he answered; 'he came here when the column was first put up, and here he stayed for wellnigh forty years.'

'What was his name?' I enquired, finding that the old *custos* was more inclined to speak of his predecessor than himself.

'James Sharman. He was with Lord Nelson at Trafalgar. It was he who helped to carry the admiral from the upper deck to the cockpit. He came home in the Victory, and afterwards joined several other ships, until he bore up for Greenwich Hospital; but not liking to be shut up there, Sir Thomas Hardy—who, you mind, was Lord Nelson's flag-captain—got him appointed to look after this column; and a good berth it is. He entered the navy as far back as 1799, and was afloat wellnigh twenty years. He came here, as near as I can remember, in 1819. He was as brave a seaman as ever stepped. I mind hearing of a gallant act of his, after he had been here about ten years. It was at the end of November; and the day was fast closing in, when the Hammond, a brig bound from Newcastle to London, drove on shore during a heavy gale, just a little way to the south of where we are standing. As she was heavily laden, and the water is shallow thereabout, she grounded more than a hundred fathoms from the beach. In a short time the wreck parted, and both her masts fell, carrying away, as was supposed, the whole of the crew. A short time after dark, however, one of the preventive men, named Smith, brought word to Sharman that he heard groans upon the wreck.

'"The groans must come from some poor fellow, and we will do our best to save him," cried Sharman; "come along, Smith."

'Taking a long rope, they hurried back to the beach.

'"Now you hold on to the rope, and I'll make the other end fast round my waist; and I'll see what I can do," cried Sharman.

'Without a moment's delay he plunged unto the surf, which three times carried him off his legs and sent him back on shore. Again he tried, and this time the sea drove him right against the wreck. The night was so dark that he had a hard matter to find out where the poor fellow was. At length he found a man clinging to the breast-work. The poor fellow told him that just before three men who had clung on until then had been washed away, and if he had come a few minutes sooner they might have been saved. As to swimming to shore, that he was certain was more than he could do. On this Sharman, taking the rope off himself, made it fast round the seaman's waist, and shouted to Smith to haul in, while he himself trusted to his strong arms to hold onto the rope. They thus mercifully got safe to shore.'

A more appropriate spot than this could not have been fixed on for a monument to Nelson, who was born at Burnham Thorpe, of which his father, the Rev. Edmund Nelson, was rector. His mother was Catherine, daughter of Dr. Suckling, Prebendary of Westminster, with one of whose sons, Captain Maurice Suckling, he first went to sea, on board the Raisonnable, of sixty-four guns. His education was obtained, first at the High School at Sanwich, and afterwards at North Walsham. After the misunderstanding with Spain had been settled, he left the Raisonnable, and was sent in a West Indian ship, commanded by a Captain Rathbone, who had been in the navy with his uncle. So great a dislike for the Royal Navy was instilled into him by the merchant seamen, that it was many weeks after he had joined the Triumph—to which on his return he had been appointed—before he became at all reconciled to remaining in it. How different might have been his lot had he not got over his prejudices! though, wherever he might have been, he would have contrived to make his name known.

On leaving Nelson's column, we proceeded along a road parallel with the river, having on our right the new barracks and on our left the Naval Hospital, which is placed in a fine airy situation, with the Denes in front and the sea beyond. It was here that Nelson, when the fleet came into Yarmouth, visited the poor wounded seamen, and going along the wards, spoke a kind word to each. It was by acts such as these that the admiral won the affection of his men, who used to say of him, 'Our Nel is as brave as a lion, and as gentle as a lamb.'

We presently found ourselves on the quays, running for a mile along the bank of the river, and which are considered equal to any in the kingdom. Opposite to us, on the south shore, a modern town has

A YARMOUTH ROW.

sprung up; and we here saw a number of vessels building, the chief of them, judging from their size, intended for the deep-sea fishery.

We had heard that Yarmouth was likened to a gridiron, and we now saw the reason. Comparatively few broad streets run north and south; they are, however, joined by one hundred and fifty or more narrow passages, called rows, which run east and west, like the bars of

T

a gridiron. In many of them the houses project beyond their founda-
tions, so that the inhabitants can almost shake hands with their
opposite neighbours. Most of the rows are paved with pebbles
brought up from the beach. Uncle Tom observed that the word 'row'
is probably derived from the French *rue*, a street. In many of them
we observed curious pieces of old architecture. They are now
numbered, but used to be called after the names of some of the
principal inhabitants. One is called George and Dragon Row; and
in it we noticed a somewhat tumbledown cottage, built in what is
denominated the 'herring-bone pattern'; the bones or frame being of
wood placed in a zig-zag fashion, filled up with masonry. Another
row is Kitty Witches Row. One end is scarcely three feet wide. It
is supposed that this row was inhabited by women, who used to go about
at certain seasons of the year, dressed in fantastic fashions, to collect
contributions. Yarmouth carts are formed probably after the model
of the most ancient vehicles in the kingdom. They are long, narrow,
and low, the wheels being placed under the seat, so as to occupy as
little space as possible. The shafts are fastened to the axles, and two
or three perpendicular pieces of wood—the hindermost being the
longest—support the seat, on which a person can recline at his ease.
It will thus be seen that wherever the horses can go, the cart can
follow.

Passing a very fine Town Hall we reached the end of a remarkably
handsome bridge, which unites Southtown to Yarmouth. We then
turned to our right through some narrow roads; and having crossed
a broad street, we found ourselves in an open space in front of the
Church of St. Nicholas, one of the largest parish churches in the
kingdom. Turning back and passing the fine Fisherman's Hospital,
we entered the market-place, which occupies nearly three acres of
land. About the centre of the market-place there are some smooth
stones in the form of a cross, which mark the spot where the town
cross once stood. It was formerly adorned with the pillory and
stocks, but they have long disappeared. The freemen of the town

have the right of selling here free, with one stall. At the north end of the market is an avenue of lime-trees, which adds to its pleasant foreign appearance. In the yard of the Fisherman's Hospital we saw a figure of Charity ; and the cupola above is adorned by a statue of the Apostle Peter, who, in former days, was looked upon as the patron of fishermen.

THE TOLL HOUSE, AND ENTRANCE TO YARMOUTH GAOL.

We went to see the Toll House and Gaol, which are the oldest buildings in the town. We entered a hall by an external staircase, leading to an Early English doorway, which has the tooth ornament on the jambs. Opposite to it is an enclosed Early English window, with cinquefoil heads and shafts in the jambs.

T 2

We were shown an ancient iron chest, called a hatch, in which the Corporation of Yarmouth kept their charters and valuable documents. Among the contents are the tallies or cleft sticks upon which the accounts were formerly kept, the stick being notched according to the amount of money advanced, one part being given to the creditor, and the other to the debtor.   The same plan is used in the present day by the hop-pickers in Kent, the overseer having one stick, while the picker keeps the other, and notches it each time a basket is emptied. Beneath this Toll House is the ancient Gaol or House of Correction. Up to the present century this gaol was as defective as that of prisons generally.   Under the ground is an apartment called the hold, with iron rings fixed to a heavy beam of wood crossing the floor.   To this beam—in olden times—prisoners were wont to be chained.   The sufferings of these unfortunate persons stirred up the heart of a Christian woman, Sarah Martin, residing in Yarmouth.   Though compelled to support herself as a dressmaker, she devoted much of her time, as did John Howard and Elizabeth Fry, to visiting her suffering fellow-creatures.   For twenty-four years she thus laboured, visiting day after day the prisoners and malefactors in the town gaol.   There was no one on earth to reward her, no one to thank her; but she trusted in God, and gave Him the praise that she was thus able to labour in His service.   By her instrumentality many who were looked upon as hardened wretches by their fellow-men were brought to the foot of the cross as penitent sinners.   When she lay dying, a friend asked, 'What shall I read?' her answer was one word, 'Praise.'   To the question, 'Are there any clouds?' she answered, 'None: He never hides His face; it is our sins which form the cloud between us and Him.   He is all love, all light.'   And when the hour of her departure was come, her exclamation was, 'Thank God! thank God!'

We read this account of the humble dressmaker near the spot where she laboured, and from whence her spirit took its flight to be with Him whom she had served on earth.

Between the old walls and the sea a new town has sprung up, with

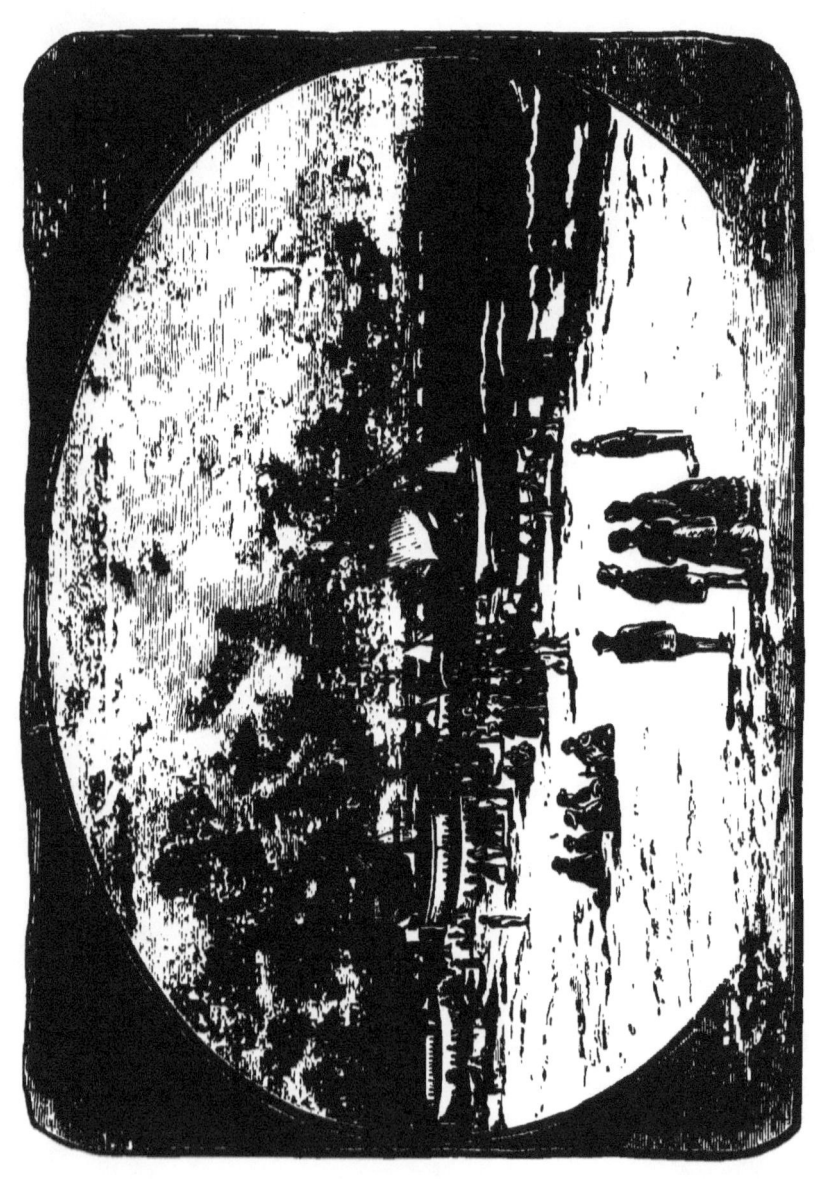

THE BEACH, YARMOUTH.

fine terraces facing the water, and a battery at either end; running out from it, over a narrow part of the Dene, into the ocean are three piers. The one known as 'the Jetty,' from its jutting out into the sea, is between the others. It is composed of strong oaken piles driven into the soil and braced together with wooden beams, further secured by iron fastenings. During heavy weather, at high tide, the sea breaks completely over the end, while at low tide it is left almost completely dry. Of late it has been considerably extended. We walked to the end, to have a look at the town, with its towers and windmills rising from amid the smaller houses. Near the beach we visited the Fishermen's Chapel, to which an Institute is attached, containing a library, reading-room, &c.

Along the shore are several high wooden structures with platforms on the top. They are built to enable the pilots or boatmen to take a survey of the roadstead and the sands beyond, that they may see any vessel requiring their assistance.

Near these structures were two or more handsome boats drawn up on the beach, which are called yawls. They can be launched when no ordinary boat can put to sea, and they are principally used for rendering assistance to vessels in distress. They are from fifty to seventy feet in length, and each carries from ten to twenty men.

An old boatman told us of a very disastrous accident which occurred some years ago to the Increase, to which a man named Samuel Brock belonged. A signal of distress was seen flying on board a Spanish brig in the offing, when the Increase, with a crew of ten men and a London pilot, put off to her assistance.

The yawl, having reached the brig, put three hands on board to navigate her into Yarmouth Harbour. She stood back for the shore. On passing the Newarp Floating Light, a signal was made requesting them to take a sick man on board, which they did, and then continued their cruise with a strong breeze, under three lugs. They were taking a snack of food, when, having imprudently trimmed the ballast to windward—a most dangerous practice—a tremendous squall took the sails aback, and in a moment capsized her. Brock being a good swimmer, struck out to get clear of his companions, his ears assailed by their cries, mingled with the hissing of water and the howling of the storm. After a moment or so he swam back to help an old man to get hold of a spar; he then himself got on the boat, and stood upon its side; but finding that she was gradually settling down, he again struck off. By this time he supposed that all his companions were lost; and he began to think of the awful position in which he was placed, the nearest land being fully six miles distant. He remembered that it was half-past six just before the boat went over, and that as it was now low water, the tide would be setting off the shore, making to the southward, and that, therefore, he must swim fifteen miles before the ebb would assist him. Just then, a rush horse-collar, which had served as a fender to the boat, floated by. He got hold of it, and putting his left arm through it, was supported until he had cut the waistband of his cloth trousers, which then fell off. He in a similar way got rid of his frock, his waistcoat, and neckcloth; but he dared not free himself from his oilskin trousers, fearing that his legs might become entangled. He now put the collar over his head, but although it assisted him in floating, it retarded his swimming, and he had to abandon it. He had gone some little distance, when he discovered one of his messmates swimming ahead of him. The wind having gone down, no cries were heard, and the moon shone calmly on the water. Ere long he beheld the last of his companions sink without struggle or cry. Should he give in also? Not for a moment would he yield to such a thought; and he prepared himself for the desperate struggle.

For some time Winterton Light, to the north of Yarmouth, served to direct his course; when the tide carried him out of sight of it, a star served to guide him. At length this was obscured by the clouds, from which flashes of lightning, with crackling peals of thunder, burst forth. Still he swam on, until again the moon shone forth. Having cut off his heavy boots, he swam more easily. And now Lowestoft Light came in sight, and he saw the checkered buoy of

St. Nicholas Gat, opposite his own door, but still four miles away from land. He had been five hours in the water. Here was something to hold on by; but he reflected that his limbs might become numbed from exposure to the night air, and that it would be more prudent to swim on. So abandoning the buoy, he steered for the land. Not long afterwards he heard a whizzing sound overhead. It was a huge gull which had made a dash at him, mistaking him for a corpse; a number followed, but by shouting and splashing he drove them off. He was now approaching Corton Sands, over which the sea was breaking, and he much doubted whether he could live through it; but in a short time he was driven over them into smooth water, and the wind and swell coming from the eastward, he regained his strength. Some distance to the southward, he saw a brig at anchor. He was in doubt whether he should make towards her or continue his course to the shore. There was a great deal of surf breaking on the beach, and he might not have strength to climb up out of its reach. Also, if he swam to the brig, he might fail to make himself heard by the crew. However, on reflection, he determined to make for the brig. He got within two hundred yards, but nearer it was impossible to get. He now sang out with all his might. Happily, his voice was heard by the watch, a boat was lowered, and at half-past one, having swum seven and a half hours, he was on board the Betsey, at anchor in Corton Roads, nearly fifteen miles from the spot where the yawl was capsized. On being lifted on deck he fainted; and it was not until long afterwards, by careful attention from the captain and crew, that he was brought round. He suffered great pain in several parts of his body, and it was with difficulty that he swallowed some warm beer. He was landed at Lowestoft, and five days afterwards was able to walk back to Yarmouth. We were shown the knife with which he was enabled to cut off his clothes and boots. A piece of silver was fixed to it, on which were engraved the names of the crew of the yawl, and the words, 'Brock, aided by this knife, was saved, after being seven and a half hours in the sea. 6th October, 1835.'

It was a remarkable thing that for some time previous he had been without a knife, and only purchased this two days before. Nearly half the time he was exposed to the full sweep of the North Sea; the other half he was partly sheltered by the Newarp and Cross Sands.

Between this and Yarmouth Roads is another long sandbank, at the south end of which is the Nicholas Gat; then comes the Corton Sandbank, over the end of which he was driven. He was described to us as a strongly-built man of five feet five. Though Captain Webb and others have swum far greater distances, few Englishmen have ever performed such a feat as this under similar circumstances.

Afterwards we inspected the lifeboats, which are kept in houses built to shelter them from the weather. They belong to an institution called the Norfolk Association for Saving Life from Shipwreck, and are similar in construction to those already described. They are fitted to carriages to convey them along the beach or down to the harbour.

We went through a number of sheds where were some fine luggers, used for the herring and mackerel fishery. Their crews were getting them ready for sea. Each vessel is from forty to fifty tons burden, and carries a crew of ten men.

The herring usually arrives on the Norfolk coast about the last week in September, for the purpose of spawning, and they are then in the best condition to become the food of man. The name 'herring' is derived from the German *heer*, an army, to which they are likened in consequence of the vast number which keep together., They are mostly caught at a considerable distance from the coast; but they do not always appear in the same place. Formerly it was supposed that they were migratory; but it is now believed that they keep within the deeper parts of the ocean until they rise nearer the surface in the autumn to deposit their eggs. For some years they have appeared near the surface as early as the last week in August. A herring seldom measures more than fourteen inches in length; but we were told that one was caught some years ago seventeen and a half inches in length, seven and a half in girth, and that it weighed thirteen ounces! Each lugger carries from sixty to a hundred nets;

TOWING OUT LUGGERS FROM YARMOUTH HARBOUR.

each net is about fifteen yards long, and is floated by corks placed a few feet apart. The united nets form what is called a train fleet, or drift of nets. The depth to which they are sunk is regulated by ropes seven or eight yards long, called seizings, of which there are two to each net. They are made fast to a stout warp, running along the whole of the train, which is upwards of a mile in length, and supported near the surface by kegs, called 'bowls.' The warp is useful in taking the strain off the nets, and in preventing their loss, in case the nets should be fouled, or cut by a vessel passing over them. The meshes are about an inch square.

HERRING FISHING.

Drift fishing is carried on at night. The nets are 'shot' a little before sunset, the vessel keeping before the wind, with only enough sail set to take her clear of the nets as they are thrown overboard. When all the nets are out, about fifteen more fathoms of warp are paid out; and by this the vessel is swung round, and then rides head to the wind, a small mizen being set to keep her in that position.

One of the masters of a lugger showed us the way the nets hang in the water; the whole train being extended in nearly a straight line, the big rope to which the corks are fastened being uppermost, and the body of the net hanging perpendicularly in the water, forming a wall of netting more than two thousand yards long and about eight yards deep. The strain from the vessel serves to keep the net extended, and the whole—vessel and nets together—drifts along with the tide.

During the day the fish keep near the bottom; but as night closes in, should the weather be fine, they swim nearer the surface, and attempting to swim through the barriers of net on each side of them, a large number become entangled or meshed, their gills preventing their return when once their heads have passed through the meshes.

After waiting two or three hours, the first net is hauled on board, when, if it is found that a number of fish have been caught, the whole of the net is hauled in by means of a capstan and the warp to which the nets are fastened. The fish are then shaken out, and the vessel beats up again to the spot from which the net was first shot, and the process is repeated.

Mackerel nets have larger meshes, being twenty-four or twenty-five to the yard. They are not so deep as the herring nets, but they are twice as long, often extending to a distance of nearly two miles and a half. Occasionally in one night a single boat has taken from twelve to fourteen lasts of herrings, each last numbering ten thousand fish; but of course the catch is uncertain. One boat, however, has been known to bring in the enormous quantity of twenty lasts. Some few years ago upwards of nine thousand lasts, or nearly one hundred and twenty millions of fish, were caught by the Yarmouth luggers. Several vessels bring in one hundred lasts each.

As is well known, immediately the herring leaves the water it dies; hence the phrase, 'dead as a herring.' To preserve the fish, salt is immediately thrown upon them in the boats; they are carried to the fish-house in open wicker baskets, called swills, where they are delivered over to a man called a 'tower,' when they are placed on the salting floor. If they are to be used at home, they remain for only twenty-four hours; but if for the foreign markets, for several days. They are afterwards washed in fresh water, and strung up by splits passed through their gills, one tier below another, to about seven feet from the ground. Oak-wood fires are then kindled under them for fourteen days, if intended for the foreign market; but if for home use, only twenty-four hours. The first are called red-herrings, and the latter are known as bloaters. When sufficiently cured, they are packed in barrels, each containing about seven hundred fish. Between thirty and forty thousand barrels are sent to the Mediterranean, but a far larger quantity is used at home. Upwards of two hundred boats, carrying two thousand men, are employed in the herring fishery; but many more are engaged on shore in curing the fish.

Hearing that the deep-sea fishing was going on, papa and Uncle Tom agreed to accompany one of the cutters which was about to rejoin the fleet; and as we had seen more of Yarmouth than of most places we had visited, we returned on board to get ready to sail with our friend.

Before long the cutter appeared, and we stood out of the harbour after her. We sailed in company for two days, when on Sunday morning, shortly after breakfast, we made out the fleet, with most of the vessels near us hove to, a steamer being among them, stationary, like the rest. In the distance were many other vessels, some standing towards the fleet, others sailing in different directions, and a few ships passing by. On getting near enough to distinguish their flags, we found that several of them carried the 'Bethel' flag, a notice that service was to be held on board. Both the yachts therefore hove to, and under the guidance of our friend we pulled on board one of the vessels. We were gladly received by the master, who was going to conduct the service. The crews of several other vessels having come on board, he invited us to join them, which we willingly did, although the space was somewhat confined. Several hymns were

THE 'SHORT BLUE' FLEET IN THE NORTH SEA.

sung, the fine manly voices of the fishermen producing a good effect. A chapter of God's Word was read, and a gospel address was given. After service, the men returned on board their vessels with books and tracts, which had been distributed among them.

We remained until the following day, that we might see the fish caught. Our friend the skipper gave us a great deal of information about trawlers. The Yarmouth fleet consists of several hundred vessels, ranging from fifty to seventy tons. They have increased rapidly. Fifty years ago, there were none belonging to Great Yarmouth. They only form a small portion of English and Irish trawling vessels. Many hundred sail leave the Thames, the Humber, Scarborough, and Lowestoft, to fish in the North Sea; while several other places send out fifty or sixty vessels to the English or Irish Channels, manned by some thousands of fishermen. It is calculated that they supply the English markets daily with three or four hundred tons of fish.

The beam trawl consists of a triangular purse-shaped net, about seventy feet long, forty wide at the mouth, gradually diminishing to four or five at the commencement of the cod, as the smaller end is called. This part of the trawl, about ten feet long, is of a uniform breadth to the extremity, which is closed by a draw-rope, like the string of a purse. The upper part of the mouth is made fast to a beam about forty feet in length, which keeps the net open. This beam is supported by two upright iron frames, three feet in height, known as the trawl heads, or irons; the lower being flattened, to rest on the ground. The under side of the net is made with a curved margin. The outside is guarded from chafing, when the trawl is being worked over the bottom, by pieces of old net. The meshes vary in size according to the part of the trawl. Near the mouth, they are four inches square, and in the cod, an inch and a quarter. The trawl is hauled along by a bridle, that is to say, by two ropes of about fifteen fathoms each, which are fastened to the ends of the trawl heads, and unite at a warp, one hundred and fifty fathoms long, which serves to haul the net along. Trawling, as a rule, is carried on in the direction of the tide, although sometimes across it, but never against a stream. It is usually kept down for one tide, and its rate of progress is generally from half a mile to two miles an hour faster than that of the stream. The fish caught are turbot, skate, soles, though others are occasionally taken in the net. The trawl can only be used with advantage on smooth ground; and, of course, a sandy bottom is preferred, not only from that being the usual resort of several valuable kinds of ground fish, but from the less danger there is on such a surface of tearing the net to pieces.

Formerly, the fish as soon as they were caught, were sent to market in fast-sailing cutters, but now steamers are generally employed; the fish, as soon as collected, being packed in ice. The trawlers themselves stay out for six weeks at a time, in all seasons of the year. They are remarkably fine vessels, and capable of standing a great deal of rough work; and a hardier set of men than their crews can scarcely anywhere be found. Steam trawlers are gradually coming into use, being independent of wind and weather, and one boat is capable of doing the work of several ordinary vessels.

Shrimp Boat

CHAPTER XIII.

TEERING for Harwich after we had left the fleet, we passed, at a distance, the handsome town of Lowestoft, from which a considerable fishing-fleet sails, and then Aldborough, an ancient seaport, with a number of new houses near it. When off Orford, on the Suffolk coast, papa told us that we were crossing the submarine telegraph line which runs from thence to the Hague. We had also passed another, which extends from Cromer to Emden.

Catching sight of the pretty little village of Felixstowe—the houses facing the sea on the north side—and of the neat watering-place of Dovercourt on the left, we stood in between Landguard Fort, on the north shore, and the long breakwater which runs out from the south, when we crossed the mouth of the Orwell at the point where the Stour falls into it, and came to an anchor off Harwich, among a considerable number of vessels, the guard-ship rising like a giant in their midst.

Though the town is small, the port has long been famous. We saw several steamers start for different parts of the Continent. If I was asked what was the chief article of sale in the town, I should say, Shrimps.

We made a short excursion up the Stour, the banks of which are richly wooded; and we also pulled up to Ipswich, where the Orwell may be said to commence, for the river above the town is confined in a narrow canal-like channel. On our return, while at anchor in the harbour, an oyster-dredging vessel brought up close to us, and papa, who was always on the look-out for information, invited the skipper to come on board.

He gave us a good deal of curious information about the oyster. They are obtained by means of a dredge, which consists of a flat bag, the under part made of strong iron rings looped together by stout wire. The upper side is merely a strong netting, as it is not exposed to so much wear as the part which is drawn along the ground. The mouth of this bag is fastened to an iron frame, with an opening about four inches deep, extending the whole breadth of the bag. The lower part of this frame is flattened and turned forward at such an angle as to enable it to scrape the surface of the ground. To the ends of the scraper two stout iron rods are firmly welded; these, after curving upwards, form the narrow sides of the mouth, and extend forward four or five feet, when they unite at a handle, to which a stout warp is made fast. The free end of the bag is secured to a stout stick, which forms a convenient hold when the contents of the dredge are being turned out. The weight of the dredge keeps it at the bottom, and but little skill is required in working it. A good-sized boat can work two dredges at one time, one from each quarter.

Oyster beds are often valuable property, and they are rented by various companies. Rules have been made for the preservation of oysters, and to allow of new beds being formed. Oysters require nursing, and unless the beds were carefully preserved and reconstructed, they would disappear. The beds are level banks of no great depth, which are seldom or never uncovered by the tide. The first important business, when preparing a bed on which the oyster may spawn, or spat, as it is called, is to sprinkle over it broken plates and pans and tiles, with empty shells and such like substances, to which the embryo oyster immediately attaches itself. This broken stuff is called 'skultch.' The oyster deposits its spawn in July; and a month afterwards the young oysters can be seen sticking fast to the skultch in confused clusters. Here they remain for two or three years, until they become about the size of a shilling; they are then taken up and spread evenly over the surface. After another year they are once more dredged up and scattered on the beds, where they are to remain until full-grown. Seven years are required to bring an oyster to maturity; but many are dredged up and sold when only five years old. The muddy shores of Essex are highly favourable to the breeding of oysters; and those are considered very fine which are dredged from the beds at the mouth of the river Colne.

'You see, sir,' said the skipper; 'oysters ain't fit to eat except in certain months. They are only prime from October to March. In April they begin to sicken, they are of a milky white colour, though fit enough to look at; then they become of a dirty grey colour, and then change to black by July, when they cast their spawn. After this it takes them two months to get well again, and they ought to have another month to fatten up, which brings us to October. It always makes me angry-like when I see people eating oysters in August; but there are poachers at all times ready to fish them up; and there would be many more if they were not sharply looked after. It is a curious fact, that while the beds on the coast of Kent make very good nurseries for oysters, they do not grow as large and fat as they do on the Essex coast. A little fresh water don't hurt them; but snow water kills them, as it does other fish, outright. To most people, one oyster is just like another; but there are many different sorts, and each sort has a fancy for a particular place. The oyster gives us work for most months in the year; for when not fishing to sell, we are either dredging up the young oysters or laying them down again.'

It is calculated that one spawn oyster produces eight hundred thousand young; and if we suppose that of every five hundred oysters, only one hundred breed during the season, and if the spat of only one of this latter number is shed, notwithstanding the great loss, the yield will be ten thousand young oysters.

The oyster has many enemies besides man. There are creatures in the sea which are very fond of them; among these are the sea urchin, the 'five finger,' and the 'whelk-tingle.' This creature sticks to the shell, through which it pierces a small hole, and sucks out the delicate morsel. One thing, however, is very certain—that the supply of oysters has very greatly fallen off of late years; but whether the fishermen are answerable for this, it is difficult to say.

Besides the numerous oyster-beds in shallow waters, there are deep-sea beds both off the English and Irish coasts. Upwards of three hundred vessels, each of about twenty-five tons, and carrying six men, hail from Colchester, Rochester, and Jersey, engaged specially on these deep-sea beds. One is ten or twelve miles off Great Grimsby, and others exist in the English Channel. Most of the owners of the beds of the shallow estuaries have a large capital invested. One company alone spends three hundred pounds a month in wages, besides rent and other expenses, and six hundred a year in watching against poachers. It sends fourteen hundred bushels to a single dealer in London, seven thousand to Kent, and ten thousand to Ostend and Dunkirk.

This gave us some notion of the vast trade carried on in oysters alone. We were told that they sell retail for the sum of twopence each. I wonder people can venture to eat them.

We had a look at Dovercourt, filled with visitors, and with a bran-new aspect, contrasting with venerable Harwich. We also managed to pull up a narrow creek to Felixstowe, which I should describe as consisting of a long row of Swiss-like cottages, with a few more substantial-looking residences perched on the cliffs above.

Our stay at Harwich was short, though we had no longer any fear of not getting round to the Isle of Wight before the equinoctial gales commenced. We sailed early in the morning, papa being anxious to get across the mouth of the Thames, either as far as Ramsgate or Deal, to avoid the risk of being run down by vessels standing up or down the river during the night.

'But would they dare to do it?' asked Dick, when papa made the remark.

'They would not intend to do so; but should the wind fall light, we might not be able to get out of their way. I shall not forget the remark made by a skipper on board a large steamer, when I was on my way to pay a visit to some friends in Edinburgh. We ran stem on into a schooner, which sank immediately; and although I hurried forward I was only in time to see her masts disappear. " Serves them right!" exclaimed the skipper, who was like myself a passenger. "Serves them right; they should have kept a brighter look out!" The poor fellows managed to scramble on board and to save their lives.'

A short distance further we came off Walton-on-the-Naze, the 'Naze' being a nose or promontory, with the sea on one side and a shallow backwater on the other. We had to keep a bright look out while standing across the mouth of the Thames, having nearly a dozen steamers in sight gliding swiftly along, and sailing vessels of all sizes, from the magnificent Indiaman, or Australian merchant-ship, of a thousand or more tons, down to the little coaster, measuring no more than forty or fifty; while yachts with sails white as snow were darting hither and thither. Besides these, there were not a few barges with yellow or tanned sails, coming out of the numerous estuaries to the north of the river, some even bound round the North Foreland, their deep weather-boards enabling them to beat to windward in a way which, considering their build, at first looks surprising. We agreed that we should not like to go to sea on board one of them, laden almost to the gunwale, so that the water must wash over their decks; but the fact is, they are completely battened down, and are like casks; so that the only place the sea can get into is the little cabin aft, or the forepeak, in which the crew, consisting of a couple of men and a boy, are compelled to live. The wind holding fair, we passed the North Foreland, standing out boldly into the sea; then sighted Broadstairs and Ramsgate. We ran inside of the ill-famed Goodwin Sands, and came to an anchor in the Downs off the low sandy beach of Deal.

The town extends a considerable way along the shore, and a fine pier runs off from it. At the south end is a castle in a good state of repair, although it would be more picturesque if it were a ruin. About a mile further to the south we saw Walmer Castle, where the Lord Warden of the Cinque Ports resides. It was here that the Duke of Wellington spent the latter days of his life. We went on shore, and had a good deal of talk with some of those magnificent fellows, the Deal boatmen, who are probably the most daring seamen and skilful pilots of any along the coast of England.

Deal has a thoroughly salt-water smack about it. 'Boys and even girls seemed to be born seamen,' as Dick observed; taking their part, if not in navigating the boats, in launching or hauling them up on the beach, and attending to them; while the older part of the community are resting from their labours. We were amused at a scene we witnessed on the beach. Two old men, aided by a big girl and a boy, were engaged in hauling up a lugger by means of a windlass, which they worked round and round with wonderful energy, putting to shame a young fellow who sat on a coil of rope idly smoking his pipe.

We were satisfied with a few hours spent at Deal. When once more under weigh, we passed the South Foreland, towering up high above our heads; then rounding the cliffs on which Dover Castle stands, three hundred and twenty feet above the sea, we stood into the harbour.

To the south of us, sheer out of the water, rose the Shakespeare Cliff, where samphire was wont to grow; while between it and the castle appeared the old town on either side of a steep valley, the heights, as far as we could see them, covered with modern houses, churches, and other public buildings.

DOVER.

On landing we went over the castle, which resembles, in some respects, that of Gibraltar, as the fortifications are of an irregular form, to suit the nature of the ground. Excavated far below in the chalk rock are numerous galleries, from which heavy guns would thunder forth an unmistakeable warning to any foes attempting to enter the harbour, or to flaunt their flags within range. Until a few years ago both the inner and outer harbours were dry at low water but now a fine new harbour has been formed.

Dover, papa reminded us, is one of the original Cinque Ports, so called from their number—five. They consisted, in the time of William the Conqueror, of Dover, Sandwich, Hythe, Romney, and Hastings. To these were afterwards added Winchelsea and Rye. These ports had peculiar privileges given to them, on condition that they should furnish the shipping required for the purposes of state. When ships were wanted, the king issued to each of the ports a summons to provide its quota. In Edward the First's time, the number they were bound to supply was fifty-seven fully equipped ships. The period of gratuitous service was fifteen days, after which they received payment. The chief officer of the Cinque Ports was called the Lord Warden. It was considered a high dignity, and was long held by the Duke of Wellington.

Many of their privileges have now been abrogated, as the ports have long been relieved of their responsibilities. It would certainly astonish the inhabitants of Winchelsea or Dover if the Queen should inform them that they must send half a dozen ironclads to complete the fleet off Spithead!

Sailing as close as we could under Shakespeare's Cliff, we passed Folkestone, standing partly in a hollow between two cliffs, and partly up the side of that on the west. Then we rounded the headland of Dungeness; and sailing by Rye and Winchelsea, we passed Hastings, renowned in history, a portion, looking old and venerable, joined to the spic-and-span new town of St. Leonard's.

Running past Eastbourne, we arrived off the bold, wild-looking point of Beachy Head. The weather becoming threatening, the wind, which had hitherto been off shore, began to shift, and drew more and more to the westward, the sky having anything but a pleasant appearance. Dark clouds gathered in dense masses on the horizon, and there was every indication of a heavy gale. Although so near the end of our voyage, there appeared a probability of its being continued for several days longer.

Papa having hailed Uncle Tom, it was agreed that we should stand close-hauled on the starboard tack away from the land, and endeavour to fetch Spithead.

We sighted two small places, Seaford and Newhaven, and could make out Brighton, covering a wide extent of ground along the sea-shore, and reaching the slopes of the hills and downs beyond.

'By standing on we shall have Shoreham under our lee; and we can but run in there, if we find it impossible to beat to the westward against the gale,' observed papa. 'It is not exactly the port in which one would choose to be weather-bound, but we may be thankful if we get there.'

The bright revolving light at Beachy Head shone forth astern. We were gradually sinking it lower and lower; at length we lost sight of it altogether. It might be our last night at sea, and I begged papa to let us remain on deck.

He laughed. 'You may, as long as you like to keep awake; but you must take care not to topple overboard.'

Dick and I for some time walked the deck, believing that we were keeping watch, and, of course, looking out on every side.

'The wind's drawing more round to the south'ard,' I heard Truck remark. 'If we go about, we shall soon catch sight of the Owers, and one more tack will take us into St. Helen's.'

I was very anxious to see the light,. because we had seen it before starting to the westward, and it would show us really and truly that we had gone right round England. I continued pacing up and down, in spite of the pitching of our little craft, for I knew if I were

BEACHY HEAD.

to stop for a moment, I should fall asleep. Of course we kept a sharp look out, not only for the light, but for any vessels which might be running up Channel or beating down it. At last I heard Truck say:

'There's the light, sir;' and I made out, a little on our starboard bow, the Owers Light.

'Hurrah!' I exclaimed; 'we have been right round England!'

'I can't make it out,' said Dick, in a drowsy voice. 'We've been sailing over the plain sea all the time, except when we mounted the locks at the Caledonian Canal. I suppose it is all right though.'

Dick could say no more. I had to take him by the shoulders and help him down the companion ladder. So sleepy was he, that he could scarcely pull off his clothes, and would have turned in fully dressed if I had not helped him.

Next morning, when we awoke and turned out on deck, we were in sight of many a well-known scene. Ryde astern, Cowes on our port quarter; while with a fresh breeze, running past Calshot Castle, we stood up the Southampton Water, and our voyage was over.

After breakfast, Uncle Tom, Jack, and Oliver, came on board; and together we thanked God for having preserved us from the dangers, seen and unseen, to which we had been exposed. We had indeed had a pleasant time of it, and very naturally did not think of any of the anxious moments we had occasionally gone through.

Uncle Tom and Jack had to return home at once; and they took Dick with them, to send him to his aunt and uncle.

'The next few days won't be so pleasant,' he said, making a long face. 'However, we shall meet at the end of them; and won't we spin long yarns to the fellows at school!'

Papa, leaving us on board, went at once to his agents, to whom he had written, requesting them to make inquiries about Nat's friends. After some time he returned, saying that no information had been received, and that he would take Nat home with us.

Of this we were very glad. It made some amends to us for having to go on shore and quit the pleasant life we had so long been leading on board. We shook hands with Truck and all the crew, and in a short time were seated in the railway-carriage rattling up to London.

We have ever since been expecting to hear of some of our little guest's relatives coming to look for him; but, as yet, no one has appeared; and as papa would never think of turning him adrift, we believe that he will become one of us; and, after he has been some years at school, perhaps go into the navy, for which, strange to say, he has a wonderful fancy.

OXFORD: HORACE HART, PRINTER TO THE UNIVERSITY

www.ingramcontent.com/pod-product-compliance
Lightning Source LLC
Chambersburg PA
CBHW020809060726
47498CB00017B/1185